# I'm Not an Artist

# I'm Not an Artist

## Reclaiming Creativity
## in the Age of Infinite Content

Giovanni Aloi

BLOOMSBURY VISUAL ARTS
LONDON · NEW YORK · OXFORD · NEW DELHI · SYDNEY

BLOOMSBURY VISUAL ARTS
Bloomsbury Publishing Plc
50 Bedford Square, London, WC1B 3DP, UK
1385 Broadway, New York, NY 10018, USA
29 Earlsfort Terrace, Dublin 2, Ireland

BLOOMSBURY, BLOOMSBURY VISUAL ARTS and the Diana logo are trademarks of
Bloomsbury Publishing Plc

First published in Great Britain 2025



Cover design: Elena Durey and Giovanni Aloi
Cover image: Giovanni Paolo Panini, *Gallery with views of modern Rome*, 1759.
Oil on canvas, 230 × 303 cm. Louvre Museum, Paris.



A catalogue record for this book is available from the British Library.

A catalog record for this book is available from the Library of Congress.

ISBN:   HB:      978-1-3504-1797-7
        PB:      978-1-3504-1877-6
        ePDF:    978-1-3504-1794-6
        eBook:   978-1-3504-1795-3

Typeset by RefineCatch Limited, Bungay, Suffolk
Printed and bound in India

To find out more about our authors and books visit www.bloomsbury.com
and sign up for our newsletters.

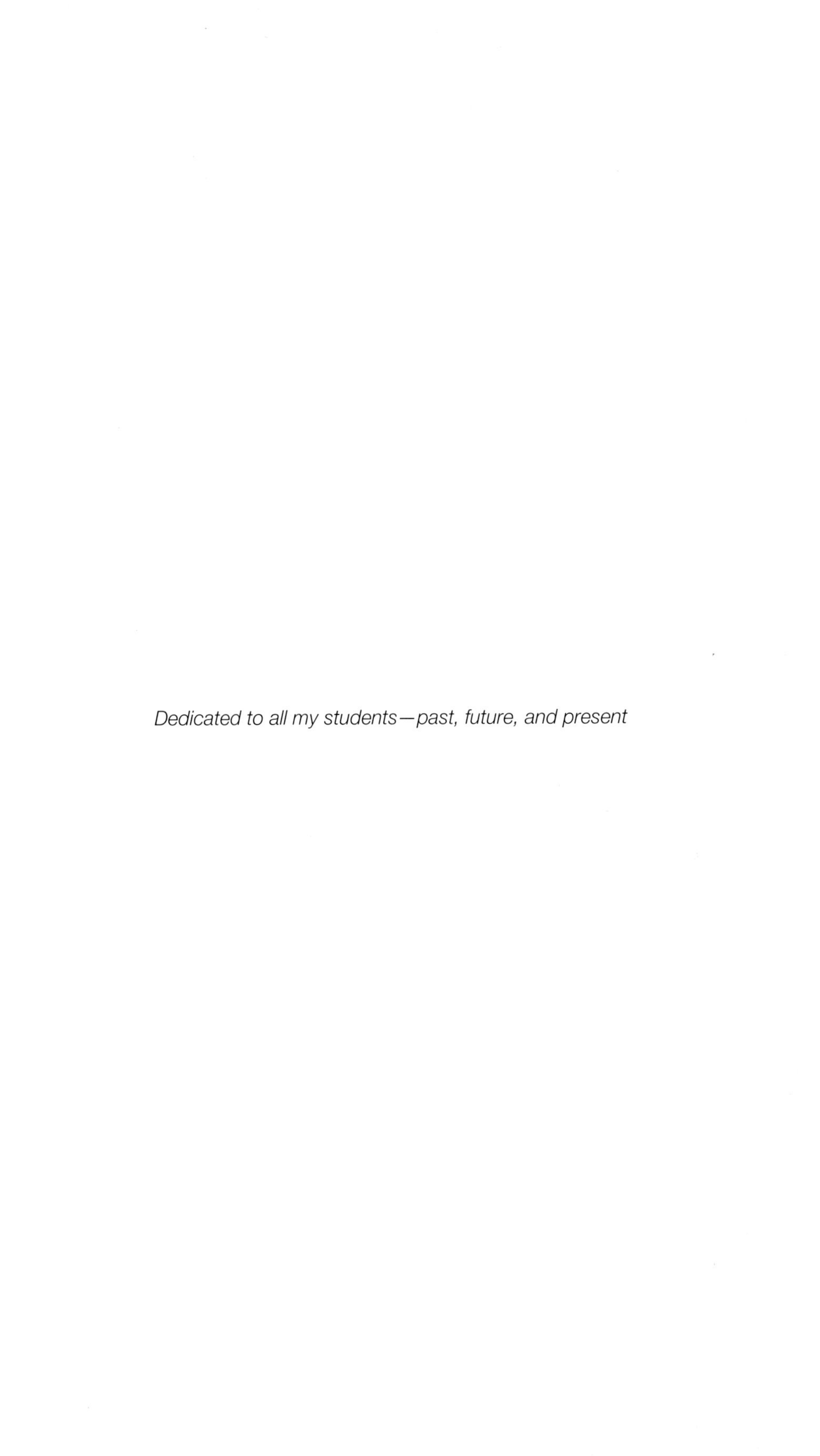

*Dedicated to all my students — past, future, and present*

# Contents

# Note on the Author

Dr. Giovanni Aloi is an author, educator, and curator specializing in the representation of nature and the environment in art. He is the Editor-in-Chief of *Antennae: The Journal of Nature in Visual Culture*. Aloi is the author of *Art & Animals* (2011), *Speculative Taxidermy: Natural History, Animal Surfaces, and Art in the Anthropocene* (2018), *Why Look at Plants? The Vegetal Emergence in Contemporary Art* (2019), and *Lucian Freud – Herbarium* (2019), and the editor of *Posthumanism in Art and Science* (2020), *Vegetal Entwinements in Philosophy and Art* (2023), *Estado Vegetal: Performance and Plant Thinking* (2023), *Botanical Revolutions* (2025) and *Lawn* (2025). Aloi has contributed to BBC radio and PBS TV, worked at Whitechapel Art Gallery and Tate Galleries in London, and is currently USA correspondent for *Esse Magazine*. He has curated exhibitions in the US and Europe, and is co-editor of the University of Minnesota Press series *Art after Nature*.

This work allowed me to channel my anger – not only at the great loss of MLK Jr., but at the lack of representation of Black artists, especially Black women artists. I was an artist, but I still needed a job so I could pay my mortgage and put my girls through college. I worked as a social worker, designed enamelware and jewelry with Curtis Tann, and did some costume designs for the Inner City Cultural Center. I taught and lectured and traveled, but I always still made my art. I've never been an artist for the sake of making art to sell. I just like to do what I want and if it sells, fine.[1]

**Betye Saar, 2021**

The way I see it, you can either spend your life pretending you're something you're not, in the hope that deception will earn you a spot in bed next to the roses and dahlias and other floral fancypants; or you can sprout right where you are. Take root like you mean it. Laugh and grit your teeth and cast your seed and bloom your bloom because *you* know it's beautiful. That slash of sunlight you worked so hard to reach will be all the sweeter because you earned it. You chocked back the poison sprayed down on you; you dodged the spades and blades bent on turning you under. You grew stronger through it all.[2]

**Luke Ruggenberg, 2020**

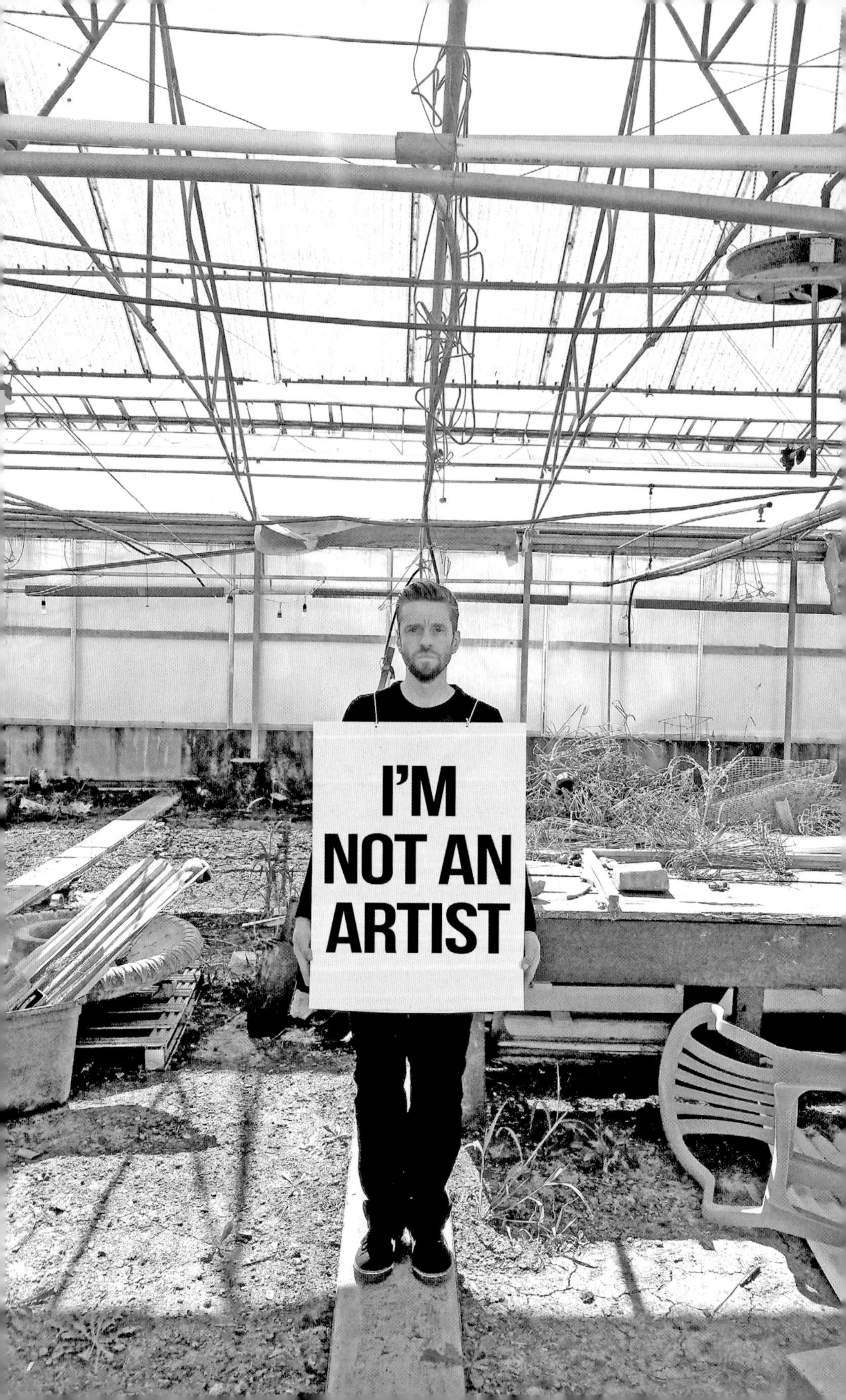

I'M
NOT AN
ARTIST

# Introduction

After hours spent tantalizing each other in the dead of night, two leopard slugs (*Limax maximus*) crawl up a tree and curl into a tight hug. Only then, together, they secrete a viscous thread from which they suspend in mid-air. Clutching over the abyss—love-trapezists in the dark—they gently twirl. As they gain speed, white, translucent organs flare out from the sides of their bodies, tightly intertwine, and slowly unfold into the shape of peony petals. Leopard snails are hermaphrodites. Sperm trickles through the mucous membranes. Both snails will carry eggs. In unison, just as quickly as they unfolded, the reproductive organs retract. The whirling slows as the hug unwinds. Strained, they let go and fall to the ground.

*  *  *

A small mound of blueberries, a cluster of white shells, Coca-Cola bottle caps, a scatter of teal petals, and shards of glass form a constellation surrounding a tall structure intricately woven from twigs. Shimmering in the dappled light that filters down through the eucalyptus canopy, the colors shine amid the earthy tones of the forest floor like an unfinished Byzantine mosaic—vibrant accents arranged to attract attention in a world where chromatic exuberance could spell death. Although little seems to happen at first, the artificer of this architectural marvel returns to tidy things up and add more found objects to his Derek Jarman-esque garden. Dressed in olive-gray and tan plumage, crowned by a fierce, bright orange crest, *Amblyornis subalaris*—also known as the striped gardener bowerbird—begins work on his plot at the earliest signs of spring.

Each bird has a pointedly personal sense of style. Composition and color palettes vary from individual to individual. Like the gardens we tend, those arranged by bowerbirds are a kind of self-portrait—mirrors of personality, character, and inclination. But the bowerbird's garden is not simply a secret retreat. The bird arranges and composes with an audience in mind. Male rivals keep a close eye on each other's creations. They can get jealous, or sometimes even flirty. Theft of ornaments is not uncommon and in extreme cases vandalism occurs, too. Once everything is set, female bowerbirds stop by to appraise the skills and sophistication of prospective partners. If suitably seduced by the arrangement, a female might take a closer look. Encouraged, the male bursts into a frenzied choreography of desire. But female bowerbirds are discerning connoisseurs—more often than not, they glance over, preen their feathers, and fly away.

**Image 1 (facing page).** Giovanni Aloi, *I'm Not an Artist*, 2019, photo concept Giovanni Aloi, photography Chris Hunter. © Giovanni Aloi

# Animals Don't Make Art

"Do animals make art?" This question annoyingly resurfaces with impeccable regularity in popular culture. Western philosophy and art history have never been in doubt: the answer is no. And the odd chimpanzee, elephant, pig, and even dolphin who've painted questionable abstract canvases—admittedly with some commercial success—haven't changed that verdict one bit.[1]

Despite our growing acceptance that humans are animals (as proposed by Darwin in *The Descent of Man*, 1871), many of us still find that idea demeaning.[2] Faced with the truth, we prefer to settle for a more comfortable iteration of the concept: if we humans *are* indeed animals then we certainly are the best of all species, always, at everything—no doubt about it. The idea that animal intelligence can compare, or even exceed, ours poses an enormous threat to our inflated human egos. The "animals don't make art" claim is simply a manifestation of this profound insecurity. What's worse is that, over time, it has been used to sanctify art as an exclusively human, and highly ennobling, activity. The assumption is that other animals don't make art because they lack talent, skills, and self-reflexivity. Their instincts entrap them. We believe that animals are endlessly enslaved by their biological needs. So, where does that leave us, human-animals, and our presumed exceptionalism?

Scientists have debunked these misconceptions for over a century, but they continue to proliferate among art historians. For a telling example, look no further than Laurie Schneider Adams's *The Methodologies of Art* (1996), which, in its introduction, boldly claims: "All the creative arts—including the visual arts—separate the human from the nonhuman."[3]

According to Schneider, spider webs and bird nests are the result of some mysterious genetic programming. These stupendous engineering feats are, according to her, made without any real clue, observation, or consideration—animals simply don't know what they are doing. Schneider, who has never studied birds or arachnids, even goes so far as to claim that animals have no understanding of their environments.[4] This could not be further from the truth: spiders measure distances (without tape measures), tie and cut threads (without knives), and fling themselves into the air to secure supporting web-strands to branches and other scaffolds. Their materials are wholly bio-crafted, produced by a special set of glands. What can a human build only with a substance produced from their glands? We idolize the embodied evolutionary genius that has given us opposable thumbs but we dismiss the same process when it has fashioned spider's backs and bird's beaks into incredibly apt weaving instruments.

Without hands or the aid of machinery (created by their ancestors), a bird can build a nest in two days. Thousands of twigs, hair, fibers, grass blades, and artificial materials are carefully sourced, transported, and woven into place. Now, think of the cursing that accompanied the assemblage of that IKEA bookcase . . . Crafting webs or nests requires discernment, not to mention the ability to judge the suitability of a location and its exposure to the elements, as well as considering safety from predators. Animals don't just build nests anywhere at random, hoping for the best. Of course, sometimes their judgment, like ours, can be off. But that's another story . . .

Art historians have for centuries championed the fictitious notion that the "artistic impulse"—as some like to call it—is innate in the human: a godly quality we call "genius." In animals, the same quality is called "instinct": a "programmed behavior." Seemingly innate creative expression elevates humans, but it reduces animals to unreasoning machines. Even if it appears at first peripheral to the subject of this book, I contend that this deeply biased perspective is actually central to the issues that plague the art world today and that predetermine the societal roles artists are confined to play.

Let's strip the picture of its contextual frame: the leopard slugs we encountered a few pages ago, in essence, stage a performance piece complete with suspense, climatic peaks, and a dramatic finale worthy of Martha Graham Dance Company or Shen Wei's conceptual prowess. As Deleuze and Guattari had already remarked in 1991, the bowerbird acts like an artist—we could go as far as claiming—in the style of Elsa Baroness von Freytag-Loringhoven, Kurt Schwitters, or Betye Saar who regularly made art with found objects.[5] Or even like experimental film director Derek Jarman, who in the late 1980s constructed a whole garden, around his Dungeness cottage, out of washed-ashore things.[6]

But as much as I disagree with Adams as well as other art historians and philosophers who intentionally devalue the creative intelligence of animals,[7] in the end, I must concede that perhaps animals *don't* make art. At least not in the sense that we now conceive art in the West. Not because they are not intelligent enough or because they lack consciousness—but just because art is a human construct in which animals truly have no interest. Animals don't make art because what we call art today is the material sedimentation of cultural, historical, and economic relations. But perhaps more importantly, because Western art has become an inbred system of fetishization that animals would not know what to do with. The cabinets, the galleries, the museums, the collections—at the core of Western art, as film critic André Bazin argued, lies a "mummy complex":[8] the preservation of beauty and youth, the desperate desire to stop the passing of time. If one thing truly separates human from animal creativity, it is our positioning toward the rest of the natural world. Animal creativity is steeped into the *now* of the seasons' flow. In opposition, our determination to extrapolate ourselves from nature's rhythms, to immortalize, has alienated us and it has greatly reduced our creative potential. It has crafted and perpetuated the figure of the artist's genius as a lone, self-obsessed monolith. Both outcomes, I argue in this book, are detrimental to the very core of what bowerbird, snail, spider, and artist have in common: *creativity*.

The exceptionalism that Western thinkers have attributed to art has been implicitly utilized not just to belittle the inventiveness of animals, but also to devalue the art forms of numerous civilizations, from Africa to Asia, Oceania, and South America, that were previously considered "primitive" and thus less than human (when human only meant white, male, and preferably cisgender).[9] The misogyny and racism that still pervade the art world today are ingrained in this genealogy rooted in colonialist ideologies. Over time, colonialism and capitalism have deliberately mistaken creativity with art and art with creativity. The two are not the same, although there can be no art without creativity. Creativity always comes first. Creativity is the driving force that governs all life on Earth. Only if we can bring ourselves to abandon the supremacy of the myth of art as a mark of anthropocentric distinction, new ways of being an artist will become visible to us. Dismantling the myth of the artist is our first step.

## Artist Mythologies, Genealogies, and Responsibilities

*I'm Not an Artist* is a book about art, artists, art history, and the art market as well as the role that creativity plays in our lives and how our creative potential becomes limited as we trap ourselves in antiquated power systems and superfluous professional identities. Current discourses on identity politics, diversity and inclusion, multidisciplinary approaches, collaborative practices, and the growing critique of the colonialist foundations that underpin our cultural institutions, have radically changed our conception of art. It is now time for creative individuals to engage in an important and honest process of self-critical reconsideration.

Curator Okwui Enwezor noted that radical questionings of the artistic personality tend to coincide with social and political crises that "force reappraisals of conditions of production, re-evaluation of the nature of artistic work, and reconfiguration of the position of the artist in relation to economic, social and political institutions."[10] The Covid-19 pandemic and the worldwide social unrest that followed George Floyd's murder are without doubt the kind of epochal turning point Enwezor refers to. The devastating cultural earthquakes that have rocked the art world in the wake of the Hamas/Israel war are a further demonstration that a deep cultural crisis is still in full swing.[11] It is in the aftermath of the devastation caused by these events that new and old paths might become visible. It is in the trail of destruction that we might redirect our ambitions and envision new futures. But will we seize the opportunity to build the nonelitist, multicultural, and fairer art world we truly need? Will we dare to forsake the virtue signaling of social media posts to finally dismantle the ideologies that, up until now, have defined our life journeys, aspirations, identities, and beliefs? Unfortunately, amid widespread dissent, it seems that institutions are simply keen to return to business as usual. Modernism was haunted by the question, "What is art?" Postmodernism resolutely asked, "What is an institution?" Today, honestly asking ourselves "What is an artist?" might just help us reconfigure art for the twenty-first century along with its institutions.

The word "artist" is the tip of the iceberg. Much more than a label or a title, it is an ideologically, dogmatically, and discursively overloaded archetypal myth. Centuries ago in the West, it simply defined the identity of a white man who painted or sculpted for the church or the very rich. But what does it mean today? What does one hope to accomplish by becoming "an artist"? When can one legitimately claim to have become one? Is it a full-time job, a vocation, a lifetime pursuit? Who is a failed artist? What is artistic success? Is it not perplexing that over the past century we have come to accept that a urinal tipped on its side can be art, but we still cannot get our heads out of that paper bag we call "the artist"?

Archetypal myths are primordial—legends that hold enormous power over us. Like clouds, they invite us to look up into the sky but cast dark shadows onto the ground. They conceal reality. As timeless stories, myths anchor our dreams to a past that never truly was, while promising impossible futures. Carl Jung, the psychoanalyst who deeply delved into the intimate relationship between art and religion, argued that myths satisfy the psychological need for contact with the "collective unconscious"—a kind of hive-mind in which our human instincts and ancient core ideas deposit and sediment.[12] Residing within the collective unconscious, Jung identified twelve mythical archetypes that we refer to as models—"universal images that have existed since the remotest times."[13] Alongside the mythical figure of the mother, the wise old man, the caregiver, the outlaw, and others stands that of the "creator/artist." There's truth in Jung's theorization, but ironically the foundations of his theory are not based on firsthand observation. He wrote:

> Analysis of artists consistently shows not only the strength of the creative impulse arising from the unconscious but also its capricious and willful character. The biographies of great artists make it abundantly clear that the creative urge is often so imperious that it battens onto their humanity and yokes everything to the service of the work, even at the cost of ordinary health and human happiness.[14]

Myths only breed myth—Jung's artist myth is crafted out of biographies. As a result, his mythologized artist-model is a terrible cliché: a timeless, mercurial egotist, driven by uncontrollable instincts masterminded by authors and poets. Biographies are nothing more than dramatized fiction with, in the best-case scenario, a backbone or at least a rib or two, of truth. But their real mission is to immortalize and aggrandize. From murkiness to glitzy, they often intentionally omit the grit of the administrative banality that all artists can't escape through their rise to fame. The Romantic myth of the artist as a tortured, misunderstood, and nonconformist genius-rebel who stands outside society is a work of fiction. Art historians, collectors, novelists, and more recently film directors have carved, embroidered, and perpetuated the stereotypical idea of the artist simply because it sells. So why is this myth dangerous? Myths have a tendency to naturalize—their legendary roots reach so deep into our minds that they eventually camouflage as truth. They sediment in our thoughts from a young age and, before we realize it, they have molded the landscapes of our future.

*I'm Not an Artist* desacralizes the mythical figure of the artist, not as a simple gesture of deliberate spite but because the artists I admire the most have already rejected this title, or at least its myth, and its archetypal aura in the knowledge that it hinders—rather than enhances—their creative potential. I am not the first (and certainly won't be the last) to take issue with the mythical notion of the artist. "Every man is an artist,"[15] Joseph Beuys proudly proclaimed in the 1950s in an attempt to dismantle the persistent conception of exclusivity associated with it. But discontent predates the radicalisms of post-Second World War, revolutionary conceptualists. Left-wing artists John Heartfield and George Grosz were among the very first to wish the term "artist" gone as early as 1920:

> He who wishes his business with the brush to be regarded as a divine mission is a scab. Today the cleaning of a gun by a Red soldier is of greater significance than the entire metaphysical output of all the painters. The concepts of art and artist are an invention of the bourgeoisie and their position in the state can only be on the side of those who rule, i.e. the bourgeois caste. The title "artist" is an insult. The designation "art" is an annulment of human equality. The deification of the artist is equivalent to self-deification.[16]

These words ring true today as global economies struggle to recover from the pandemic, as social justice finally gains impetus, wars threaten global stability, and cultural institutions worldwide crumble. In this context, appraising the power of the word "artist" is part of a broader process of decolonization. Decolonizing knowledge, institutions, and practices entails a thorough and often complex deconstructive approach aimed at identifying the concealed legacy of colonialist ideologies that we still carry with us: sexism, racism, discrimination, patriarchy, hetero-/cis-normativity, and settler-mentalities among others.[17]

Archetypal labels embody all this and therefore, today, they have become uncomfortable. This was clearly expressed by the director of the 18th Venice Biennale of Architecture, 2023, Lesley Lokko. In the press release, Lokko said:

> We have deliberately chosen to frame participants as 'practitioners', not 'architects' and/or 'urbanists', 'designers', 'landscape architects', 'engineers' or 'academics' because it is our contention that the rich, complex conditions of both Africa and a rapidly hybridising world call for a different and broader understanding of the term 'architect'.[18]

Let's then imagine a world without artists! Identity-related labels define who we are and limit what we can do. Some might claim that the "artist" title, like a magic cloak, gives them license to do what others can't. This might be true in some environments. But the word still entraps just as much as it might free. Artistic expressions are the fiber of our lives. They help us rethink, reenvision, and articulate problematic legacies in new and constructive ways. However, artistic expressions have, like almost everything else in our lives, been packaged, commodified, and branded. If we acknowledge that criticality has become a core value in contemporary art, then we cannot afford to ignore the colonialist and capitalist systems ingrained in the myth of the artist that still permeates the minds and identities of so many of us.

Although it wasn't necessarily born in the West, the myth of the artist was institutionalized and commodified there in ways that today globally define museums, schools, books, music, films, adverts, fashion, as well as the art that younger generations can and want to make. The boldness of Michelangelo, Leonardo's genius, Caravaggio's mercuriality, Monet's obsessiveness, Munch's alienation, Van Gogh's torturdness, Kahlo's vulnerability, and Basquiat's anger—the artist myth is a deadly cocktail. How can we truly position ourselves in a critical way if we remain unaware of the cultural genealogies that we implicitly perpetuate? To blindly endorse the artist model means to subscribe to its values, its histories, and its exclusionary and discriminatory approaches.

Institutional critique has run its course and yielded comparatively little of concrete usefulness.[19] In the 1960s, artists fiercely accused museums, galleries, and the market of "cultural confinement," but an intricate game of self-interest never allowed them to completely break free. The same is still true today. The top-tier museums, blue-chip commercial galleries, and art schools have also entrapped creativity into a game of toxic and narcissistic dependencies. The financial crisis and mass layoffs early in the pandemic revealed the extent to which crucial issues have been allowed to fester since the 1990s. Not only, since then, have museums and universities failed to sufficiently diversify staff, programs, and collections and adequately represent diversity, but their directors enjoy the benefits of corporate pay scales while educators, curators, and the vast majority of artists—who actually create content—scrape the bottom of the barrel.

Today, the mainstream art world is defined by deeply unjust, inequitable, and exploitative neoliberal ideals and logics. Insiders know all too well that, despite its efforts to portray itself as a compassionate and benevolent environment, beneath the surface the art world is dominated by reckless and greedy institutions and investors that act like corporations. How did we get here? Why do fierce criticism and accusations only result in very slow, rather than momentous and radical, change? At least in part, artists, curators, and art historians are to blame. Enough of accusing institutions as if they were untamable monsters. We must also hold ourselves accountable. It is time to recognize that, as a creative force, we have actively contributed to the politics of exploitation, extraction, and exclusion that have shaped the art world. We must be the change we want to see.

## From Myth to Ecologies

*I'm Not an Artist* emerges from my experience as an LGBTQIA+ educator, curator, editor, and maker who has studied and worked in higher education as well as some of the most influential museums in the United Kingdom and the United States for over twenty years. I am an immigrant, first-generation college student of working-class background who, out of necessity, has always worked full-time to support his studies. Much of the knowledge I share in this book was developed through firsthand engagement in the mainstream art world and learning the workings of the art market directly from industry specialists. I've seen artists rising to stardom, but I've also watched students and colleagues damage their lives (and the lives of others) in pursuit of unachievable or antiquated career models as they blindly followed the myth of the artist. Hand on heart, much of this unnecessary disappointment is caused by art schools. My colleague James Elkins has written extensively on how art schools fail art students. His polemical *Why Art Cannot be Taught* (2001), which I highly recommend, takes to task the shortcomings of institutional art teaching, particularly focusing on the structure and function of evaluation processes that end up hindering creativity.[20]

While Elkins's book looks inward at the flawed pedagogical approaches of art schools, *I'm Not an Artist* looks outward at how art schools fail to adequately prepare and guide artists, art historians, and curators to understand who they can be in the contemporary art world. Students are never taught how the market truly works, what successful artists do to lead rewarding, long-lasting, and financially sustainable careers, how being a professional artist entails substantial amounts of administrative pragmatism and diplomatic maneuvering, how networking really works . . .

A coincidence? Over the past ten years, many art schools around the world have closed, drastically downsized or merged. Enrolment figures are down. Art schools are in crisis.[21] The issues I address in this book have emerged, in part, from conversations with colleagues and class discussions with students. It is from them that I have learned how uncomfortable they feel with an outdated artist label they are now paying exorbitant fees to acquire. As a nobiliary title and badge of honor, the title "artist" today conjures up self-indulgent and aggrandizing stereotypes that often reflect onto terribly arrogant attitudes—purity, rarity, and preciousness—ideas that crumble in a world stifled by glaring and no longer ignorable social injustice. Nowadays, the widely held belief that an artist is freer (whatever that means) or more authentic than other creative people seems steeped in narcissism. That the artist is implicitly a nonconformist rebel sensitive to things others remain pathologically blind to reeks of pompous delusion. Why do we continue to implicitly fetishize the romantic myth of the artist in popular culture, allowing its clichés to determine our creative potential, since it belongs to the obsolete category of colonial heroes?

*I'm Not an Artist* is written for anyone who might be considering a career in the arts—aspiring artists first and foremost, but also art historians, curators, or art critics—or who already have a career that's not yet working out as they hoped. Or for current students who feel confused about their art school experience; for parents who are thinking about remortgaging their homes to send their late teens to art school; and for anyone wishing to support them in an informed and realistic way. If none of the above applies to you (yet) this book is also written as an alternative, accessible, and irreverent introduction to the art world. My hope is that it might empower and help readers to understand and engage with art beyond the trite clichés of mainstream culture. Most importantly, this book explains what the myth of the artist is, how it developed, how it can harm people's lives, and how to avoid it.

In 1973, Joseph Beuys clarified what he meant when he said, "Every man is an artist":

Only art is capable of dismantling the repressive effects of a senile social system that continues to totter along the deathline: to dismantle in order to build A SOCIAL ORGANISM AS A WORK OF ART. This most modern art discipline – Social Sculpture/Social Architecture – will only reach fruition when every living person becomes a creator, a sculptor, or architect of the social organism.[22]

Beuys's conception of the social organism implied an important perspective that aimed to desacralize the idea of the artist as a romantic hero in favor of a new social model of collaboration and interconnection. Unfortunately, the art world has been eager to commodify, rather than assimilate Beuys's ideas. This is why this book explains the art market and the art world as an "ecosystem." This approach is derived from my research and publications on the subject of nature and ecology in art,[23] as well as from the work of prominent contemporary thinkers like Donna Haraway, Bell Hooks, Amitav Gosh, Robin Wall Kimmerer, Anna Tsing, Vandana Shiva, Timothy Morton, and others who have over the past couple of decades decentralized the fictitious certainties we have inherited from colonialism to make room for new models of being in this world.[24]

Already in 1992, French philosopher Félix Guattari had clearly evidenced the all-important links that tie environmental, social, and mental ecologies. In *Chaosmosis: An Ethico-aesthetic Paradigm*, Guattari exhorts:

> How do we change mentalities, how do we reinvent social practices that would give back to humanity—if it ever had it—a sense of responsibility, not only for its own survival, but equally for the future of all life on the planet, for animal and vegetable species, likewise for incorporeal species such as music, the arts, cinema, the relation with time, love and compassion for others, the feeling of fusion at the heart of the Cosmos?[25]

So much is at stake in this essential and desperately needed process of reconfiguration. Thinking ecologically means to prioritize conceptions of collaboration, interdependency, and reciprocity. It means to acknowledge that, in ecosystems, all "participants" play equally important and indispensable roles. Ecosystemic conceptions help us reshape notions of relativity, scale, and time. Ecosystems are not perfect. They are not stable. We have to relinquish all ideals of purity and perfection—notions dear to the Western classical canon—in order to conceive an ecosystemic art world in which we can all fully and meaningfully exist. Ecosystems are by nature unbalanced, and survival entails struggle, awareness, and adaptation— they are not utopias. Like bacteria, fungi, plants, and animals that dwell in ever-evolving and overlapping worlds, creative individuals must develop a detailed understanding of their environments in order to thrive, especially when circumstances become adverse. Furthermore, ecosystemic notions encourage us to be present and form symbiotic connections with others, rather than conforming to institutional hierarchies. As Timothy Morton puts it, "the ecological thought is the thinking of interconnectedness"[26]: it is a process and a becoming; a frame of mind that can allow artists to reposition themselves, their practices, and, in the process, tilt the axis of the art world.

The artist myth, at its core, is anti-ecological; it is thoroughly anthropocentric—it positions the exceptionalism of human genius at the center of the world, alone, and above everything else. It will be impossible to survive in today's ecosystemic art world with the artist myth firmly planted in one's minds. Many artists learn this to their own cost. Understanding the art market is essential to avoid becoming its next victim. Whichever kind of artist one wishes to be, whatever kind of art one makes, there are many ways to have a fulfilling and sustainable creative life. Art school teaches students how to make art but not how to be artists.

## Overview

This book is organized in two parts. You can begin reading from either one. Start from the first to develop your knowledge about the myth of the artist through time and learn what art history books often omit. Canonical art history celebrates artists on the grounds of their influence and artistic innovation. Instead, this book focuses on their ingenuity, industriousness, and the behind-the-scenes strategizing that helped them lead fulfilling careers. In this section, I unashamedly follow the "power and money trail" to deconstruct the myth of the Western artist genius. Aspiring and up-and-coming artists must understand the power of this mould in order to break it and make clear and informed choices about the directions of their careers. I thus map power networks between dealers, collectors, art historians, institutions, and artists to reveal the economic and social structures that have perpetuated the artist's myth. Who crafted the business models others followed and why? Who mythologized who and how? Who reinvented the role of the artist during the last century and to what end? What can less advantaged creative individuals learn from the strategies that made other artists famous?[27]

The second part of the book focuses on the contemporary art world and the contradictions, hypocrisy, and paradoxes that characterize the relationship between artists, the education system, the art market, and money in the age of free infinite content. Often, books on the art market quickly become too technical and indecipherable to the nonexpert.

Toward the end of the book, I discuss the personal challenges and conundrums that creative individuals face today. I break down the capitalist-hierarchical structure that defines the art world in order to reclaim creativity from a system that no longer values it in a genuine sense.

*I'm Not an Artist* concludes with a series of short conversations with contemporary practitioners of all kinds who discuss the myth of the artist and their personal approaches to creativity. In the context of this book, their voices are as important as mine. These conversations were led after this book was written. I wanted their voices to complement or contradict mine, to expand the scope of my argument. Although I boldly pronounce the word "artist" redundant in this book, I purposely refrain from proposing a substitute because I believe that it would be both arrogant and wrong of me to attempt to replace an outmoded paradigm with a new one. Every creative individual, collective, and community is now in charge of crafting new, ever-evolving, and fluid models. I hope that this book will give its readers, especially the younger ones, the confidence to try their hands at creating their own unique models, together. In the end, that's all that counts.

And just to avoid any misunderstanding, this book is not an attempt to tell a global art history. Its predominantly Western focus is intentional and necessary to dismantle the artist's myth. At a time in which emphasis on alternative and neglected histories of art is predominant, this book might seem out of sync with contemporary discourse. However, the opposite is true—the Western myth of the artist haunts artists of all colors, nationalities, and genders around the world. We certainly no longer need to focus on the Western tradition to celebrate its presumed superiority and greatness, but we should not forget it quite as quickly either. Leaving it behind us in a rush will allow it to haunt us for eternity. More deconstruction of its power tropes is needed before we can break free from the myths that still rule the system. In a provocative way, this book is a contribution to that essential and often painful process.

Finally, this book is not against the arts, art schools, or the humanities. The opposite is true: my arguments are born out of the love I have for all the creative individuals I work and collaborate with every day. It is not my intention to dissuade anyone from pursuing a creative career in the arts—I have so far had a highly rewarding one myself. Those who claim that there's no money or future in it are likely ill-informed. But they are right about one thing: there's little payback in the romantic artist model that might lead people to consider this field in the first place. We just need to steer clear of the "A-word." It is toxic. This book is an invitation to reinvent entirely what being an artist means and pursue that, whatever form it might take, with utter conviction. My aim is not to discourage dreaming, but rather to give guidance on how to dream better and safer, and with our eyes wide open.

# Part I

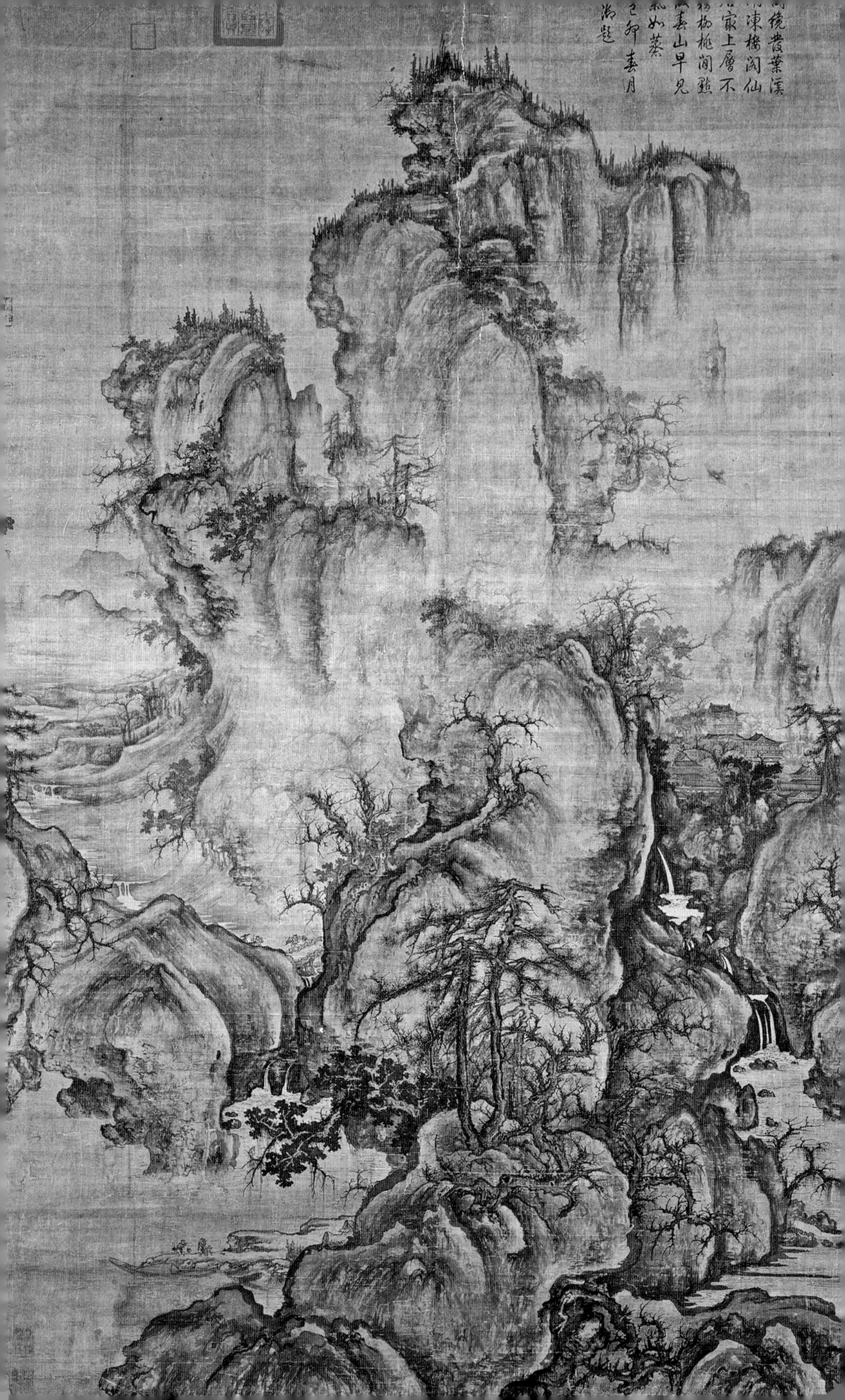
繞蒼葉溪
凍橋閣仙
寂上層不
柏枇間點
叢山早見
和如蒸
己卯春月
御題

# 1 Becoming an artist: Constraints and Freedom

# Words and Visions: The Birth of a Myth

Guo Xi (1020–90 CE) painted at a brightly lit desk by a window. On the left side sat an ornate Duan stone from Guangdong Province. Inksticks made of dried, charred pinewood and resin laced with animal glue lay nearby, waiting to be ground on the top end of the stone and then mixed with water. A small lake of viscous, black ink lay at its center—the reflective surface brimming with creative potential. Nearby were brushes of all sizes—neat clumps of deer, goat, rabbit, and wolf hair tightly fastened to polished bamboo handles. On the desk's right side were seals, paste boxes, brush washers, bowls, and stands. The center was covered in thin sheets of paper made from rice, wheat straw, sandalwood bark, hibiscus stalks, and seaweed. During the Song Dynasty (960–1279 CE), Chinese paper was a sought-after commodity across the lands we today know as Japan, Vietnam, Thailand, and Indonesia.[1] Together, inkstone, brushes, ink, and papers outlined the *wenfang sibao* (Four Treasures of the Scholar's Studio).[2]

Near the top corners were two small porcelain incense burners. Guo Xi often burned agarwood—a healing resin that drips from deep wounds in the heartwood of the aquilaria tree. A dusky scent, accented by a hint of spice, filled the room as he painted in solitude with the utmost concentration.[3]

Like other well-known artists of his time, Guo Xi was a court professional, a member of the literati, who respected the Chinese tradition of monumental landscape painting but also valued innovation. In this period, painting and calligraphy became indissolubly intertwined. Images on scrolls were known as *wu-sheng-shih*, meaning "silent poetry." The same brushes that traced pictograms also outlined the delicate contours of branches, petals, and feathers. Calligraphic brushwork inspired the aesthetic flair of painterly compositions. It is from the poetic entwinements between the two art forms that, at this time, the matrix of the artist myth emerged.[4] From then on, being an artist meant to reveal the *ch'uan-shen*, or "spirit of things"— this skill forever distinguishing the work of the enlightened man from the mere artisan.

The most celebrated Chinese artists of the Northern Song Dynasty (960–1127 CE) were scholar-officials firmly positioned within the intellectual elite (and, not surprisingly for the time, all male). They studied for the imperial examination, an extremely rigorous and lengthy series of tests that only a meager one percent of applicants ever passed. Memorization of Confucian texts, poetry, religion, and literary classics was essential.[5] For those who succeeded, the reward was a higher social status: mandarin.[6] Loyal to the Confucian teaching that the acceptance of limitations leads to happiness, the mandarins advocated for a return to ancient philosophies through the study of calligraphy and painting—something they believed would in turn heal a society they increasingly perceived as corrupt. The literati were well aware of the power of their work.[7] The Chinese "bureaucrat-scholar model" spread to Japan, Korea, and Vietnam, influencing art-making across much of Asia for centuries. Making art became an important mark of cultural and social distinction.

Since the beginning of the Tang Dynasty (618–907 CE), neo-Confucianism affirmed the centrality of male authority in both government and culture. Women were fetishized as beautiful and fragile objects—their feet bound with cloth permanently restricted their movements as well as their minds. The popular Chinese saying "A woman without talent has virtue" eloquently captures the idea. Fathers, husbands, then sons: women were first and foremost the possession of the men in their lives. As in the West, most women were systematically excluded from publicly practicing art, and when they did, their work was implicitly deemed inferior.[8] The emperor's concubines were an exception—as in Japan and India, they could paint a narrow moralizing repertoire of illustrations like the ones in *Ladies' Classic of Filial Piety* (*Nü hsiao ching*).[9] On rare occasions, women learned painting under the tutelage of their open-minded, literati husbands. It is under these circumstances that Guan Daosheng (1262–1319 CE) rose to unprecedented fame. Guan's father encouraged her talent from an early age and Zhao Mengfu, her husband, helped her study traditional styles. She started by painting orchids—a symbol of purity, fragility, and rarity that symbolized female virtue. But it was her bamboo paintings that sealed her status as a truly great artist.[10] Bamboo was traditionally a masculine emblem. The plant's ability to bend without breaking and its resilience to the winter cold incarnated masculine virtue.

An inscription left on a scroll reveals that Guan fully grasped the groundbreaking political importance of her work: "To play with brush and ink is a masculine sort of thing to do, yet I made this painting. Wouldn't someone say that I have transgressed? How despicable; how despicable."[11]

Both Guo Xi and Guan Daosheng reflect the ideals of Zhang Yanyuan, a Tang Dynasty art historian who felt that art must respect morals and ethics, and that uniqueness and innovation are central to it. The author of the first-ever survey of Chinese art, Zhang mostly wrote biographies. This choice set the blueprint for what became the foundation of the artist's myth through a form of fetishization that elevated the artist on the grounds of their unique personalities and unparalleled innate gifts.[12]

The artist as a cultural elite. The artist as poet. The rule-breaker artist-hero. The artist confined by their gender. The artist-intellectual as hermit. The self-fashioned pioneer. The noble artist who should not be mistaken for a craftsman. All these facets that shaped the lives of Guo Xi and Guan Daosheng, and of those that followed, compose the contradictory portrait of the artist as anything but free. Although the blueprint of the artist's myth that haunts the contemporary art world has developed in the West, it is in China that its early roots can be most easily discerned in the intimate relationship that binds word and image: the words woven into images by artists; those that art historians crafted to engrave nuanced truths into mythologies, and those the viewer endeavors to decipher upon beholding the artwork.

## From Medieval Anonymity to Renaissance Divinity

Just as in China, so in the West, women were categorically excluded from making art. Recent research has highlighted the important, and often overlooked, roles wealthy

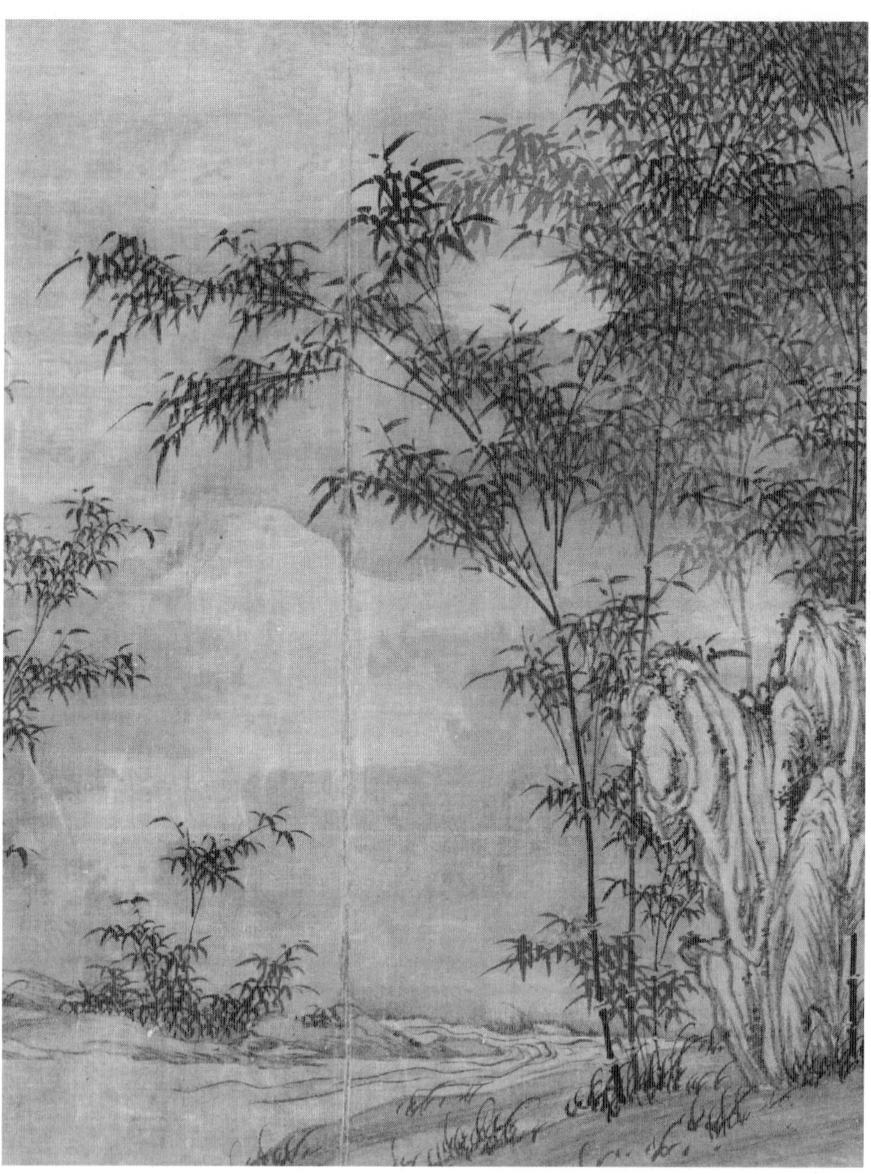

Image 3. Guan Daosheng, *Bamboo Groves in Mist and Rain*, Section of a handscroll, Indian ink on paper, 1308, National Palace Museum, Taipei. Public Domain

women played in the patronage of art and architecture across Europe—contributions that in the context of medieval creativity amounted to much more than simply financing works of art. In fact, the distinct roles of commissioner and artist, with which we have become familiar, only truly split around the seventeenth and eighteenth centuries.[13] During the Middle Ages (476CE to the beginning of the 13th century) and Renaissance

(13th century to the 1520s), patrons paid for materials; thus they also had control over theme and composition. How much gold, blue, or purple should be used—the most expensive colors—was up to them, not the painter. At this time, works of art largely expressed the client's taste rather than the character and genius of the maker.

As the first art historian of the West, Giorgio Vasari, tells us, medieval artists were trained to subdue, rather than inflate, their egos. Medieval art making was a collaborative endeavor—anonymous votive offerings; humble gestures designed to perpetuate God's glory.[14]

Painters, carvers, and sculptors had been, for centuries, considered lowly manual laborers. As such, unlike their counterparts in the Chinese literati, European artists often emerged from humble backgrounds. Art was made in the hustle and bustle of workshops—the same places where tables, chairs, and chests of drawers were hammered together. However, in time, medieval education split between the mechanical and the liberal arts. Mechanical art emphasized collaboration; the liberal arts elevated the individual. These liberal arts were organized around four subjects concerned with structures and measures (arithmetic, astronomy, geometry, and music) and three based on language (grammar, logic, and rhetoric).[15]

It was in around 1400 that Florentine artist Cennino Cennini began to advocate for the inclusion of painting and sculpture among the liberal arts.[16] His *Libro dell'Arte* (The Book of Art) was the first handbook for the medieval apprentice. It explained materials, methods, and techniques essential to professional development. Cennini's work elevated art from the dusty floors of workshops into the ranks of intellectualism. And, like Zhang Yanyuan five hundred years before, Cennini exhorted craftsmen to pursue innovation.[17]

About 150 years after Cennini's book, Giorgio Vasari's *Le Vite de'più eccellenti pittori, scultori, e architettori* (The Lives of the Most Excellent Painters, Sculptors, and Architects) laid the foundations of the "myth of the artist-genius" in the modern West. Constrained by technical limitations to publish a book without images of artworks, Vasari, like Zhang, harnessed the enthralling narrative powers of biography to keep his readers keen. Interlacing truth with fiction, and sprinkling every other page with gossip, he wove an unprecedently heroic tapestry of artistic exceptionalism. By emphasizing the educational journey of each artist, Vasari refashioned the manual aptitude of the craftsman into the learned and refined skill of the artist. The myth of the Western artist was born, emboldened in the very structure of Vasari's book.

Major artists were given their own chapters. Lesser-known ones were grouped together. This tiered structure instilled a competitive protagonism that still pervades the art world today. No longer the anonymous collaborator in the workshop, the artist was immortalized as a unique prodigy—their personality, not just their works, a sign of social distinction. According to Vasari, Raphael was modest and well-mannered. But Michelangelo truly embodied the soul of the Renaissance artist: equally excelling in painting, architecture, and sculpture, he was a gift from God—his mission to show

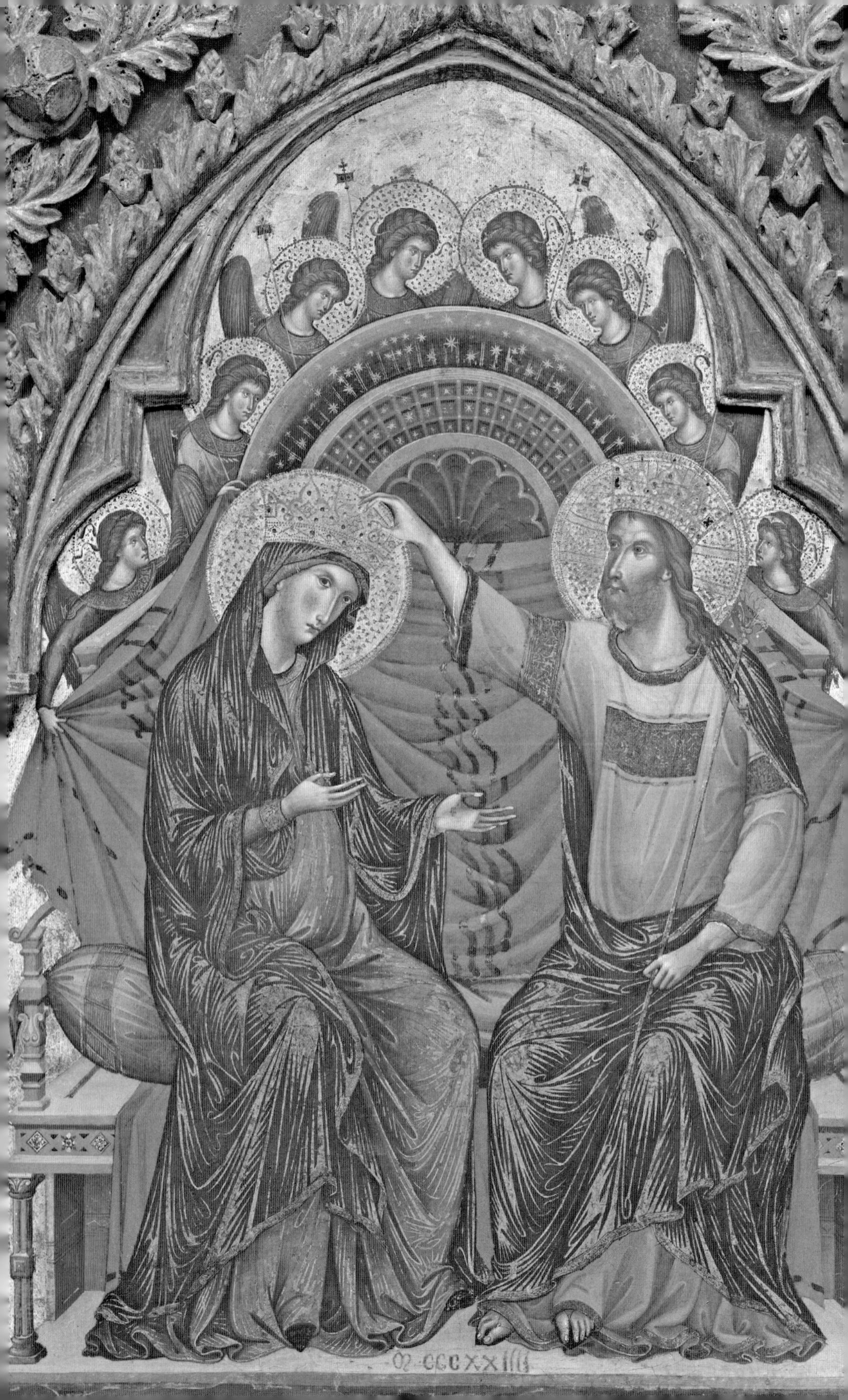
M · CCC · XXIIII

other artists how art could approach divine perfection.[18] There exists a profound and often overlooked link between the written word, art, and religion that played an important role in the canonization of the artist as a divine being. In the eleventh canto of "Purgatory" from the *Divine Comedy*, Dante and Virgil meet a group of people condemned to carry heavy stones on their backs: the prideful. Among them is Oderisi da Gubbio (d. 1299), a miniaturist who in life was motivated by competition and fame more than love for his work. Oderisi tells him how the fame of Cimabue (d. 1302) was swiftly supplanted by Giotto whose solid figures relegated the flatness of the Byzantine tradition to the past. Sorrowfully, the artist admits to Dante that he has squandered his life since fame is fleeting.

God, wealth, fame—to some, becoming an artist was a way to have it all. In a culture where devotion was seen as a vital virtue by the aristocracy, an artist like Giotto, who painted Saint Francis with the fullest humanity, would by association acquire celestial attributes. Michelangelo's Sistine Chapel drove that point home like nothing else, further endowing the myth of the artist with a near-godly aura.[19]

Beginning with Cennini and finishing with Vasari, the extraordinary transformation from humble craftsman to otherworldly artist-genius took a little over 150 years. If the purpose of the medieval craftsmen was to cast light on God's master plan, that of the Renaissance artist was to breathe immortal life directly into it.

## Shamanism: The Root of the Artist's Superiority Complex

The idea of the divine artist was only rediscovered and repackaged, not crafted from scratch, during the Renaissance. Artists had been central to magical rituals and divining sacrifices for millennia, as shamans. Female shamans, or "shamankas," existed among the Tungus people, the Buryats, Yakuts, Ostyaks, and among the Kamchadals in Siberia and Northeast Asia, in Tibet and Afghanistan and ancient China and Japan, South Africa, and the Philippines and the Western coasts of the Americas.[20] Among North American Indigenous people, "medicine women" were as common as medicine men especially among the Dakotas and the Creeks, and both also were powerful presences in Inuit cultures.[21]

Over 30,000 years ago, prehistoric shamans drew images on cave walls to tell stories from the otherworld, speak with animals, heal, and escort the souls of the dead on their final journey. Hallucinogenic-induced trances and ecstatic mystical experiences granted access to invisible realms. The shaman translated the evanescence of a transcendental state of mind into a decipherable language for the common mortals.[22] Carving, drawing, dancing, performing, and narrating: shamans were the first multimedia artists in the world.

Image 4 (facing page). **Master of the Washington Coronation, *The Coronation of the Virgin*, tempera on poplar panel, 108.3 × 79 × 1.5 cm (42 5/8 × 31 1/8 × 9/16 in.), 1324, Samuel H. Kress Collection, National Gallery of Art, Washington DC. Public Domain**

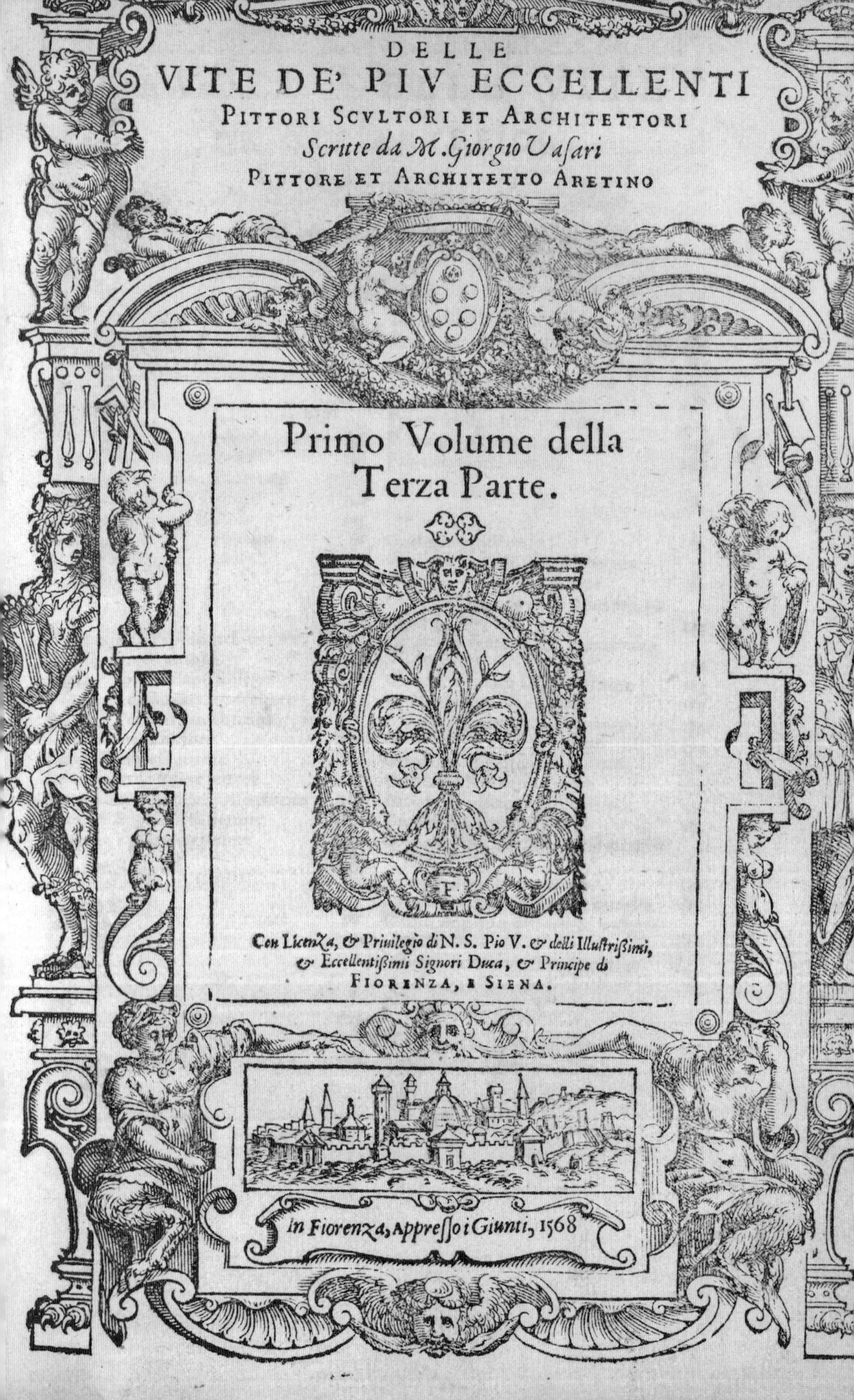

DELLE
VITE DE' PIV ECCELLENTI
PITTORI SCVLTORI ET ARCHITETTORI
Scritte da M. Giorgio Vasari
PITTORE ET ARCHITETTO ARETINO

Primo Volume della
Terza Parte.

Con Licenza, & Priuilegio di N. S. Pio V. & delli Illustrissimi,
& Eccellentissimi Signori Duca, & Principe di
FIORENZA, E SIENA.

In Fiorenza, Appresso i Giunti, 1568.

Medicine men, shamans, and witch doctors held highly regarded roles in their societies. Being a shaman was a matter of mystical vocation. Surviving terrible adversity, such as a life-threatening illness or near-death experience, enhanced the credibility needed to be one.[23] The metamorphosis from common mortal to quasi-divine being took place under the guidance of an expert shaman. Adepts of the supernatural, shamanic vision penetrated reality beyond surfaces and across time.[24] Perhaps more significantly, the art they created reminded everyone of their uniqueness. Two characteristics unite the shaman, the African artist, the Italian Renaissance painter, and the Chinese mandarin: their creativity and their desire to elevate their social standing through art.

## The Rise of the Artist Star: Myth, Power, and Money

So how did ancient artist-shamans lose their prestige over time? Largely responsible for the setback in the West was Plato's theorization of art. Plato saw painting, sculpture, and performance as reductions of reality. In his eyes, artisans and craftsmen—who produced functional objects—were more valuable. According to Plato, art was superficial, because

> a painter will paint a cobbler, carpenter or any other artist, though he knows nothing of their arts; and, if he is a good artist, he may deceive children or simple persons, when he shows them his picture of a carpenter from a distance, and they will fancy that they are looking at a real carpenter.[25]

If works of art only provide false knowledge of reality, then all artists are nothing more than masters of deceit: liars. In a sense, Plato was onto something: after all, shamans made claims to truth that common mortals could not verify. He thought that all art was a dangerous illusion. Thus, bundled in with shoe and furniture makers, painters and sculptors were for centuries commonly referred to as "technites": hands able to make work.[26]

Contrary to what art history would have us think, the separation of the artist from the craftsman that took place during the Renaissance was not a matter of natural evolution but one of mythology, writing, power, and money—a concoction that still defines artistic careers today.

By the end of the second half of the fifteenth century (High Renaissance), Italy found itself in a period of remarkable turbulence. Its political fragmentation into small and powerful city-states was a hotbed of governmental instability. The wealth that tensely held them together arose from the colossal devastation imparted by the Black Death (1346–53). Killing, some claim, up to 200 million people worldwide, the plague radically redistributed wealth, reconfigured social structures, and initiated a deep

Image 5 (facing page). Giorgio Vasari, *Le vite de' piu eccellenti pittori, scultori . . .*, Giunti, Florence, 1568. Public Domain

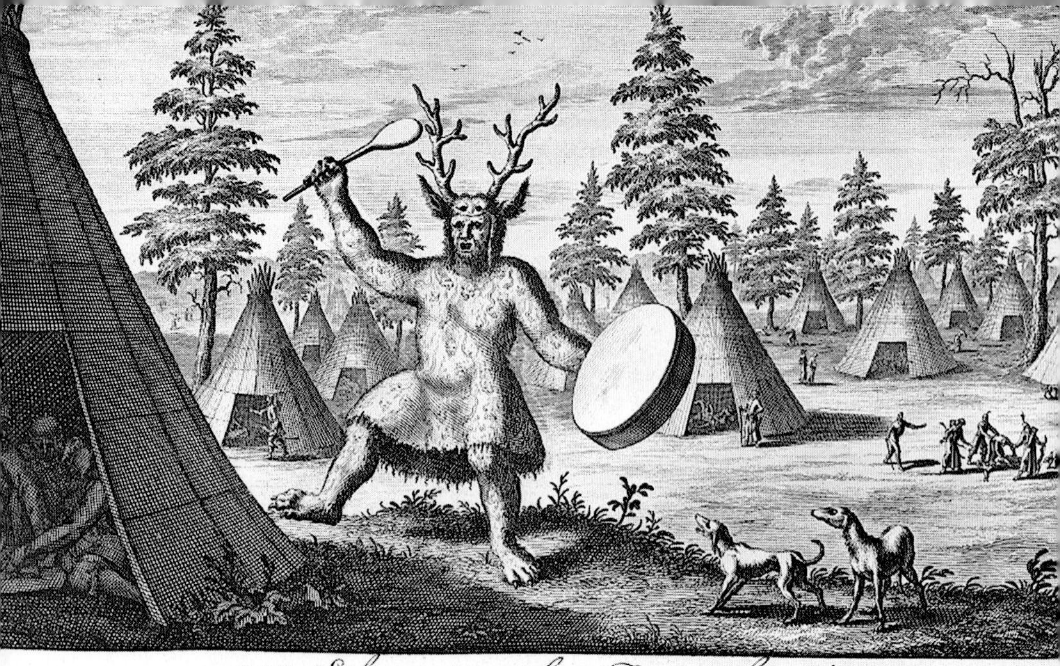



Image 6. Depiction of an Evenki Shaman wearing antler headdress (after Witsen 1785: 655). Public Domain

existentialist rupture from which a new philosophical current emerged: humanism.[27] In the West, the "artist as an intellectual" emerged at this point from the ruins of a dilapidated old order.

The new money of merchants and businessmen who craved social affirmation shaped the economic and cultural life of the Renaissance. In an increasingly competitive and hierarchical society, social status symbols became essential. Ostentatious and grand, they needed, at a glance, to communicate the wealth and intellectual sophistication of the owner. Painting perfectly fit the part: a miraculous vision frozen in time. Renaissance artists enormously benefited from the rise of the new merchant classes as well as from thriving banker families such as the Medici. The best artists quickly learned how to play the game. Aware of their growing social kudos, they set their eyes on money and luxury.

This new social reality—in which fortunes could be made as fast as they could be lost—came along with new and aspirational life models. Life in Renaissance cities was tough. Sudden brawls, violent robberies, spiked drinks, and simmering vendettas—everything was at risk in a world where petty disagreements were often settled with knives and poison.

Most of urban Europe was an open sewer. Gutters were engulfed with all kinds of putrid matter—human, animal, as well as rotting waste. The rat-infested streets reeked of feces and urine. Those who could afford them wore necklaces made of entwined lavender, or as in Germany, they carried an apple stuffed with fragrant spices to fend off the abhorrent stench.[28] It's hard to blame artists for wanting to escape this grim reality. Despite Cennini's advice that successful artists should be motivated by a genuine passion for their work rather than monetary gain, by the late fifteenth century, successful painters had—for good reason—evolved into smart entrepreneurs.

Art history has taught us to worship the artist-genius as a kind of magical and transcendental power. But the reality is very different. Sheer talent is never enough, and successful careers often emerge from careful networking, masterminding, and endless strategizing. Leonardo's letters provide a wonderful illustration of this, revealing more of the artist's ferocious ambition for riches and notoriety than of a pure love of painting.

Born out of wedlock to respected Florentine notary Ser Piero and a young peasant woman, Leonardo, as an illegitimate son, should never have accessed any form of education. But when his father saw the youngster's gift for drawing, he placed him in Andrea Verrocchio's studio, where he picked up painting at the age of 14. By the time Leonardo turned 20, he had become a master artist in Florence's prestigious Guild of Saint Luke and established his own workshop.

Despite his growing popularity, Leonardo—an astute self-promoter—quickly gained a reputation for leaving work unfinished and patrons unhappy. Much of his time was spent sketching out the most lethal weaponry ever imagined, rather than painting heavenly works.[29]

Following the fall from power of his main patron, Ludovico Sforza, in 1499, the artist traveled across Italy, confidently hiring himself out to feuding powers in Rome

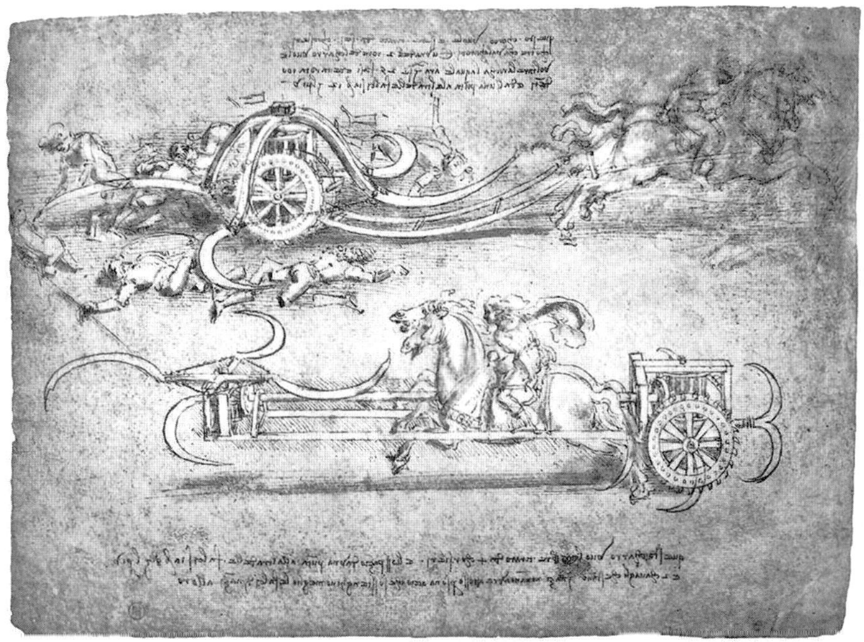

Image 7. Leonardo da Vinci, *Assault chariot with scythes*, 1485. Public Domain

and Venice. Constantly dissatisfied by his patrons' disinterest in his deadly war machines, he eventually settled for a very comfortable and prestigious role as court painter to King Francis I of France. Such was the esteem in which Leonardo was held that he was given exclusive use of Manoir du Cloux, the king's lavish summer home, where the artist died in 1519 with the *Mona Lisa* by his bed.[30] Throughout his life the man did anything he could to retain a social status that wasn't his by birthright — including painting when he couldn't care less.

Women's path to fame and riches was far more treacherous: Renaissance society was still steeped in patriarchal power, the role of the artist star was exclusively male. While records show that women were particularly active in the Flemish textile industries and northern France, the rise of painting and sculpture as quintessential artistic media of the Renaissance reasserted their inferiority. It comes as no surprise that, out of Vasari's 133 artists' biographies he included in the *Lives*, only one should be of a woman.

To get noticed, women had to invent their own career paths from scratch. Properzia de' Rossi was a true Renaissance woman — well-versed in painting, music, dance, poetry, and classical literature.[31] Her biography in Vasari's book adds up to little more than disconnected but intriguing fragments. De Rossi was a rebel — twice charged with disorderly conduct, once in 1520–1 for destroying a neighbor's garden and then again in 1525 for throwing paint in the face of fellow artist Domenico del Franco.[32]

To stand out from the crowd, de' Rossi carved miniatures on peach, plum, and cherry stones. At the time, sculpture was considered a male pursuit. Traditional tools and materials were costly. Cheaper than full-size marble sculptures, against all odds, her marvelously detailed miniatures eventually gained her artistic respect among prestigious commissioners. It wasn't long before recognition of her talent led de' Rossi to contribute a bas-relief for the doors of the Basilica di San Petronio in Bologna, the most important building in the city. Unfortunately, the plague took her life in 1593, the same week that Pope Clement VII, an admirer of her work, requested to meet with her.[33]

## When Art Became Institutionalized

In an ever-more competitive art world, the merchants' and workers' associations, or guilds, quickly went from protection to conservativism. Their bureaucratic structures prevented innovation by internally, and very thoroughly, regulating styles and methods in artistic production. Guilds often determined prices, set wages, prohibited competition, and approved or disapproved projects. For centuries, they had promoted security, stability, and conformity. But the new model of the Renaissance artist star didn't fit well in the guilds' mold.[34] An alternative soon emerged. In January 1563, Cosimo I de' Medici, ruler of Florence, founded the Accademia e Compagnia delle Arti del Disegno (Academy and Company for the Arts of Drawing). Modeled upon the academies of ancient Greece, the Accademia provided a theoretical education including mathematics and anatomical dissection, along with the traditional practical training typical of workshop apprentices. Painting, sculpture, and architecture were grouped together under the concept of Fine Arts for the first time. Cosimo's

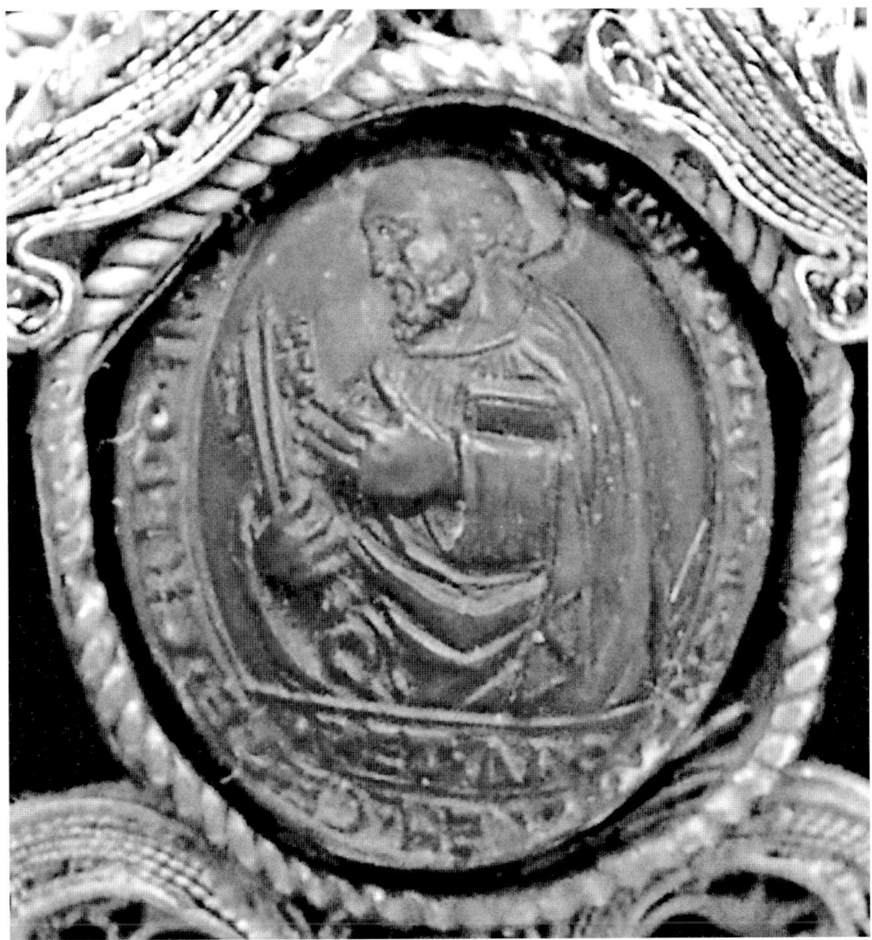

Image 8. Properzia de' Rossi, Carved plum stone, part of the Silver filigree and carved peach and plum stones Grassi Family Crest, 1510–30. Museo Civico Medievale, Bologna

involvement underscored its credibility, laying the foundations for the institutionalization of art education in Europe.

Soon after, the Venetian Accademia di San Luca, which opened its doors in 1593, followed the Medici model. Academies quickly overshadowed the guilds with matters such as settling professional disputes and appraisals for prestigious commissions.[35] For better or worse, the academies canonized the artist as a trained and qualified professional. Art became institutionalized. Local governments seized the opportunity to standardize subjects and styles. The power relations became further entangled.[36] Nepotism ran rife: Vasari became director of the Accademia e Compagnia delle Arti del Disegno and he appointed his favorite artist, Michelangelo, as its first teacher.

Aware of their influence and power, each player in this game validated one another's authority through the publication of influential books, the commissioning of prestigious works, and participation in political and cultural negotiations. This is where the power matrix of today's art world started to form. As part of this power complex, many artists also came to realize the importance of the signature. Vasari's catalog of Renaissance masters compelled artists to sign their works in order to avoid future misattribution. Signatures became brands. Someone's reputation turned into currency.

During the second half of the sixteenth century, in response to Martin Luther's (1517) condemnation of the corruption that pervaded the Catholic Church, the true political power of art was unleashed upon the West for the first time. The Protestant Church saw art as an unnecessary and expensive distraction from liturgical teachings—the sinful source of corruption as well as ethical and materialist contradictions. Recognizing the propagandistic potential of visual representation, the Catholic Church heightened its involvement in the arts to reclaim the faithful and regain control of Europe.[37]

At the Council of Trent (1545–63), the world's longest meeting, the Catholic Church spelled out a new institutionally approved artistic agenda. Art had to be first and foremost a teaching tool for the clergy. The ambiguous compositions of Mannerist masters must be replaced by a sense of clarity in color and narrative. The artist's interpretative freedom was discouraged in favor of a literalist approach to scriptural accuracy.[38] For as radically new as it might seem, this type of relationship between artists and political/religious power was quite common in other parts of the world.

The histories of Chinese, Japanese, and Indian art show the strong correlations between a ruler's personal stylistic and philosophical inclination and the art produced during their reigns. Chinese emperor Huizong of the Song Dynasty was a talented artist and art collector. In the eighth century, he established the Hanlin Imperial Painting House, the academy for which he devised the curriculum and promoted attention to realism in art.[39] Later, in Japan, the art of the Momoyama Period (1574–1615) was stylistically defined by the taste and lofty imagination of feudal lord Toyotomi Hideyoshi (1537–98).[40] In India, Jahangir, the Mughal emperor from 1605 to 1627, was a lover of Western painting and actively promoted the use of Renaissance central perspective among his court painters as he advocated the importance of realistic representation in the depiction of animals and plants.[41]

Although art history has taught us to look at art as pure human expression, styles and schools have always emerged from the intricate entanglements between ruling religious and political powers. While on the surface it might seem that these conditions today no longer apply, the reality is very different.

## Why Have There Been No Great Women Artists?

The myth of the artist is intrinsically exclusionary. Not just in the West, women have been for millennia forbidden from engaging in cultural pursuits. However, it wasn't always so. The oldest institute of higher education was founded by Fatima al-Fihri in Fes, Morocco. Al-Qarawiyyin opened its doors in 895 CE and focused primarily on religious studies and the teaching of grammar and rhetoric. Al-Qarawiyyin admitted both male and female students.[42] The prestigious University of Bologna, Italy, founded in 1088, produced the first female graduate: Bettisia Gozzadini in 1237.[43] The United States established an unprecedented first as Oberlin College, Ohio, became the first to enroll women, Indigenous and African American students in the 1830s.[44] While Oxford University, founded in 1096, admitted women in 1879, it excluded them from graduating until 1920.[45]

In 1971, Linda Nochlin's groundbreaking essay, "Why Have There Been No Great Women Artists?", traced a genealogy of female exclusionism from art training in Europe between the seventeenth and eighteenth centuries.[46] Addressing the sociological context in which artists were trained, Nochlin pointed out that, since the Renaissance, women had been forbidden to study the naked body. Women were thus excluded from making what back then went by the name of "great art": historical, mythological, and religious subjects in which the naked human body was ubiquitous. Unable to enter prestigious competitions, such as the Prix de Rome, or apply for important scholarships, women artists—diminished and marginalized—turned to the "lower" ranks of art genres like still-life compositions.

Scholars of sixteenth-century Italian academies were the first to rank genres in art. A hundred years later, André Félibien, court historian to Louis XIV, set the rule in stone:

> He who produces perfect landscapes is above another who only produces fruit, flowers, or seashells. He who paints living animals is more estimable than those who only represent dead things without movement, and since man is the most perfect work of God on the Earth, it is also certain that he who becomes an imitator of God in representing human figures, is much more excellent than all the others.[47]

Félibien's words profoundly changed the course of Western painting. The work of Maria van Oosterwijck, Rachel Ruysch, and the botanical illustrator Maria Sybilla Merian is a testament to the undisputed talent of women artists who painted still-lifes. But images of flowers and fruits appealed to the less learned, new wealth of mercantile classes and thus carried less social prestige. This patriarchal thread entangled in gender and social biases largely prevented the recognition of women as "great artists" in the West until the 1930s.

The situation was not that dissimilar in other parts of the world. Still, between the sixteenth and the nineteenth century, becoming a successful female artist often required the support of a man. In Korea, Shin Saimdang was trained by her maternal grandfather, who treated her like a grandson. Saimdang is today remembered as one of the earliest and finest Korean female artists. Her bold and original style of embroidery, coupled with a countercurrent penchant for painting weeds and pests, made her stand out to later generations of artists, eventually boosting her fame.[48]

In Europe, Artemisia Gentileschi's rise to fame, during the male-dominated Italian Baroque, unraveled under similar circumstances. Her father, Orazio Gentileschi, a respected artist in his own right, trained his only daughter as he would have done a son. With him, she studied history and mythology masterpieces of the past. Orazio was well connected to other influential artists like Caravaggio and to wealthy patrons—a substantial advantage for Artemisia. As it was in China centuries before, this was one of the few opportunities for women to enter the artistic profession. But despite their evident talent and creative abilities, women were generally undervalued, if not ridiculed. A letter Gentileschi wrote to a patron leaves no doubt of this: "You think me pitiful because a woman's name raises doubts until her work is seen"; "I will show Your Most Illustrious Lordship what a woman can do"; "You will find the spirit of Caesar in this soul of a woman."[49] At the age of 18, Gentileschi was raped. While her assailant was found guilty, her reputation was irreparably damaged. The gory scenes of Judith cutting off the head of Holofernes that Gentileschi made thereafter have often been, perhaps erroneously, read as a metaphorical castration of the male aggressor and an assault on patriarchal power.

Throughout the last century, Western art history has worked hard at erasing the pioneering contributions of female artists. It is disheartening to note that exactly four hundred years after the publication of Vasari's *The Lives*, across the pages of Ernst Gombrich's 1950 monumental *The Story of Art* again only one woman artist can be found: Käthe Kollwitz.[50] Today, art historians like Ferren Gipson, Kathy Hessel, Whitney Chadwick, Catherine McCormack, and many others are setting the record straight, recovering, reconsidering, and reinstating the work of women in the deeply biased and incomplete history of art that we have all learned at school.[51]

## Museums: Exclusionary Displays

During the sixteenth and seventeenth centuries accessing works of art from which to learn was a substantial problem for women and people of color who were also excluded from the academies in Europe. As rulers in India, China, and Japan had done before, academies in Italy collected the works of teachers and alumni. These early institutional archives were carefully curated to preserve the power of patriarchy and to further consolidate the canon: the ideal standard in art. Collecting art had always been the prerogative of the very rich. Exotic animals, rare plants, precious stones, artifacts—these were the status symbols of the past.

Some of the oldest collections originated in Chinese courts, but Aztec rulers also collected precious artifacts. In Europe, collecting the relics of saints validated the holiness of the Christian Church. Nails of the cross, hair strands, nail clippings, bones, and teeth were highly sought-after possessions in central Europe throughout the Middle Ages.

By the end of the Renaissance, the European aristocracy was deeply invested in owning extravagant cabinets of curiosities filled with naturalia and art. Organized according to the taste and interests of the aristocratic collector, cabinets of curiosities made sense of a wondrous and ever-expanding world. The discovery of the Americas and the intensification of commerce with the East propelled an inexhaustible desire to collect wonders. Colonialism only deepened this desire leading to the looting of other

Image 9 (facing page).  Artemisia Gentileschi, *Judith Slaying Holofernes*, 1620–1, oil on canvas, 162.5 x 199 cm. Uffizi Gallery, Florence. Photo: Steven Zucker. CC BY-NC-SA 2.0

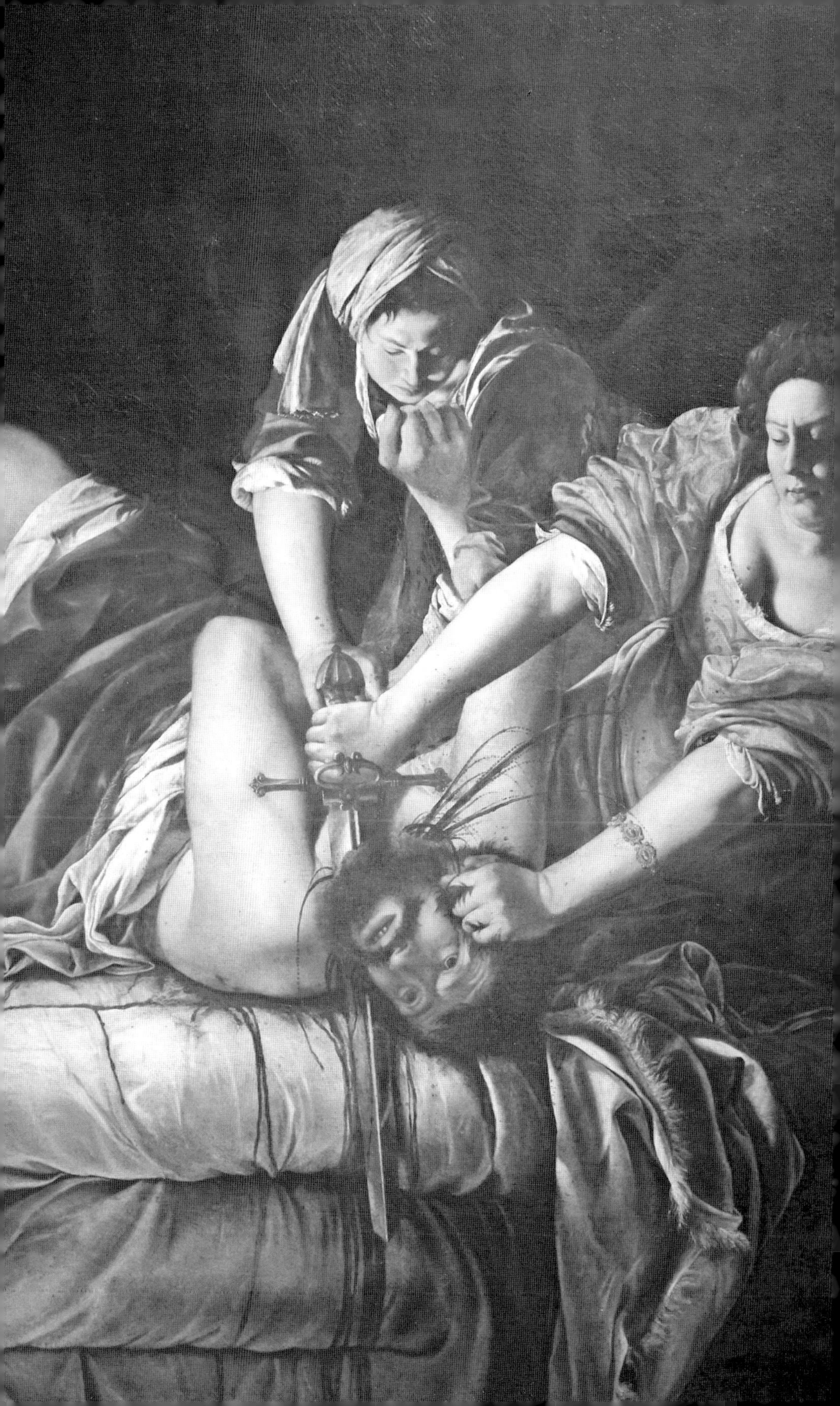

cultures' treasures and the indiscriminate killing of innumerable people, animals, and plants.

As cabinets of curiosities increased in size so did the ambition of their owners. Bigger and richer cabinets eventually led to the birth of the modern museum.[52] On the one hand, the museum fictitiously realigned time and space by organizing works of art according to the chronologies and geographies of the dominant culture. On the other, art history used the museum to amplify influences, trace genealogies of exclusion, and map lineages of superiority that impacted the careers of artists as well as our reception of African, Indian, and Chinese art for centuries.

For the first time, beginning with the end of the eighteenth century, artists could see more art than ever and read about its history. They could gain an invaluable overview of what art meant in a broader sense and acquire an unprecedented critical perspective—they awoke. It, however, soon appeared clear that museums further consolidated Félibien's hierarchy of art genres, reasserted the superiority of male artists, and systematically excluded women and BIPOC painters, sculptors, and architects. .

Coincidentally, it was during the second half of the eighteenth century that artifacts from Pompeii and Herculaneum were discovered. This spearheaded a resurgence of ancient Greek and Roman art across Europe, popularized by painters like as Antonio Canova and Jacques-Louis David. It was amid this neoclassical revival that German art historian Johann Joachim Winckelmann laid the foundations of modern art history. For decades thereafter, well-dressed gentlemen with powdered wigs descended from the prestigious Académie des Beaux-Arts to discuss the art exhibited at the Louvre in Paris.[53] But true change loomed on the horizon. The impetus of the Industrial Revolution and the social unrest that followed the French Revolution swiftly altered artists' perceptions of their duties in society and what their work should do and say. Those who dreamt of prestigious careers bolstered by stately commissions unreservedly embraced the utopian elegance of neoclassicism, while those determined to start their own artistic revolution began to dream up a new world.

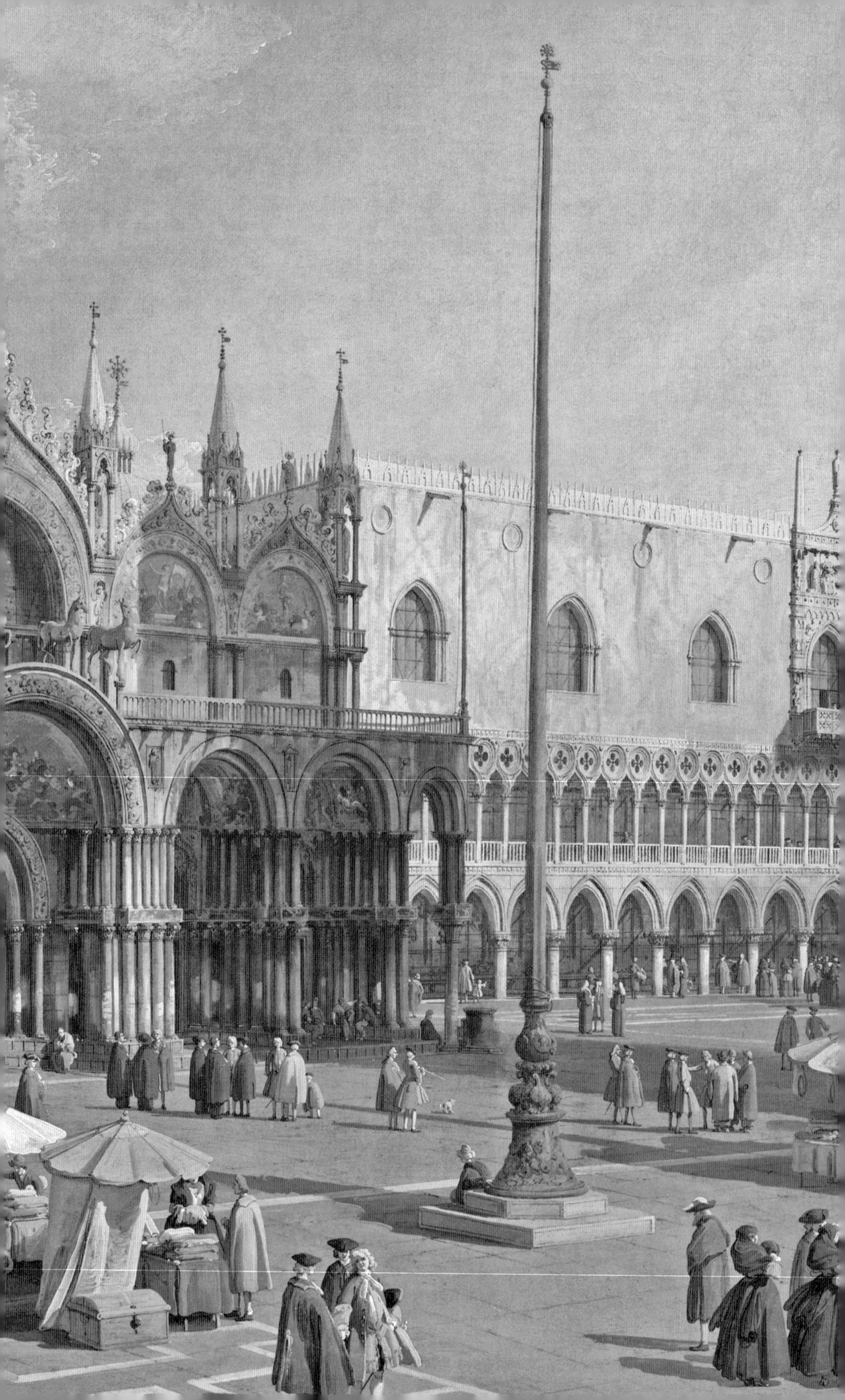

# 2  The Modern Artist: A Rebel Without a Cause?

# Postcards from the Revolution

Making money from art has always been a challenging task. During the seventeenth century, Peter Paul Rubens and Rembrandt van Rijn pushed the workshop model to an extreme. Not only, like their Renaissance predecessors, did they entrust assistants with the important task of painting most of their works to speed up production, but they also charged students to learn from them. Rembrandt would sell their work and take a cut, too.[1]

These early exploits paved the way for a definitive commercial turn in the eighteenth century—a revolution that sprang from the bottom ranks of Félibien's hierarchy. Still-life paintings of flowers, fruits, and the occasional gory skull or imperturbably serene landscapes became the first big hit in a new mass art market. Much more modest in size than history, mythology, and religious paintings, and far less personal than portraits, these subjects had broader appeal. The rise of the art market, a potentially lucrative alternative to the commission model that for centuries had tied art to royalty, aristocracy, and the church, offered new opportunities but it also came at a cost.

Venetian artist Giovanni Antonio Canal, better known as Canaletto, painted a dazzling array of meticulously detailed and ready-to-carry-out vistas of his city. These were specially made for the young aristocrats who could afford the Grand Tour, a cultural journey throughout Europe that frequently lasted several months to many years and allowed (mainly) male artists to come into contact with ancient antiquities and Renaissance art. In a pre-photographic world, Canaletto's hyper-realistic paintings of the Grand Canal and prominent Venetian churches were the forerunners of the souvenir postcard.

To fulfill high demand, the artist worked with a *camera obscura*—a tracing device similar to a pinhole camera. It sped up drawing and improved accuracy: a great mass production strategy. Canaletto quickly amassed a fortune and gained fame across Europe, mostly thanks to British consul Joseph Smith, a banker who acted as his agent.[2] But while painting picturesque scenes of Venice earned Canaletto instant fame, his artistic reputation among the intellectuals suffered. Art historian J. G. Links noted that the artist's work was admired by those with the most unsophisticated taste—namely, early modern tourists.[3] His paintings were primarily sold across an ever-growing network of antique dealers focused on selling to the mercantile middle classes of Flanders and Italy.

Art is often extremely time-consuming and expensive to make, yet critics and art historians have always frowned at artists who have boldly courted commercial success. Across time, the accusations are always the same: commercialism is bad, and it devalues art; if too many people like it, it must be vulgar.[4] The artist myth is founded on this impossible premise—a puritan principle that has for centuries led artists to make bad decisions and that still wrecks lives and careers today.

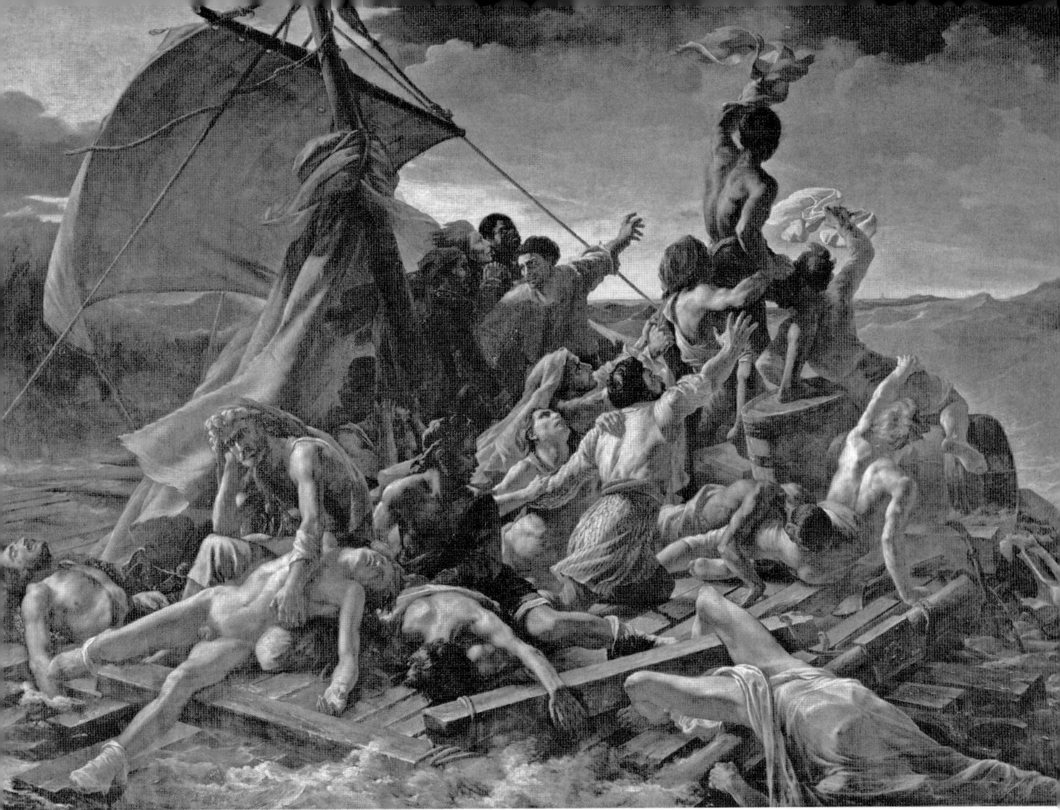

Image 11. Théodore Géricault, *The Raft of the Medusa*, oil on canvas, 1818–19, Musée du Louvre, Paris. Public Domain

## The Artist Rebel: How to Make or Wreck a Career

Théodore Géricault's family was wealthier than Canaletto's. A significant annuity came to him after his grandmother's death. This bought him the freedom necessary to create a work that forever changed the history of Western art. In 1818, at the age of 27, Géricault began work on *The Raft of the Medusa*, his most ambitious painting. Measuring over 16 × 23 feet (490 × 716 cm), the monumental canvas and the oil color needed to cover it amounted to a small fortune.

At this time in Western art, size mattered a great deal. Strict academic conventions dictated that enormous canvases be utilized primarily for historical, mythical, and religious topics; viewers relied upon these conventions to decode meaning. It is perhaps no surprise then that at Louis XVIII's Salon of 1819, upon approaching *The Raft of the Medusa*, they were puzzled, appalled, and disgusted.[5] It wasn't just the tragic scene of a shipwreck cast against a murky stormy sky, the hyper-realistic expressions of anguish and terror on the survivors' faces, or even the livid colors on the rotting corpses that caused outrage. Géricault had infringed the canon's laws by painting a contemporary event on a far too large a canvas. Those who attended the Salon were certain: what they witnessed was an illustration of a story they read on the papers a few years before.

Géricault's painting publicly shamed France. The *Medusa* sailed for Senegal in 1816, but it was wrecked by the captain's incompetent navigation. Aristocrats and politicians were taken to safety in lifeboats, leaving the other 151 passengers to fend for themselves on a makeshift raft. Géricault's massive canvas captured the moment, after thirteen arduous days at sea, when the last fifteen survivors catch a glimpse of the ship that will save their lives. The French monarchy had deemed the rescue operation too costly, and never sent help, hoping no survivors might tell the tale. But those who made it were far too keen to report horrific stories of escalating violence and cannibalism aboard the raft. A national scandal ensued.[6] Rather than entertaining with beautiful images of classical beauty, Géricault made people deeply uncomfortable. His painting asked its audience to confront reality in the most brutal of ways.

As happened to many other works of art we today admire, in its time, *The Raft of the Medusa* was a massive flop. Géricault's ambition to launch his career with this memorable work miserably failed, or so it initially seemed. He needed a plan to tip the scales in his favor. Undeterred, the following year, he exhibited the painting in London where it attracted a staggering 40,000 visitors.[7] Géricault made 20,000 francs—roughly the equivalent of $85,000 today—from ticket sales.[8] Although this sum is little in compared to today's skyrocketing art market prices, it is worth remembering that demand for noncommissioned and exceedingly unconventional paintings like these was almost nonexistent back then.

*The Raft of the Medusa* remained unsold until 1824 when, after the premature death of the artist, it was finally acquired by the Louvre—Géricault's ascension to the art historical pantheon was complete. However, throughout his career, the artist's determination to produce controversial and nonconformist works with very limited commercial appeal led to bad financial investments. In late 1821, he ravaged his savings by investing in a factory producing synthetic stones. More of his assets were lost in 1823 to a dishonest broker.[9] The artist died in poverty, his mental and physical health rapidly deteriorating in the last few years of his life following the disappointments that marred his career.

*The Raft of the Medusa*, however, marked a radical schism in the conception of the Western artist. The godlike artist-genius of the Renaissance, who brought beauty and harmony to a deeply troubled world, now had a wicked, revolutionarily creative counterpart: the artist rebel. Géricault's vicissitudes show that the new creative freedom granted by the art market came at a cost. In the early days of Romanticism (late eighteenth century), artists could no longer ignore the all-important financial question. How to support an artistic career without shackling creativity to the impositions of wealthy patrons? They were about to discover the true cost of creative freedom on their own dime.

## Realism: The Birth of the Political Artist

Two main factors impacted the rise of the Romantic artist in the first half of the nineteenth century: the Industrial Revolution and the invention of photography. Romanticism, the intellectual movement that gave us Mary Shelley's *Frankenstein* (1818), Caspar David Friedrich's sublime paintings of nature, and Ludwig van Beethoven's and Frédéric Chopin's musical masterpieces, was all about surviving a colossal existentialist crisis. A sudden loss of trust in the rationalism and optimism of the European Enlightenment (1715–89) and the rise of religious skepticism elevated a new form of heroism in which the intensity of emotion corresponded to the authenticity of experience. Romanticism was the cultural response to the Industrial Revolution and its relentless rationalization and commodification of life. It was an antidote to the unprecedented ecological and cultural degradation; a way to nurture the spirit in the face of radical change and relentless alienation.[10]

The painting that most apltly captures this condition certainly is Caspar David Friedrich's *The Wanderer Above the Mists* (1817–18). The figure of a lone (white) gentleman atop a rocky peak contemplating the vastness of nature's greatness embodies the heroic loneliness of the romantic artist and the mystery of its myth. The artist's spiritual seclusion, infused with a healthy dosage of melancholia, is not only an indicator of true exceptionalism, but also the social mark of the "artist-outcast" burdened by the weight of his brilliance.

The invention of photography further contributed to a sense of creative instability. Since 1839, when it was first unveiled in Paris to public acclaim, photography radically altered our relationship with identity, memory, history, and, of course, painting. Loved by the public, loathed by the critics, and feared by many artists, to the classically trained eye photography looked plain vulgar. Romantic artists and critics believed that authenticity resided in the essence of things, not their surfaces—but surfaces were all that photography could capture. Shackled to reality, the new medium seemed to lack the emotional depth typical of what people pompously liked to call "great art."[11] Surrounded by mass-reproduced images, mechanically printed books, and machine-made utensils and garments, artists clung to their skills and manual craft—priests and priestesses of truth and authenticity in a world filled with copies of copies anyone could fabricate. Photography instilled in artists an existential crisis—it forced them to ask two critical questions: "Why still paint?" and "What should one paint now?"

In this new cultural panorama, Géricault's invitation to weaponize painting against power and the status quo began to appeal to a new movement of revolutionary artists: the French Realists. Their leader, Gustave Courbet (1819–77), believed that painters should only represent what can be seen and experienced.[12] The French Revolution and the upheavals of 1848 had shown that history is made in the present. It was in the aftermath of this phenomenal and bloody unrest that art finally became contemporary. Enough with Greek mythology and Roman battles—the time had come to immortalize the present with the same dignity reserved to the past.

Courbet, and other realist artists, despised the hierarchy of genres and yearned for a democratization of art. For the first time in the history of the West, artists looked at the working classes, not with disdain but admiration. No longer sought after in the Platonic perfection of classical art, truth was to be found in the honest representation of everyday life, in the struggle of labor, in the lives of those who existed in the present because they held no stakes in their futures. The realists' rough handling of brushwork and unconventional lighting conveyed, with dignity, the emotional hardship of the poor. Painting the lowest elevated the artist to the rank of ethically just

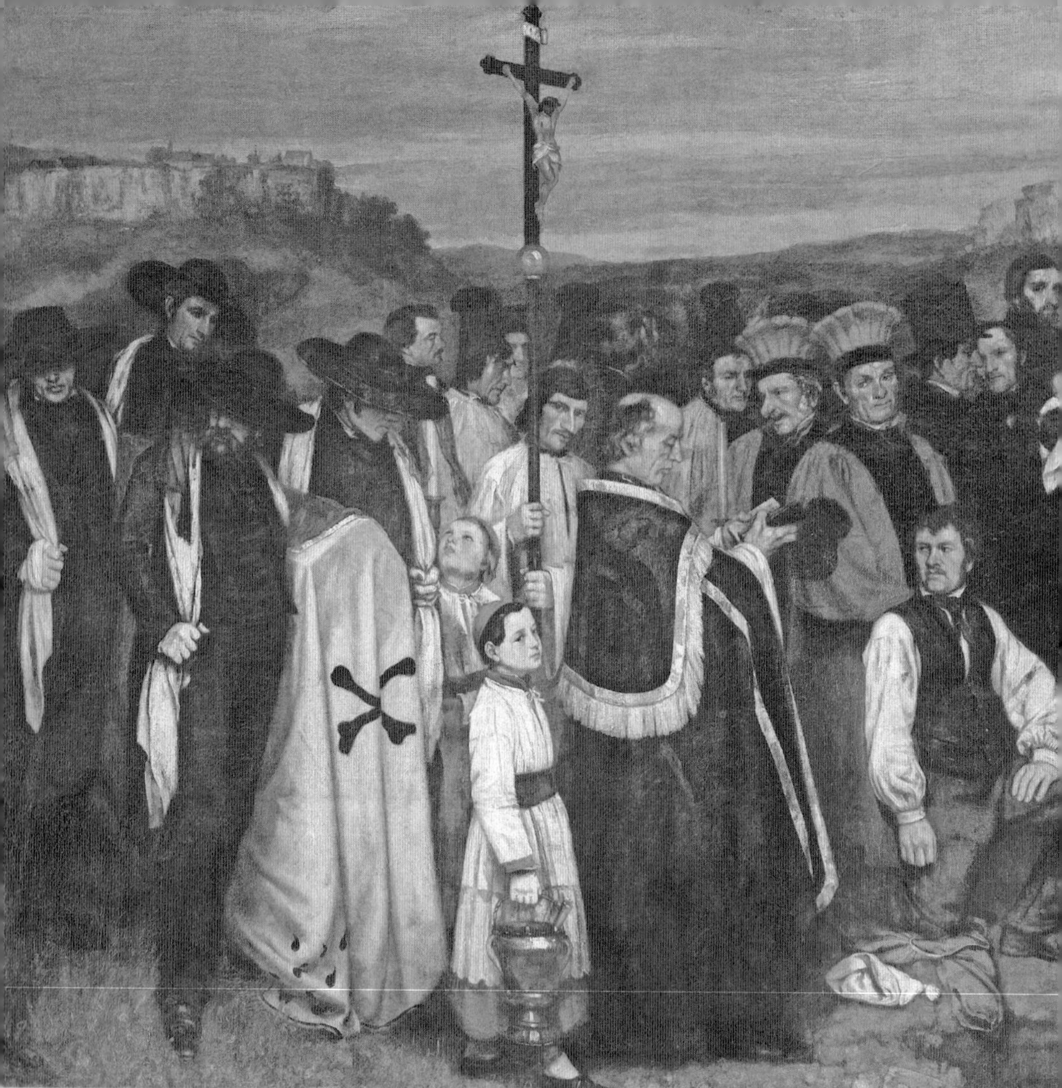

Image 12. Gustave Courbet, *A Burial at Ornans*, gouache on canvas, 1849–50. Musée d'Orsay, Paris

cultural gatekeeper. Many artists today still see this as an important aspect of who they are.

Presenting peasants and workers on colossal canvases, the realists threatened the social order and bruised the ego of the upper classes. Paintings such as Courbet's *A Burial at Ornans* (1849–50), which measures 124 × 260 in (315 × 660 cm), inflamed spirits. Like Géricault, Courbet deliberately chose a massive canvas to challenge tradition. Although it might seem laughable in comparison to the outrage generated by contemporary art today, this subversive act was highly political, and it paved the way for more artistic rebelliousness to come.

Not the funeral of an emperor, or a queen, or a pope . . . Courbet's *A Burial at Ornans* memorialized the burial of an anonymous, working-class layman. It mercilessly put on display the simplicity and sincerity of everyday working-class roughness in a provincial town. "Why should I care?" bored Parisian aristocrats could be heard scoffing.

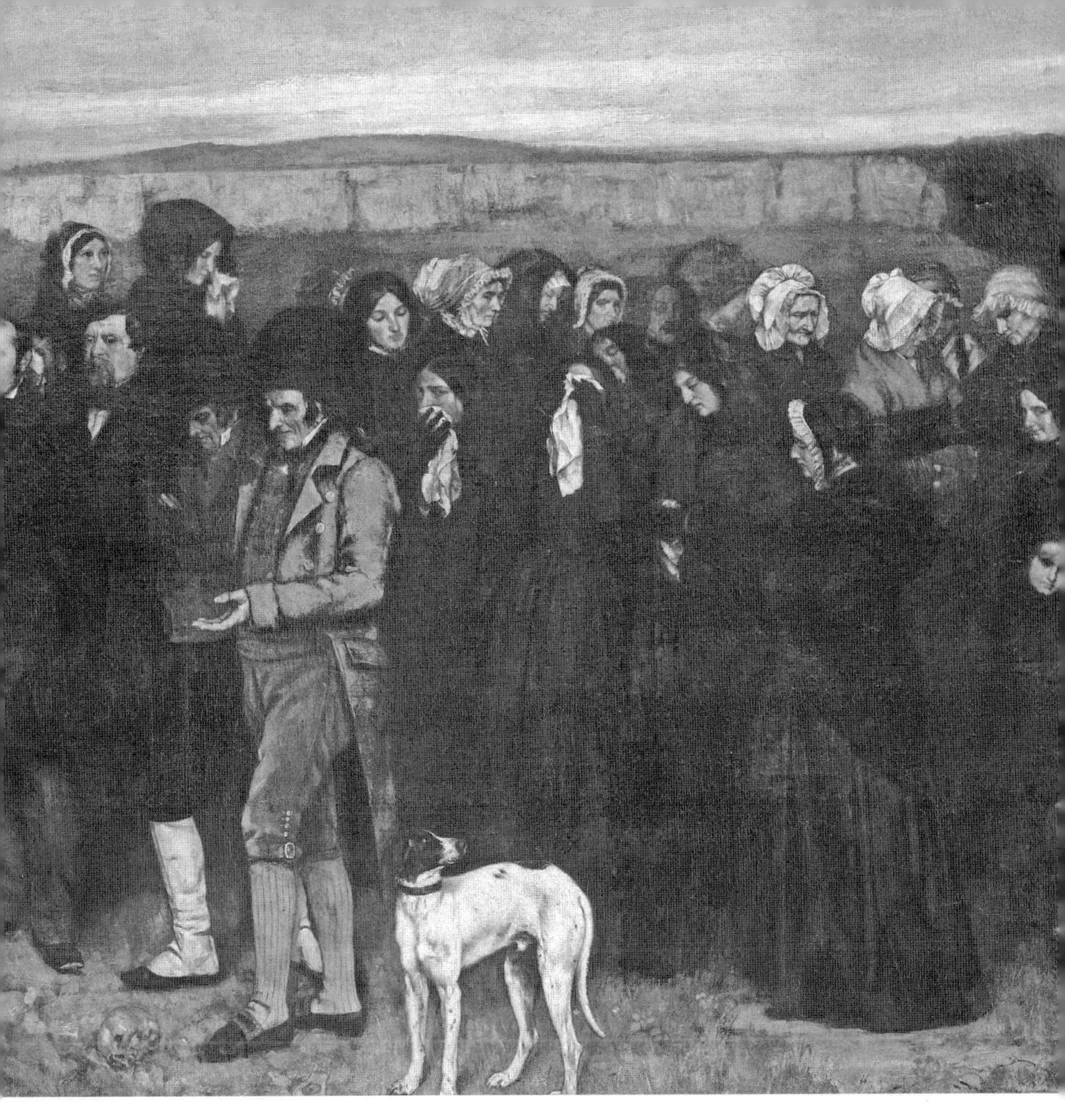

Despite their disinterest, this funeral gave birth to the avant-garde. Borrowed from military jargon, the term "avant-garde" encapsulates the realist's determination to be at the forefront of experimentation—the aim: to change people's minds. The avant-garde's militant approach sowed the seed of what, today, many contemporary artists consider to be art-activism. And by penning the first manifesto in the history of Western art Courbet essentially turned the realist movement into the first artistic political party.[13]

## Courbet and Bonheur: The Artist Entrepreneur

Unlike others, Courbet also knew how to marry politics and self-interest: "It is a serious responsibility to first provide the example of liberty and personality in art, and then afterward to provide publicity to the art which I have undertaken."[14] In this sense, too, Courbet was truly at the forefront of an important revolution that many artists today still overlook. Marketing one's work, as Courbet knew, is an essential part of the game, not a degrading and desperate maneuver to rig it.

Despite portraying himself as a rough-and-tumble character in *Bonjour, Monsieur Courbet* (1853), Courbet's lifestyle had little in common with that of the workers he depicted. He was a bohemian, well known in such fashionable Parisian hangouts as Café Momus or Cabaret Andler-Keller.[15] He understood that the power of representation was greater than what a panting's frame can hold—the artist's character mattered a great deal, and so he astutely self-mythologized. An inactive activist, despite his fiery insurrectionist rumbles, Courbet took no action during the workers' uprising of June 1848. In a letter to his family from that year, he said: "We are in (the middle of) a terrible civil war . . . I don't fight for two reasons. First, because I do not believe in wars fought with guns and cannons, and because it runs counter to my principles . . . The second reason is that I have no weapons and cannot be tempted" and "as for me, in this business, I wage my fight entirely with words."[16] Meanwhile, at the Salon of 1849, his painting of working-class men gathered around a modest dining table won a gold medal, and was purchased by the government. Courbet would be chastised today (and quite rightly so) for appropriating and exploiting the plight of a socioeconomic class to which he did not belong.

In the years leading up to the Paris Commune—a far-left revolutionary government that controlled Paris for a couple of months in the spring of 1871—Courbet continued to nurture the artistic image of a rustic cavalier, heavy-drinking peasant-philosopher. He impeccably curated his image, and perfected the art of straddling two worlds with his paintings just as much as he did in his life. He was a shrewd marketeer who keenly managed a diversified brand: the controversial pictures kept his name in the spotlight while he courted affluent clientele with completely apolitical portraits and dull landscapes.

The younger, and very radical, Courbet who stated that "there is no way around it, if you have to earn money with stuff like that [portraits] you would be better off turning a wheel, at least you would not have to give up your convictions"[17] would likely have been very disappointed in his older self.[18]

Courbet was a socialist at heart and, hugely influenced by Karl Marx and Frederick Engels's 1848 *Communist Manifesto* and philosopher/economist Pierre-Joseph Proudhon, he had some interesting ideas about how the art world should change. He openly expressed his fervent desire to democratize or even abolish artistic institutions. According to his plan, the Salon would become free of any governmental interference, and medals and awards would be done away with altogether. He even proposed the closure of all art academies in France, Italy, and Greece. Once and for all, artists would be free from the impositions of classical art, he thought.[19]

Courbet's defiance of institutional power had already become evident when he opened his *Pavillon du réalisme*. In 1855, disappointed by the rejection of two of his largest canvases at the Exposition Universelle, he bypassed the "artist-institution-client" power structure governing the art world and opened his own exhibiting venue to which he charged an admission fee of one franc. With shameless audacity, he orchestrated an advertising campaign in Parisian newspapers and invited critics and editors to secure press coverage. A total of forty canvases were exhibited in a temporary structure situated off the Champs-Elysées, a few steps from the Palais des Beaux-Arts, in central Paris.[20] Courbet still performed the tortured, mercurial, lone-soul genius part, while behind the scenes he acted as an entrepreneur acutely aware of professional power relations and brave enough to challenge the status quo. He went so far as sell postcards of his paintings and self-publish an exhibition catalog titled *Exhibition et Vent* ("Exhibition and Sale"). At the time, in France, the word "exposition" identified art exhibits, while "exhibition" was applied to shop windows and department stores. The title of the exhibition catalog also nodded to the contemporary commercial galleries that had sprung up across Paris. Often clustered around large museums such as the Louvre, art galleries of the early nineteenth century sold a bit of everything from genre paintings to art supplies and curio objects. Courbet's admission fee was also seen as a degrading alignment with popular entertainment.[21] In the end, the exhibition was a disappointment. Perhaps Courbet had gone too far. The critics mostly hated the exhibition, attendance was poor, and the artist took a financial loss. Yet, the *Pavillon du réalisme* did not fail to capture the imagination of art students such as Édouard Manet, who idolized Courbet as the artist-hero who stood against the power of the institution to free art.

A contemporary of Courbet was Rosa Bonheur—the most successful and one of the richest artist of the nineteenth century, who, unlike Courbet, was willingly forgotten by art historians and erased from the art history book for over a century. Bonheur was punished for being a woman artist but also for painting pictures of animals, a popular subject that academies and elite critics associated with the lowest ranks of art genres—a deadly cocktail at the time. Bonheur was the daughter of a piano teacher and a landscape painter. Her father, Oscar-Raymond Bonheur, was a follower of French social theorist Henri de Saint-Simon who advocated for the equality of the sexes, so Rosa was given an education and trained to become an artist. Success didn't take long to knock on her door—at the age of 19, a painting of two bunnies nibbling carrots garnered attention at the Salon and a stream of commissions followed. She exhibited every year at the Salon between 1841 and 1855, winning a gold medal in 1848. This recognition led to an important state commission, *Ploughing in the Nivernais*, which was likened by the critics to Courbet's brand of realism. The monumental canvas attracted the attention of dealer Ernest Gambart who would go on to manage Bonheur's career and make her a millionaire in her own lifetime. Gambart orchestrated the exhibition of the painting at various locations throughout the United Kingdom and secured a private viewing for Queen Victoria, a pet lover and avid collector of paintings depicting animals.

Transatlantic fame came toward the end of the 1850s with the colossal, 16.5 ft wide canvas *The Horse Fair* which was sold to American businessman Cornelius Vanderbilt for the astronomical sum of $53,000 (almost $2 million dollars today). He gifted the painting to the Metropolitan Museum of Art in New York, which propelled Bonheur to stardom.[22] In the 1860s she became the first artist to have a doll made after her—with cropped hair and wearing pants! It became a massive hit.[23] Bonheur had received a special permit by the French police that allowed her to wear trousers, then forbidden to women. She smoked cigars in public and enjoyed hunting. She was openly a lesbian—

sharing her life and home with two female partners throughout her life. A true nonconformist spirit, Bonheur lived her homosexuality with pride and fierceness at a time when only a few dared. A strong-minded and independent character, she once said, "I have no patience for women who ask permission to think."[24]

Bonheur was honored with the French Legion of Honour in 1865 by Empress Eugénie, in recognition of her lifetime achievements. However, her notoriety in her native land swiftly waned. Thoroughly engaged in her commercial fortune and a true market pioneer, in 1851, Bonheur licensed the use of reproduction of her paintings which generated a steady income stream and expanded her visibility beyond the museum circuit.[25] As it had been for Canaletto before, her artistic legacy suffered from the commercialization of her work.

While her recent rediscovery is a positive step in the right direction, over a hundred years of erasure have severely impacted Bonheur's influence. How different would art history be if her uncomformist, queer, and extremely successful role model had been allowed to inspire a slew of new artists?

Perhaps the first truly modern artists, Courbet and Bonheur understood the importance of self-promotion, commercialization, and fame like no one before them. "When I stop being controversial, I'll stop being important," said Courbet at the height of his notoriety. Bonheur was a little more uneasy with the attention her work garnered. She retreated to country life, near the Fontainebleau Forest, where with the money earned by her work she purchased a chateau, a house, and a farm. True pioneers, both artists were chastised by the establishment for disrespecting conventions and challenging the power of institutions. But most importantly, they understood that the world was rapidly changing and that artists had to change with it—enough of naked Venuses and imperial equestrian portraits, artists had a duty and that was to represent the now. Their role was to disrupt the peace. Nowhere had Charles Baudelaire's exhortation to sieve the heroism of the everyday from the gritty hustle and bustle of modern life been more confidently assimilated.[26] Somewhat surprisingly, that cultural change was unintentionally aided by Napoleon III, the last French monarch, known for remodeling Paris, boosting the country's economy, and his love of prostitutes.

## Manet: The Value of Controversy

In 1863, after an unusually harsh jury of twenty-four academic painters rejected two thirds of the (roughly 5,000) paintings submitted to the Parisian Salon, Napoleon III agreed to hold an alternative exhibition for those who were excluded. His official statement claimed:

> Numerous complaints have come to the Emperor on the subject of the works of art which were refused by the jury of the Exposition. His Majesty, wishing to let the public judge the legitimacy of these complaints, has decided that the works of art which were refused should be displayed in another part of the Palace of Industry.
> The Athenaeum: Journal of Literature, Science, and the Fine Arts,
> n.1855, May 16 1863, p.655, London: John Francis

Unknowingly, the Emperor was about to singlehandedly change Western art forever. The Salon des Refusés (Exhibition of Rejects) of 1863, with its 780 works by 64 sculptors and 366 painters, turned out to be the biggest misfire in the history of Western art. Held at the Louvre since 1725, the Salon des Beaux-Arts was the ultimate career "maker or breaker" of nineteenth-century artists. Since 1761, the exhibition had acquired prestige on a global scale. By the end of the eighteenth century, the Salon was sponsored by the French government and the Académie des Beaux-Arts. Both used the exhibition as an opportunity to promote neoclassical art. Winners of the Salon received a gold medal and governmental commissions.

Napoleon III thought the Salon des Refusés would reaffirm the supremacy of classical art. Exhibiting "bad art," he thought, would show people what is good once and for all. Well, he was wrong. The Salon des Refusés was a roaring success, attracting more than a thousand visitors per day. Sure, many of them laughed their way through the galleries pointing and sneering at the "crude" pictures of everyday life. The painting people laughed at the most was Édouard Manet's *Le Déjeuner sur l'herbe* (Luncheon on the grass), which depicted a naked woman at a picnic with two, fully clothed men—another woman appears to be washing her privates in the background.

While Courbet's iconographies only loosely referenced classical art, Manet's most scandalous works were an early modern version of cut and paste. The composition of *Le Déjeuner sur l'herbe* was directly lifted from Raphael's *Judgment of Paris* (1513–15). Other references included Titian's *Pastoral Concert* (1509). A year later, even more controversial was Manet's unapologetic portrait of a successful sex worker lying naked on her ruffled sheets, *Olympia* (1863). This was a mash-up of Titian's *Venus of Urbino* (1538) and his *Danaë* series (painted between the 1540s and 60s), masterpieces of classical art that the audience had been taught to unquestionably revere. Manet played a game of bait and switch: he lured the viewer with the promise of something morally worthy (as suggested by the familiar composition) and then shoved the decadence of contemporary Paris in their faces.

Manet fast-forwarded classic Renaissance masterpieces straight into 1863. He plunged mythological allure into what Baudelaire called the "heroism of modern life": the struggles, carnal joys, and social tragedies that make Parisian streets so decadently iconic.[27] His nudes had no allegorical depth, truth was smeared all over their (dirty) faces. Most viewers could not stand the proud gaze of Victorine Meurent, an artist in her own right who posed for both *Olympia* and *Le Déjeuner sur l'herbe*. Others were offended by the presence of the black maid in *Olympia*. Even more astutely than Courbet, Manet's incendiary paintings were designed to ask big questions about society and art itself. Modern art true and proper began with this resoundingly public slap in the face to classical art. Parisian crowds laughed out loud, the critics panned both works, and cartoonists parodied them in the press. The artist wasn't quite prepared to take the heat . . . "They are raining insults on me," cried a heartbroken Manet to his friend Baudelaire. A star was born, but at what cost?[28]

While Manet's fame failed to translate into financial success, his reputation among other modern artists grew exponentially. Art no longer had to please—it was now free

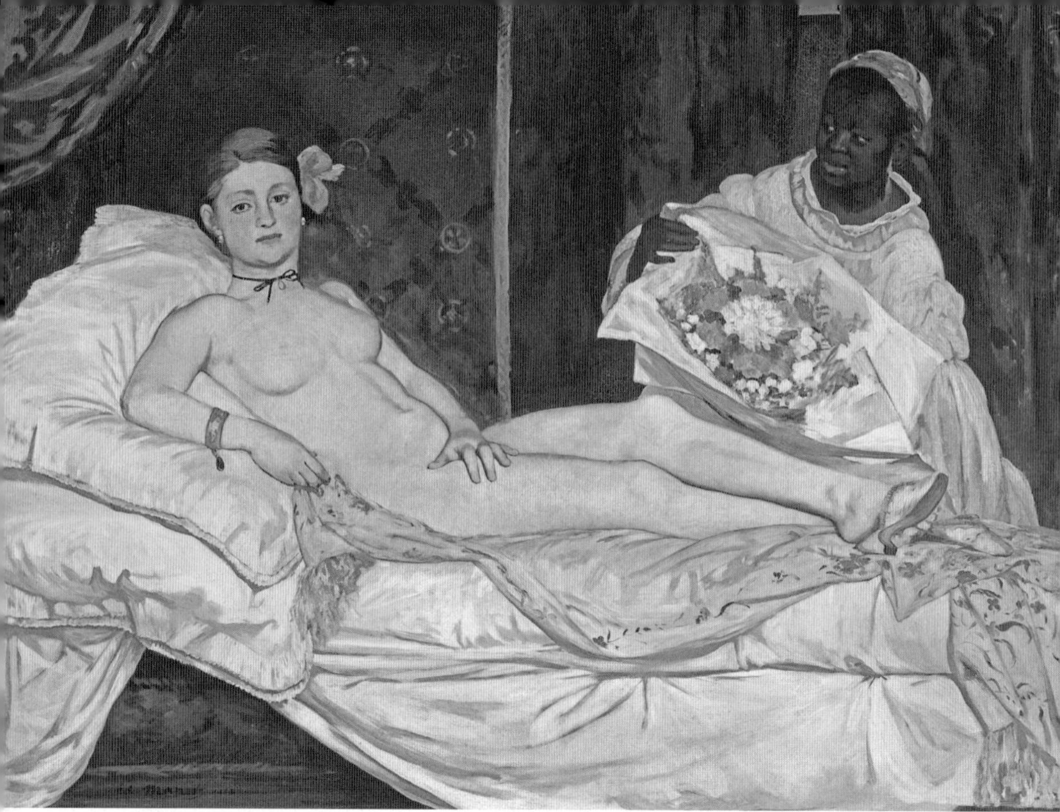

Image 13. Édouard Manet, *Olympia*, oil on canvas, 1863. Musée d'Orsay, Paris

to show the ugly truth, shock, and challenge. This pivotal turn in the history of Western art enabled the rise of the artist as a social critic, contemporary philosopher, and harbinger of a kind of truth that for the first time no longer belonged to antiquity, patrons, the academy, the church, or the state. Meanwhile, the young artists who dared to challenge the establishment continued to face the ever-present threat of financial ruin.

## Impressionist Cash: From Trickles to Waterfalls while Staring at Ponds

While it was easy for Claude Monet, Pierre-Auguste Renoir, and Camille Pissarro to prop their easels wherever they wished and paint undisturbed for a few hours, the female protagonists of Impressionism had a much harder time. Mary Cassatt and Berthe Morisot experienced closely monitored social lives. While to Renoir or Pissarro, Paris was a wondrous whirl of modern hustle and bustle, for Morisot and Cassatt the

Image 14 (facing page). Mary Cassatt, *Woman with a Red Zinnia*, oil on canvas, 1891. The National Gallery of Art, Washington DC (previous page)

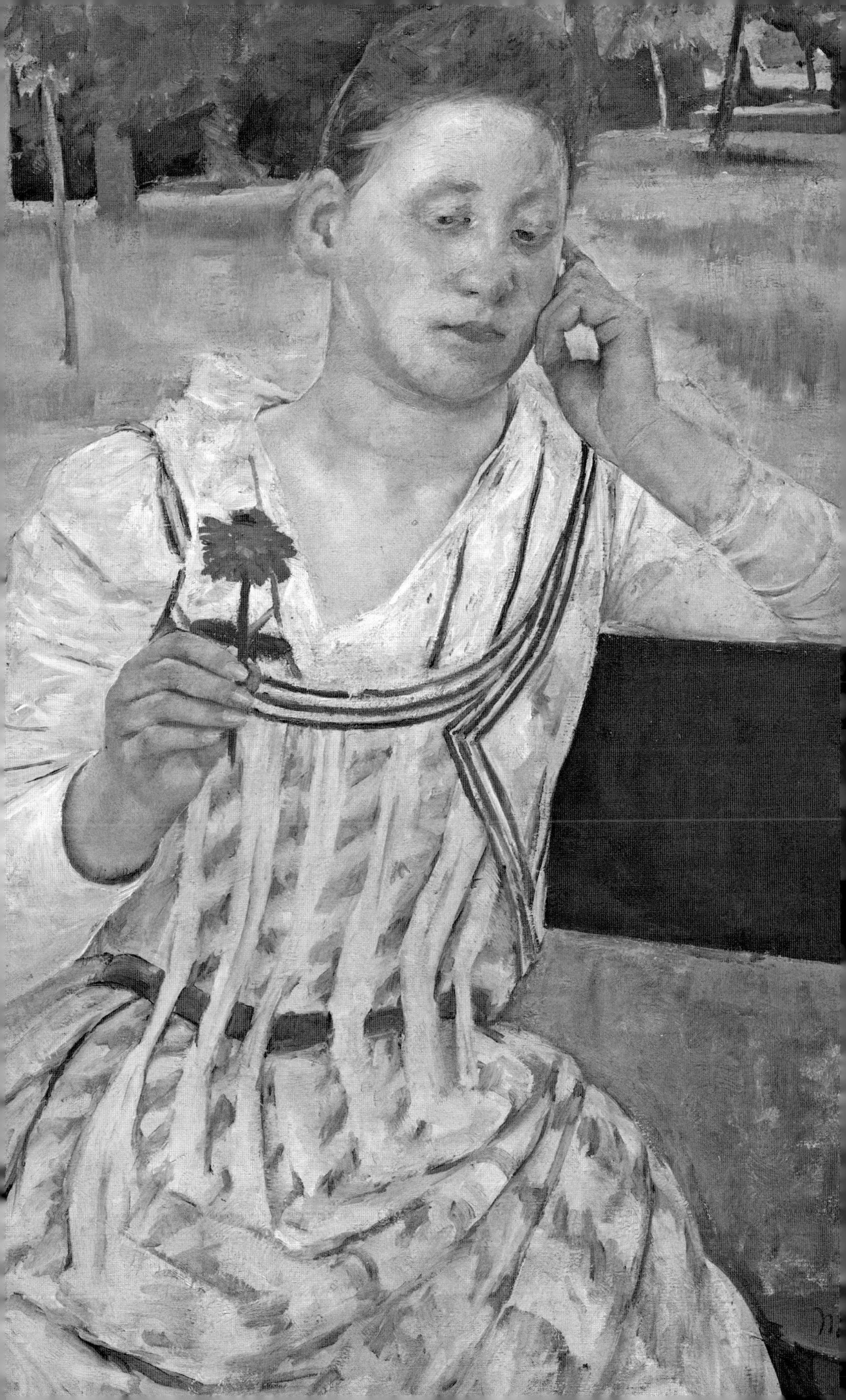

city posed a threat to their very womanhood. Women could rarely experience city life unaccompanied by a figure of authority: a father, older brother, or a husband. Lone women wandering the streets of Paris risked being mistaken for sex workers. This not only led female artists to bring Impressionism indoors, often with outstandingly original results, but also imbued their compositions with a distinctive kind of intimacy and melancholic longing. Gardens and balconies, open-air enclosures—this form of quasi-captivity was what Cassatt and Morisot frequently painted. Their women subjects are surrounded by fences and railings—symbols of societal restrictions and impositions—prisoners of patriarchal power.[29]

Initially and for many years, Impressionist paintings by either male or female artists, did not sell. Luckily, the group had learned plenty from Courbet's and Bonheur's industrious natures. The first Impressionist exhibition of 1874 was the result of a similar go-getter approach. Monet's idea to set up an independent exhibition, as Courbet had done, worked. Being good friends with the famous photographer Nadar, and that he was happy to host the Impressionists' show at his studio gallery, proved to be a significant asset. The exhibition opening was strategically set a few days before that of the Salon, to capitalize on the influx of art lovers flooding Paris. Two hundred visitors attended on the first day; a hundred per day thereafter. As with the Salon des Refusés, those who went mostly laughed; the mandatory negative reviews followed. The newly affluent, aspiring middle classes—the bourgeoisie—were simply not ready for Impressionist paintings. Instead of affirming and validating their self-importance, Impressionism baffled them with what seemed to them an unforgivable lack of skill.

But the self-organized exhibition gave the artists exposure, a very important—and currently deeply misunderstood—value in art that nineteenth-century avant-garde artists were just learning to leverage. The first exhibition made way for a lot more than giving Impressionism a break into the art world. Monet, for example, took the opportunity to set up a cooperative society of artists. Commercialism was at the forefront of his mind. His dear friend Pissarro, a self-professed anarchist, bought into the communist undertones of the idea, perhaps not fully aware of Monet's true motives.[30] The promotional spin soon followed.

Star novelist and art critic Émile Zola, who had supported the Impressionists in Parisian newspapers, asked his protégé Paul Alexis to write an article in *L'Avenir National* to put the as-yet-unnamed movement on the map. It was seen by officials as anti-government propaganda. *L'Avenir* was prosecuted and closed in a matter of months. News of Monet's proposed pseudo-political artist commune reached the Salon jury. They saw it as a provocation, an assault on their hegemony on taste and "good art." Another scandal, another page for the art history book. In their time, the Impressionists had nothing to do with chocolate boxes, coffee-table books, or calendars as they do today. They were modern rogues.[31]


Image 15 (facing page). Berthe Morisot, *The Artist's Sister at a Window*, oil on canvas, 1869. The National Gallery of Art, Washington DC (previous page)

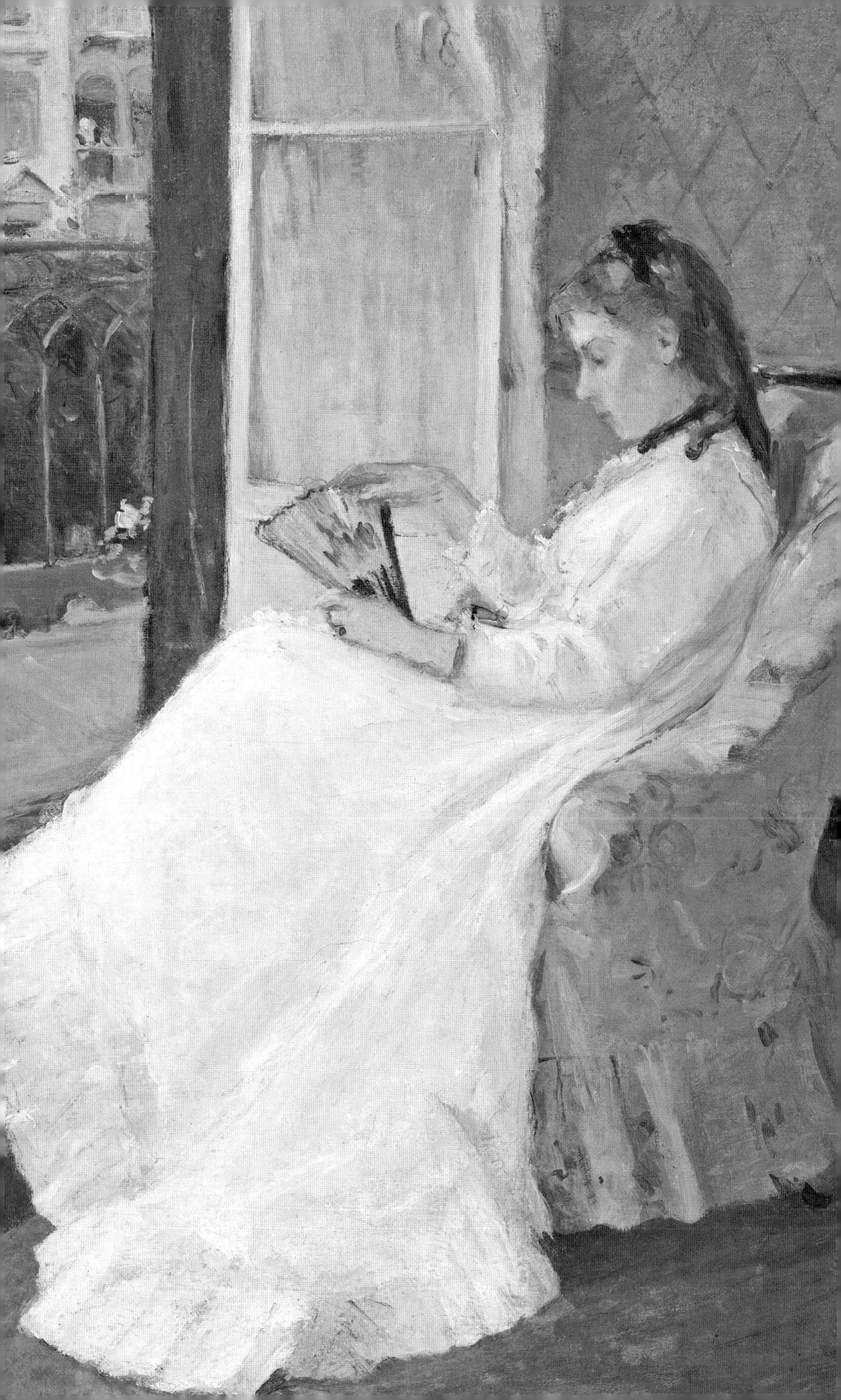

It quickly appeared clear to these artists that new alliances needed to be formed in order to fill the void left by patrons, state, and church. Art critics, historians, collectors, and dealers forged new connections as they mapped a new symbiotic ecosystem: the modern art world.

At the beginning of 1874, art critic Armand Silvestre penned a catalog essay about Monet, Sisley, and Pissarro in which he stressed the extraordinary innovativeness of the Impressionist group. The text was commissioned by pioneer art dealer Paul Durand-Ruel. Durand-Ruel planned to buy as much work by Impressionist artists as possible to build a market for them. He came up with an investment model based on the "validation factor" that would become the norm in the art market.[32]

In 1870, aware that works of art can gain value when acquired by prestigious collectors, Durand-Ruel secured a loan from a banker, Charles Edwards, and used Impressionist paintings as collateral so that, at a later time, he could legitimately advertise the lot as "The Edwards Collection," adding prestige to the paintings. The Paris sale, which took place at the glamorous auction house Hôtel Drouot, was a success. This simple marketing maneuver made the value of Durand-Ruel's paintings balloon.[33] The strategy was straightforward. It relied on the principle of social aspiration: the simple idea that if someone famous buys or enjoys something then it must be good, and that, by buying it, too, we ordinary folks can become a bit like them. Today this model has developed into a many-headed beast, with perhaps the latest incarnation being the ubiquitous social media influencer.

An astute and creative self-promoter, Durand-Ruel published journals (concealing his name) that publicized the art he sold, organized monographic exhibitions, and published catalogs. He understood that each of his activities validated and bolstered the legitimacy of the other. He thus generated the kind of exposure that promoted prestige and credibility. Taking a leaf from Courbet's "book of the artist as entrepreneur," Durand-Ruel standardized the "artist's solo show," today considered a hallmark of professional accomplishment. Durand-Ruel revisited Vasari's love for biographies and curated retrospective-style monographic exhibitions that mythologized the artists' creative journeys. This strategy also monetized the artists' unfinished studies, sketches, and preparatory drawings, turning them into desirable collectibles.

But this financial speculation was not necessarily bad for the Impressionists since Durand-Ruel would reinvest much of what he earned into their development. It wasn't long before many became "kept" artists. Durand-Ruel paid them a monthly stipend so that they could work—producing paintings that he promptly bought in bulk but for which a strong market didn't yet exist. In fact, for years, Durand-Ruel stood pretty much alone, surrounded by an openly hostile crowd of academicians and famous art critics who wasted no opportunity to despise the young art movement. *Le Figaro*'s Albert Wolff described the second Impressionist exhibition of 1876 thus:

> The rue Le Peletier is in bad luck. After the fire at the Opera, here is a new disaster that befalls the neighborhood. We have just opened at Durand-Ruel an exhibition, said to be painting. Inoffensive passer-by, attracted by the flags which decorate the facade, enters, and to his horrified eyes is offered a cruel spectacle. Five or

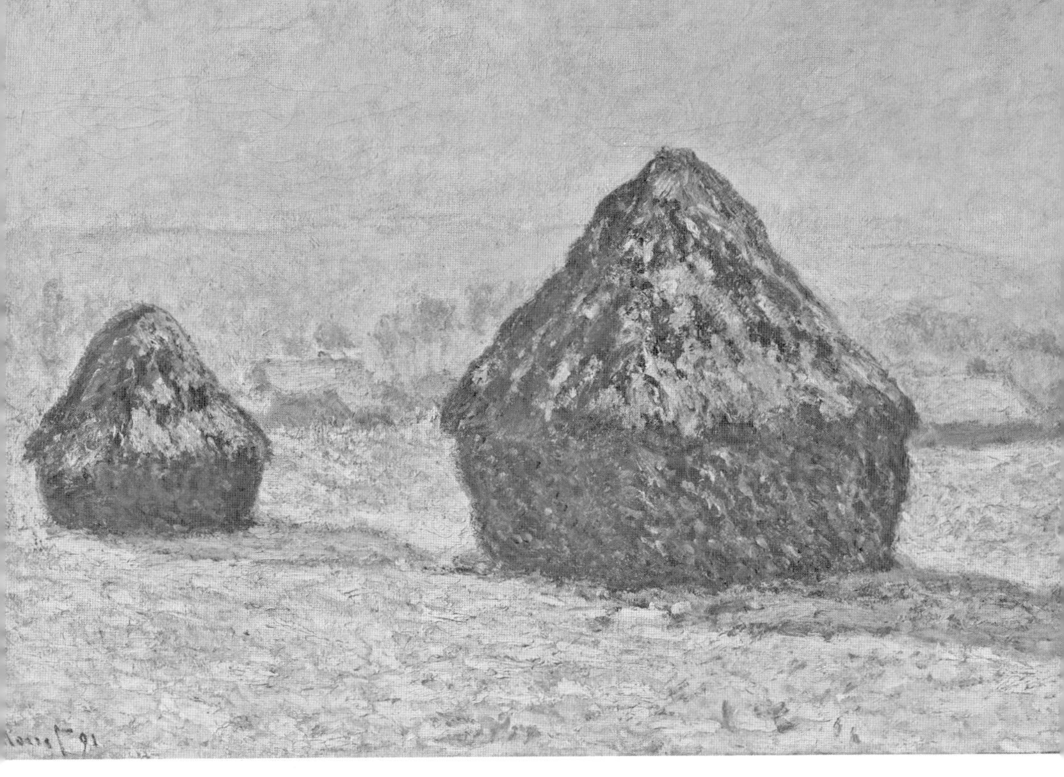

Image 16. Claude Monet, *Wheatstacks, Snow Effect, Morning*. Oil on canvas, 1891. The J. Paul Getty Museum, Los Angeles

six lunatics including a woman, a group of unfortunate people suffering from the madness of ambition, there are given an appointment to exhibit their work. There are people who giggle at these things. I have a heavy heart. These so-called artists call themselves the uncompromising, the impressionists: they take canvases, color, and brushes, throw in a few tones at random and sign everything . . . Frightful spectacle of the human vanity going astray until insanity.[34]

Durand-Ruel endured years of humiliation and risked bankruptcy many times over until, in 1885, the tide unexpectedly turned in his favor. An invitation by James Sutton, Director of the American Art Association, to exhibit some of his represented artists in New York and the diplomatic help of Mary Cassatt brought about overnight success. Claiming the exhibition was primarily for education purposes (it was not) Durand-Ruel avoided a customs tax on the three hundred canvases that traveled across the ocean with him.[35]

In stark opposition to French audiences, Americans were in awe of the vibrantly rendered views of everyday European life—scenes that many of them dearly missed. Where to Parisian eyes, the Impressionists only portrayed everyday banality, the less stuck-up Americans saw vivid memories—charming reminders of the last time they strolled down the Champs-Élysées or sat by the river Seine eating finger food out of a basket. Durand-Ruel sold forty-nine pictures for about $40,000. A year later, he was back in New York armed with more canvases and the determination to open his first American gallery. A substantial exhibition of Impressionist works held in 1905 at Grafton Galleries in London was received more positively than any previous event—evidence of the cultural feedback loop tying the United States and the United Kingdom that has characterized much of twentieth-century history.

Durand-Ruel was the first gallerist/collector/entrepreneur brave enough to forge new business models to support a new kind of modern artist. By the end of the nineteenth century, the blueprint for the modern art market we know today was, for better or worse, set in place. Without him, the Impressionist would have never happened.

The *fin-de-siècle* Parisian artist emerged from the dissipation of commissions, the dwindling of patronage, and the steadily intensifying market competition. The creative process now rested entirely in the hands of the artist—no longer the result of careful negotiations and consultations with wealthy donors and institutions, artists could finally paint what they wanted . . . But at what cost? With this unprecedented freedom also came the need to develop a distinctive identity profile, create a market, generate publicity, stay visible, and, above all, become desirable. To survive, the modern artist had to evolve into an astute artificer.

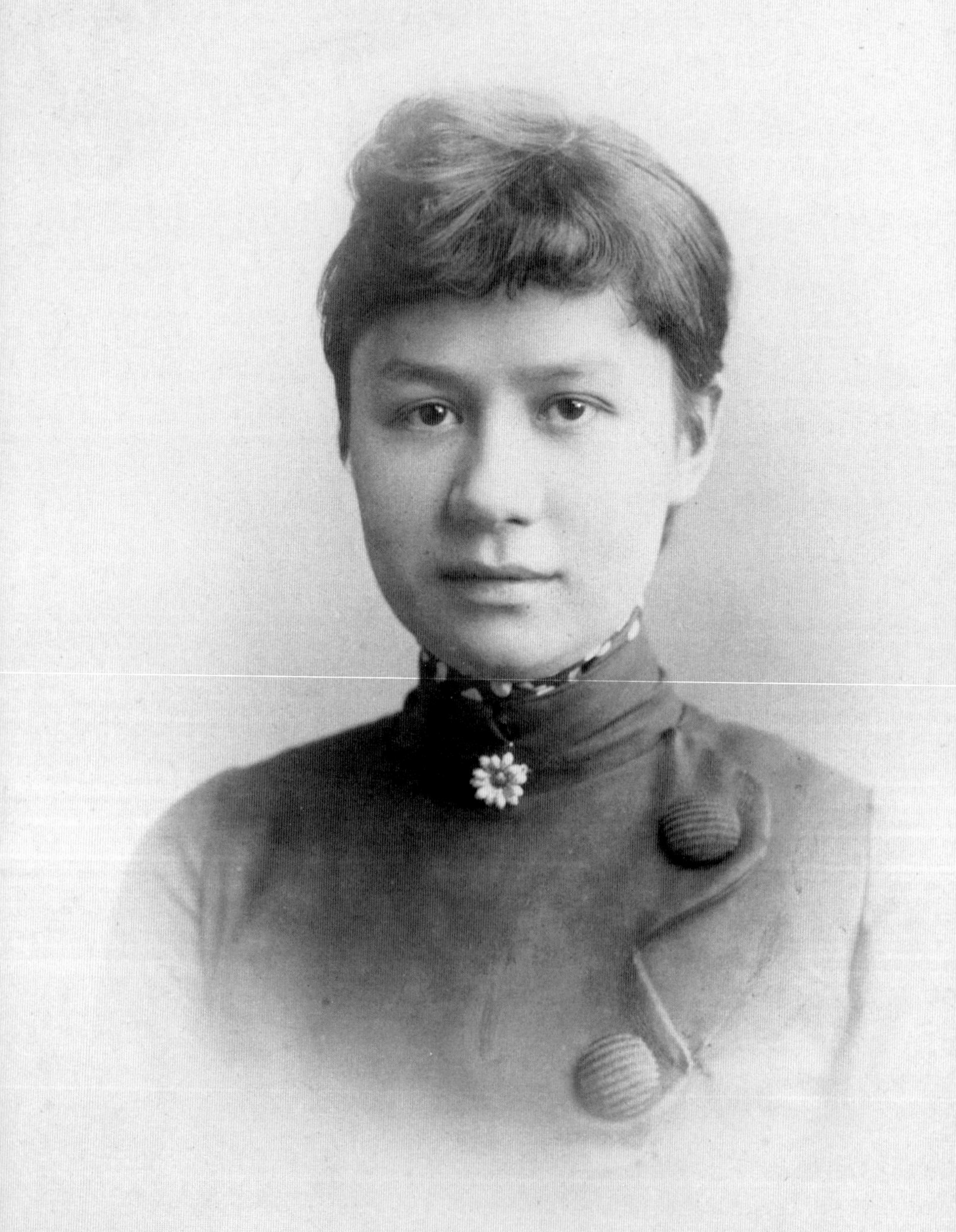

# 3  Modern Ecologies: Markets, Marketeers, and Alliances

Image 17 (facing page). Jo van Gogh-Bonger, 1889. Photograph: Woodbury & Page, Amsterdam. Public Domain

# Fearing the Mob: Elitism and Art

Cigarette smoke fills the air—wrapped in a stone-and-sparkles studded leotard a gymnast pirouettes from one side of the hall to the other surrounded by a crowd of drunken punters loudly cheering, heckling, and jeering. People dance, music plays all night. The loud chatter squeezes out even the occasional silence between the notes—the working classes play just as hard as they work. Magicians, mimes, singers, and comedians—a 9-pence ($3 today) entrance fee buys hours of entertainment.

By the 1860s, the figure of the *lion comique* started to dominate the bill, making fun of the dandies and champagne Charlies, mocking the frivolity of those who spent time people-watching instead of working, and the flamboyant fashion items they flaunted.[1] Ridiculing the upper classes exorcised their power. For a brief moment, in the fictional realm of the music hall, workers had the upper hand—booing at the effigies of those who have it easy, validated their principles.

The music, the dancers, the drinking, the excitement—every weekend, throughout the second half of the nineteenth century, the working classes invented modern mass entertainment. By the 1880s, the music hall moved from the suburbs to the heart of cities, courting middle-class audiences—they quickly garnered a pretty terrible reputation. To the upper middle classes, performance after performance, the music hall—the antithesis of the museum—eroded the integrity of the ancient arts. Above it all, looming large was the fear that financial gain took precedence over the purity of expression.

Eventually, art landed the entertainment bill. The worst crime the music hall could commit: to blur the boundaries between *tableaux vivants*, classical sculpture, painting, theater, and photography. Art appeared to have been swallowed up into a vortex of hedonistic superficiality that baffled and horrified the upper classes. It had lost its moral compass, dignity, and respectability—they thought . . . and most artists agreed with them, too.

For over two hundred years, academies, professional juries, the state, and the church (for much longer) had prevented art from "going astray." Even Charles Baudelaire, the staunch supporter of "the painter of modern life," dreaded the popularization of art. To him photography was a vulgarizing blight that indulged the "stupidity of the multitude"; its popularity "a disease of imbeciles."[2] While open-mindedly advocating for the need to "discover whether we possess a specific beauty, intrinsic to our new emotions,"[3] he also loathed mechanical reproduction as the new opium of the people. Baudelaire's contradictory stance typified the dandy: the upper-middle-class intellectual who incites the revolution from the comfort of his armchair. Remember Courbet? Baudelaire was acutely aware of the modern condition in which the nonaristocratic intellectual must sell their soul to make a living selling their art. Those who decide to push the envelope and make new, cutting-edge art implicitly entered a kind of Faustian pact; forever freed from the shackles of classicism but endlessly enslaved to an unforgiving market-master.[4] By the end of the nineteenth century, it became apparent that the only social mark of distinction left to the modern intellectual was taste. With Baudelaire, a new self-styled cultural aristocracy was born—one that in more than one way repackaged older forms of elitism into a multitude of new aesthetic and conceptual propositions that, movement after movement, intentionally made art less and less accessible to the masses. The romantic myth of the artist as misunderstood genius had at this point become a far too real, self-fulfilling prophecy.

## Markets, Marketeers, and Selling Out

Both the history of the Netherlands and the history of art were drastically altered by the economic boom that followed the end of the Eighty Years' War with Spain in 1648. Sometimes it was the family members of artists who would seize the favorable opportunity to start an art business. Johannes Vermeer was represented by his relatives who also branched out into selling the work of others. Antiques traders who specialized in maps, books, and furniture became art dealers.[5] Some would commission work for prospective clients, others traveled Europe's estates in search of hidden treasures. But regardless of what they sold and how they did it, the key objectives of the dealer were to instill interest and generate demand. Successful salespeople have always been great storytellers. They know how to fill a picture or an object with a universe of wonder. By the second half of the nineteenth century, they had carved for themselves a special place in the art world that is still just as important today.

A great exponent of this lineage, Ernest Gambart was among the first dealers to open a successful art gallery in London in the late 1850s. At around the same time, in New York, Michael Knoedler established the first free-entry gallery (a 25-cent admission charge was usual), setting a trend that would enable an ever-growing cultural circle to form around a new art market. But exhibiting and selling through a gallery rather than the official institutions proved highly controversial, at least until the end of the century. At times, marginalization leads to trailblazing originality. It was in fact a number of highly ingenious, talented, determined, and often unacknowledged, women who fueled the collecting world of early modern art. In 1901, Berthe Weill opened her Parisian gallery—with the money set aside for her dowry—as "a place for youth." This was the slogan emblazoned on her business cards. Weill launched Picasso's career by placing his drawings in important collections.[6] In the United Kingdom, Lucy Carrington Wertheim promoted the work of Henry Moore, Walter Sickert, and Cedric Morris.[7]

The growing success of commercial galleries raised eyebrows at the Royal Academy of Arts in London and the Parisian Salon. In these upper-class circles exhibiting in a commercial gallery could taint an artist's reputation and permanently thwart careers. In the early days of the art market, enthusiasm and anxiety were key ingredients of a modern cocktail. Artists, art critics, and dealers mapped uncharted territories, negotiating and forging new alliances strong enough to withstand the staunch opposition of ingrained institutional power. Risk-taking was the only way forward and affiliations could make or break careers; a bold marketing maneuver could bring a financial windfall *but still* destroy an artist's legacy (sometimes temporarily, at other times for good).

John Everett Millais, one of the most revered masters of British art, began his career in the 1850s as a member of the rebellious Pre-Raphaelite Brotherhood. Over thirty years later, he sold a work entitled *Bubbles* to the soap company A. & F. Pears for promotional use. The substantial fee of £2,200 (the equivalent of £305,000 today) included the copyright ownership and the freedom to add a bar of their soap to the original. Millais's commercial "sell-out" was demonized by the press and even ridiculed in a successful novel.[8]

Writing mythologizes. It makes or breaks artists' careers. As Zhang Yanyuan and Giorgio Vasari had amply demonstrated hundreds of years prior, writing anchors the material permanence of art to the bedrock of history. By the end of the nineteenth century, critics and art historians had become powerful players in the new art world. Durand-Ruel's savvy and manipulative use of the printed word as a promotional tool had amply demonstrated its power. The new art history and art criticism were shaped by money and interest just as much as they were by the desire to promote innovation. Rubbing shoulders with dealers and auction houses, critics and art historians became part of a complex and essential validating ecosystem. Yesterday as today, they influence taste. While some helped women artists to emerge from obscurity, the new modern art world was still dominated by male collectors who imposed their taste on mostly male dealers, who in turn worked closely with male art historians, critics, and gallery owners in order to fulfill the collectors' desires. Furthermore, the white supremacist feedback loop that throughout the last century has kept (and in large part still does) male artists at the top has also resulted in a substantial sidelining of BIPOC artists. In the United States as well as in Europe, African American artists were seriously held back by racism and prejudice. Artists determined to make a living through their art had little to no choice but to become part of this system. And to become part of it wasn't easy either.

Through sheer talent and the ability to develop strong networks of supporters and collectors, Robert Seldon Duncanson became famous in his own lifetime as America's finest landscape painter. After many years working as a house painter and decorator, in 1838, Duncanson moved to Cincinnati—then a thriving cultural center known as the "Athens of the West"—to become an artist. Self-taught and struggling to assimilate in a thoroughly white and exclusivist local scene, Duncanson established a close friendship with abolitionist Methodist minister Charles Avery who commissioned work and also introduced him to other like-minded individuals.[9] Inspired by the work of the Hudson River School, Duncanson began to focus on portraying the serene grandness of the Ohio River Valley. This new body of work attracted the attention of Nicholas Longworth, one of the richest and best-connected men in the United States. As a result of more prestigious commissions, Duncanson's fame spread to Canada (where he relocated during the Civil War) and across the Atlantic: the prestigious *London Art Journal* declared him a master of landscape painting. He became the first, most successful African American artist in the history of art. His landscapes,

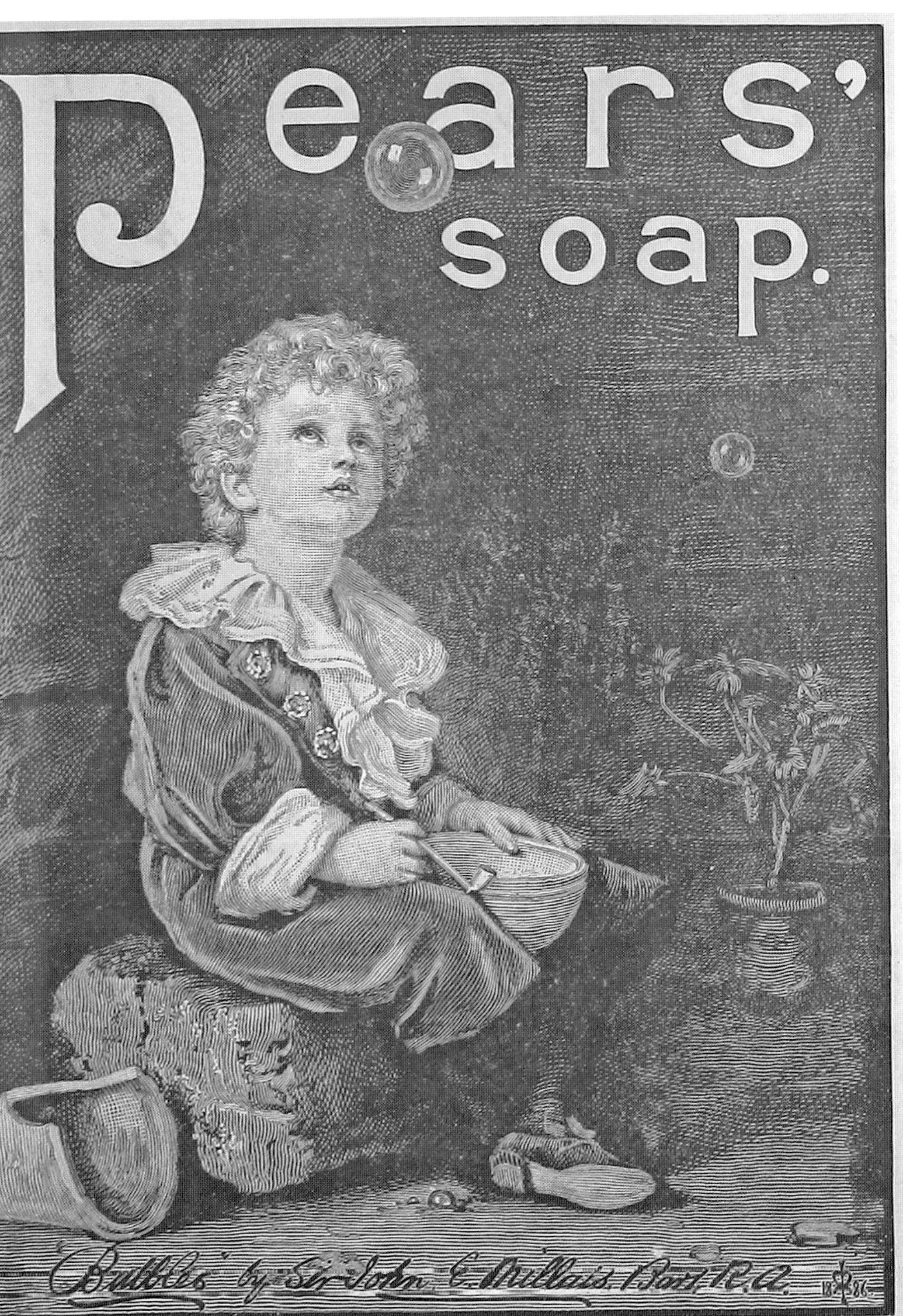


Image 18.  John Everett Millais, *Bubbles*, advertisement from Pears' Centenary Edition of *Charles Dickens' Christmas Books*, 1912. Public Domain

although inspired by a long-standing Western tradition, were imbued with an African American sensitivity that also challenged preconceptions on what and how a Black artist should paint.[10]

## Johanna van Gogh-Bonger: The First Art Market Guru

Why did Theo Van Gogh, a successful art dealer, find it impossible to sell his brother's paintings? While it is common knowledge that Theo supported his brother Vincent Van Gogh every step of the way—from buying his brushes to paying his rent—it is not well known that, before becoming a painter, Vincent was himself an art dealer. Between 1869 and 1876, he worked for the prestigious print publishing and art dealer firm Goupil & Co. (partly owned by his uncle). Van Gogh's true ambition to become an artist only matured in 1880, years after he left the company. His experience at Goupil, however, shaped his future creative life in ways that are not commonly acknowledged.

Determined to conquer both the French and English markets, he titled his works in both languages. His letters to Theo reveal that his iconic sunflowers series, which has been mythologized by art history as an unbridled moment of pure artistic genius, were masterminded for the British market where he hoped to sell them for the equivalent of 500 francs each.[11] Brightly colored and stylized, his paintings were too ahead of their time —the market for them simply wasn't there yet. It didn't take long for the artist to give up his dreams of market domination and continue to paint for his own enjoyment. So how is it that one of his paintings today can sell for over $80 million?

Van Gogh owes his colossal modern art-genius status to the wit and determination of Theo's widow, Johanna van Gogh-Bonger—his sister-in-law. Vincent passed away in 1890, leaving behind almost a thousand paintings in less than ten years. Theo died six months later. Finding herself alone at the age of 28, with a one-year-old son, and hundreds of Vincent's paintings in her basement, Jo sought the opportunity to make a living while fulfilling her late husband's wish to make his brother famous. She left Paris—it was too expensive—and strategically relocated to the Dutch town of Bassum, where she opened a guesthouse. There she befriended a circle of artists who connected her to the local art scene. As her knowledge of the scene and confidence grew, she organized exhibitions of Vincent's works in Amsterdam and abroad. Her goal was to do what art dealers do best: generate interest and demand. Fortunately, *Mercure de France* published a laudatory piece on Van Gogh's paintings by renowned art critic Gabriel Albert-Aurier just before the artist's death.[12] Leveraging the article's influence, Johanna tirelessly networked with collectors, artists, and other dealers to build the myth of Van Gogh from scratch.

Sometimes, the admiration of fellow artists can become a true asset to another artist's career. In 1892, Émile Bernard—a personal friend and great admirer of Van Gogh's work—helped her out by organizing a small solo show of Vincent's paintings in Paris. Artist/art dealer Julien Tanguy exhibited his Van Gogh paintings with several

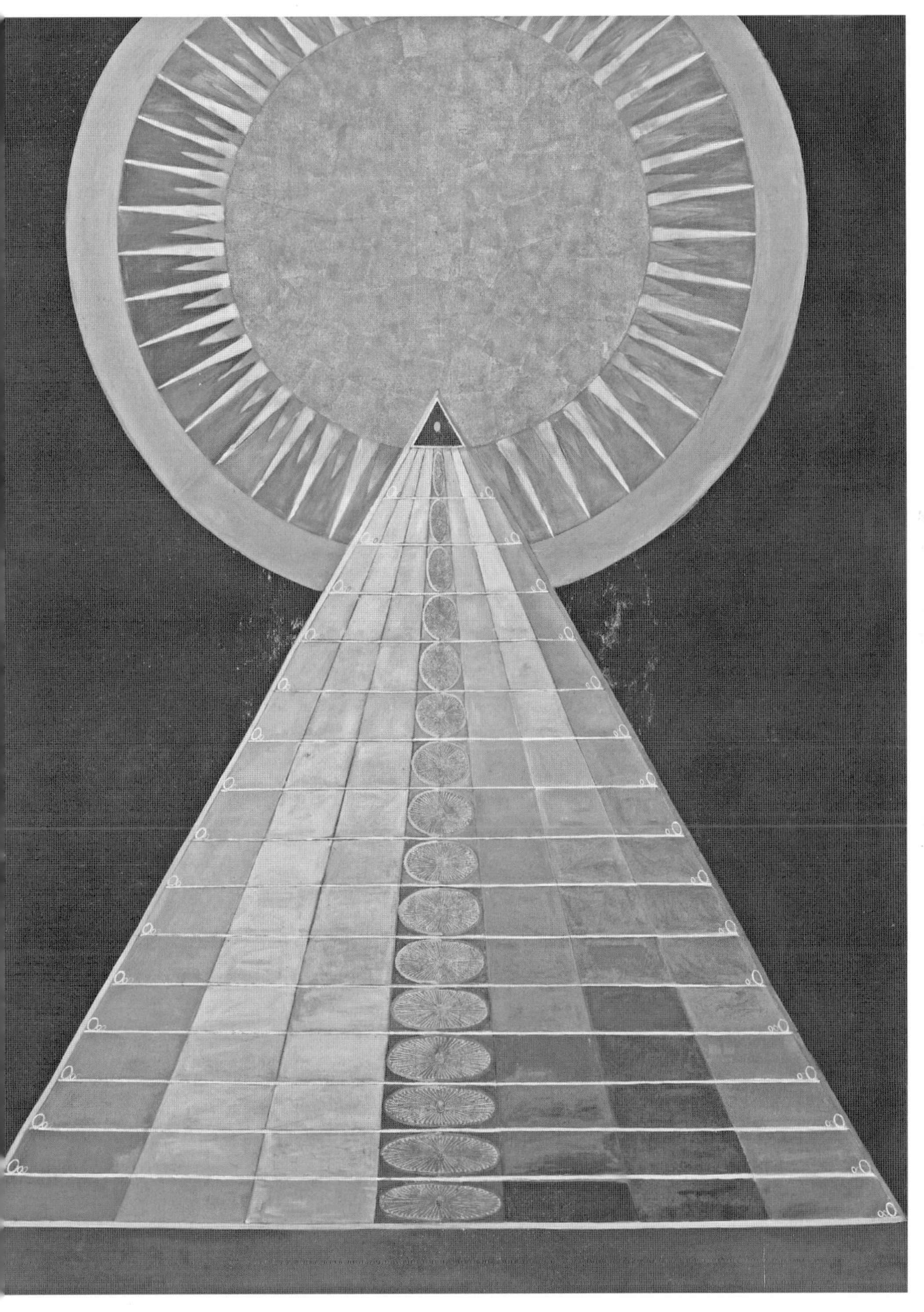

Image 19.  Hilma af Klint, *Altarpiece, No. 1, Group X*, *Altarpieces*, 1907. © Stiftelsen Hilma af Klints Verk. Photo: Albin Dahlström/Moderna Museet

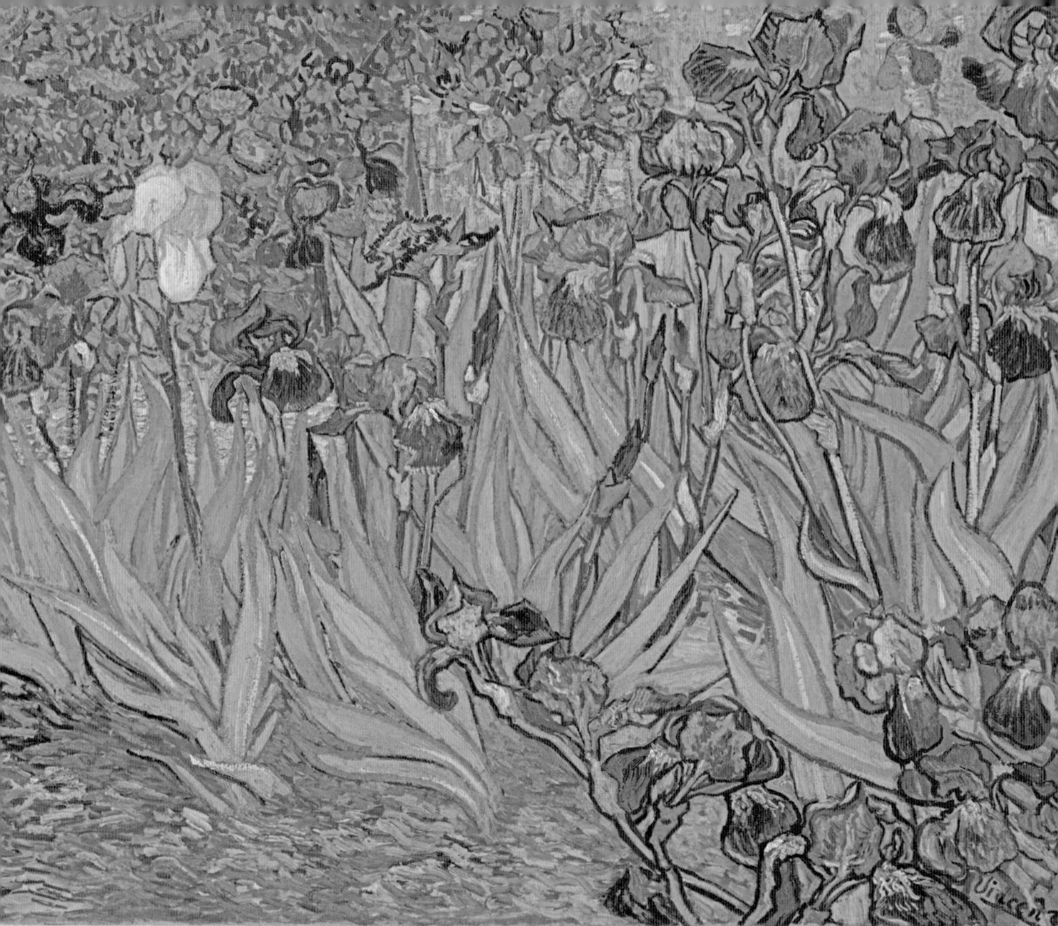

Image 20. Vincent Van Gogh, *Irises*, 1889. Oil on canvas. The J. Paul Getty Museum, Los Angeles.

consigned from Johanna. In April 1894, Durand-Ruel also became involved. Noticeably, Gauguin—once a dear friend and then a fierce rival—stayed out of it.[13]

In 1905, Jo's determination and entrepreneurial flair paid off. A massive retrospective of 480 canvases was held at the Stedelijk Museum in Amsterdam. The exhibition—the biggest and most prestigious at that point—inflated the paintings' value. However, one piece of her mythologizing puzzle was still missing. But she knew where to find it. Along with many paintings and several hundred drawings, Johanna inherited 820 letters—the intense correspondence between the two brothers. A treasure trove of personal stories, anecdotes, and commentaries along with important biographical notes and detailed sketches, Van Gogh's letters were published as a volume in 1914—an astute marketing move that sealed the artist's legendary status. Savvy, self-styled, industrious dealer-cum-editor Johanna van Gogh-Bonger cracked the art market and navigated institutional politics at a time when women were generally given very little credit in this field.[14] Her hard work behind the scenes is still paying off today, while her praise remains mostly unsung.

# Art Historians Change the Past. . . If They Want To

From a certain point in their careers, the venerated innovators of early modern art such as Van Gogh, Gauguin, and Munch pursued their artistic inclinations mostly with deliberate disregard for the art world and its politics. This enabled them to enjoy creative freedom, but they also lived tortured lives steeped with depression and financial trouble. Public recognition only manifested well after their deaths and after a critic or art historian cast new light on their work.

Unlike the Impressionists, who together plotted their artistic revolution in Parisian bars and cafés, the likes of Gauguin, Cézanne, Van Gogh, Matisse, Toulouse-Lautrec, and Seurat owe much of their fame to an art historian called Roger Fry. A specialist in Old Masters with a curatorial stint at New York's Museum of Modern Art (MoMA) and a number of well-respected essays published in art historical journals under his belt, Fry came upon the artworks of Cézanne, only three years after the artist's death, in the aftermath of substantial retrospectives of his work that had taken place in Paris, most notably at the 1907 Salon d'Automne.[15]

Aware that these artists shared something meaningful through their work, he singlehandedly masterminded the label "Postimpressionism." As he explained, "For purposes of convenience, it was necessary to give these artists a name, and I chose, as being the vaguest and most non-committal, the name of post-impressionism. This merely stated their position in time relatively to the Impressionist movement." The Postimpressionists didn't quite exist as a movement of artists who worked together pursuing a communal aesthetic goal. Rather they were retrospectively crafted—a plan that worked exquisitely well for their legacies, as well as Fry's own career.[16]

But while critics can be powerful champions of artists, they are fallible, and the failure to recognize true originality has at times lent terrible blows to artists' careers. Among the many is Hilma af Klint, a Swedish artist, influenced by the study of spiritualism, who pioneered abstract art. She went four years without touching a paintbrush after being deeply hurt by Rudolf Steiner's negative reception of her work in 1908. Disheartened, af Klint endowed her outstanding body of work to her nephew, Erik af Klint, requesting that it should remain secret for at least twenty years after her death. When the artist passed away in 1944 this clause cost her dearly. By the time the paintings were shown in public, the history of abstraction had been written and published—without the chapter about her work in it.[17]

Inserting deserving artists retrospectively in the narrative of art history has always proved hard. It is as if such an operation might tamper with the presumed integrity of a natural evolution of art. Paradoxically, paleoethology is more likely to revise its planetary chronologies based on the discovery of a new fossil than art history is willing to contemplate the canonization of a newly discovered artist (especially if female or BIPOC).

The misfortune of self-taught photographer Vivian Maier shares similarities with af Klint. Maier, a professional nanny who worked in the Chicago suburbs, took over 150,000 photographs (many still undeveloped) throughout her life. None of them was shown during her lifetime. It was only in 2007 that real estate agent John Maloof bought a box of undeveloped rolls of film and negatives for $400 from an auction house. He then proceeded to develop, print, and exhibit her work. While the originality and quality of her output is unquestionable—Maier was a modern street photographer with a penchant for the grittiness of real life—her work is edited and sequenced by Maloof and other collectors. Art historians find it difficult to engage with her work in a confident way. Where does the artist begin and the collector end? This aspect in particular has cast a shadow on academic interpretations as well as ethical considerations on the use, often for profit, of her archive. While commercial success has been substantial, Maier's work is constantly embroiled in lawsuits related to copyright ownership and has yet failed to secure a solo exhibition at a major art museum.[18]

The conditions of success that underpin an artist's career have, during the last century, dramatically changed—creative freedom in the modern art world became something artists had to buy. How did some of the biggest artists of the last century—the ones art students often cite as their models—from Frida Kahlo and Georgia O'Keeffe to Pablo Picasso, Salvador Dali, Jackson Pollock, Michel Basquiat, Andy Warhol, and Yayoi Kusama claim their spot in the artistic limelight? How did they gain the financial stability that allowed them to lead long and productive careers?

## Playing the Fame Game

Trained by his father and unsuited to art academy life, Picasso traveled to Paris in 1904. As the art historical official narrative has it, living in abject poverty, he burnt some of his works to keep himself warm at night. In his case, too, as for Van Gogh, it wasn't his sheer talent that lifted him from obscurity. He would have probably died poor and unknown if it hadn't been for pioneer art dealers Daniel-Henry Kahnweiler and Ambroise Vollard, as well as the patronage of Gertrude and Leo Stein.

It was Kahnweiler who introduced Picasso to George Braque, the artistic accomplice co-responsible for the invention of Cubism, and who actively supported the artists through their experimental journey.[19] Between 1906 and 1910, the crucial years during which Picasso transitioned from his Rose Period to Cubism were defined by the Steins, who at the time were the artist's only collectors.

Picasso was just as good at flirting as he was at professional networking. At one of Stein's exclusive Saturday evening salons, he met the collectors Claribel and Etta Cone, who also began to purchase his work as well as that of Matisse. A savvy businessman and talented artist, by the age of 28, Picasso no longer had to worry about money. Ten years later, he could safely consider himself rich. By the age of 65, he became the world's richest living artist. In 1973, upon his passing, Picasso's estimated worth was between $100 and $250 million. That's equal to today's $530 million to $1.3 billion.[20]

Image 21 (facing page). Pablo Picasso, *Man with a Pipe*, 1915. Oil on canvas. Art Institute of Chicago. © 2018 Estate of Pablo Picasso / Artists Rights Society (ARS), New York

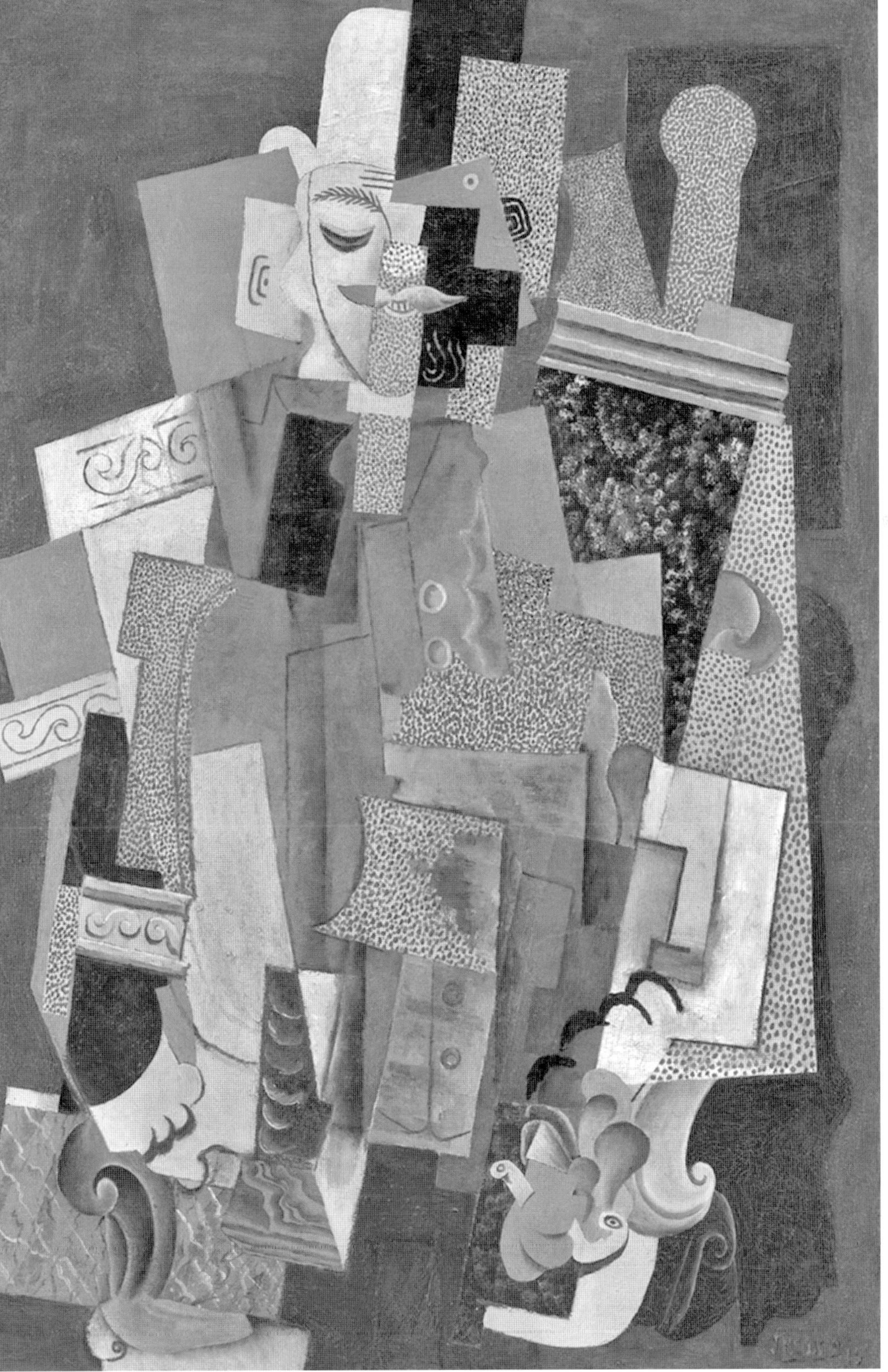

But how did Picasso become so well known? What about his art-charmed collectors around the world? The answer once again lies beyond his talent. He was the first artist to be swept up by the new printed and moving image media into a mythologizing frenzy that quickly veered toward parody and yet retained sacrality. The artist genius whose work is truly original, bold, and instantaneous; the insatiable womanizer; the mysterious and capricious child—Picasso was a living stereotype, and the media loved him.

Frida Kahlo's breakthrough happened in 1938, after the leader of Surrealism, André Breton, saw her paintings in Mexico City. Enchanted by the works and recognizing in them a raw and emotional surrealist charge, he wrote to his friend, art dealer Julien Levy, who invited the artist to hold a solo show in New York. Kahlo's haunting paintings bewitched the audience. In 1943, the artist's inclusion in the pioneering exhibition *31 Women*, curated by Peggy Guggenheim, cemented her status as one of the most exciting artists of the last century.[21]

Kahlo met Georgia O'Keeffe and her husband Alfred Stieglitz at the opening of Diego Rivera's (Frida's husband) 1931 exhibition at MoMA. They quickly became close friends. As talented women working in a male-dominated field, both Kahlo and O'Keeffe simultaneously benefited and suffered from being directly associated with successful husbands. Both Stieglitz, an art dealer and the most influential photographer of the early twentieth century, and Rivera, the most famous mural artist in the world, were extremely well connected. Having nurtured a sense of apathy for the realist tradition she had studied, O'Keeffe had already set the idea of becoming a full-time artist aside, opting for a commercial artist job in Chicago, followed by a spell

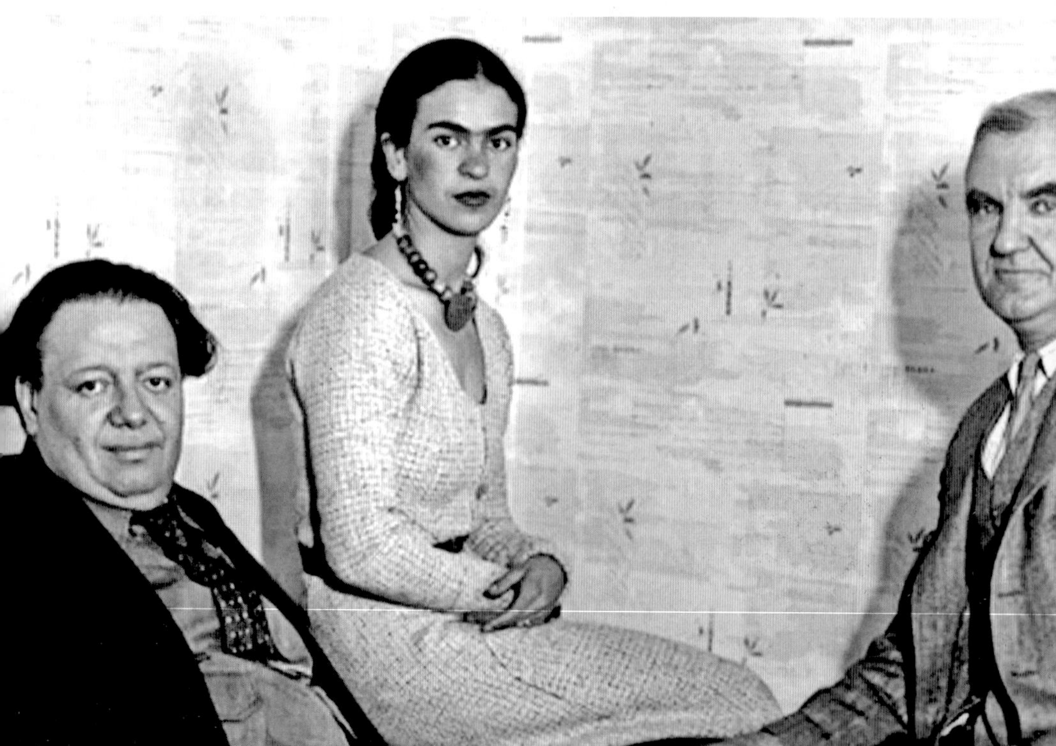

as a teacher. In 1915, feeling confident about a series of new abstract drawings, O'Keeffe sent a sample to a friend in New York who showed them to Stieglitz. He was so impressed with them that he gave O'Keeffe her first solo show in 1916.[22] However, both O'Keeffe and Kahlo were automatically diminished by the attention their notorious husbands attracted, which often cast a shadow on their talents and accomplishments.

Salvador Dalí deliberately threw his academic career under the bus when, at his final examination, he told the graduation committee that since "none of the professors at the school of San Fernando are competent to judge me, I retire."[23] This was allegedly part of a sophisticated ploy designed to free himself from familial shackles and move to Paris. Dalí knew well that making it as an artist wasn't just a matter of training and gathering qualifications, and that aspiring artists needed to network right at the epicenter of the art world in order to succeed. So, quite appropriately, his first stop in Paris was at Picasso's studio—a unique opportunity orchestrated by other fellow artists. According to art historical mythology, Dalí told Picasso: "I have come to see you before visiting the Louvre."[24] In 1929, fully immersed in his surrealist investigations, Dalí managed to strike a deal with art dealer Camille Goemans for a solo show in Paris that turned out to be a success.

But it was Gala, the artist's wife, who proved instrumental to Dali's financial stability—in the 1930s, she became his promoter and agent. Not only did she pitch his work to galleries and dealers but, in 1933, she persuaded Prince Jean Louis de Faucigny-Lucinge, along with eleven other philanthropists, to form the charmingly named collective called the Zodiac Group. They agreed to pay Dalí 2,500 francs per year in exchange for the right to choose a large painting or a smaller picture and two drawings. This financial support helped Dalí establish his career before fleeing to the United States in 1940 with a ticket purchased for him by Picasso.[25]

Once in the United States, to support himself, Dalí painted high society portraits. By the 1960s, greed—he was nicknamed *Avida Dollars* ("eager for dollars") in some circles, a telling anagram of his name—got him into trouble. Dalí had capitalized on his growing popularity by signing advertising deals with many brands—Wrigley's and Ford among others. At this point, he came to realize that his signature alone, on a blank sheet of paper, was worth roughly $40. Gala thus suggested he should pre-sign a staggering amount of plain paper—some claim 350,000 sheets—which could then be sold to forgers to paint or print at will on his behalf. While this provided the cash flow Dalí needed, the pre-signed blank sheets destroyed his prints market when a truck loaded with them was stopped by the police in 1974.[26]

Image 22 (facing page). Author unknown, undated. Diego Rivera and Frida Kahlo meeting with Anson Conger Goodyear, President of the Museum of Modern Art, in New York. Public Domain

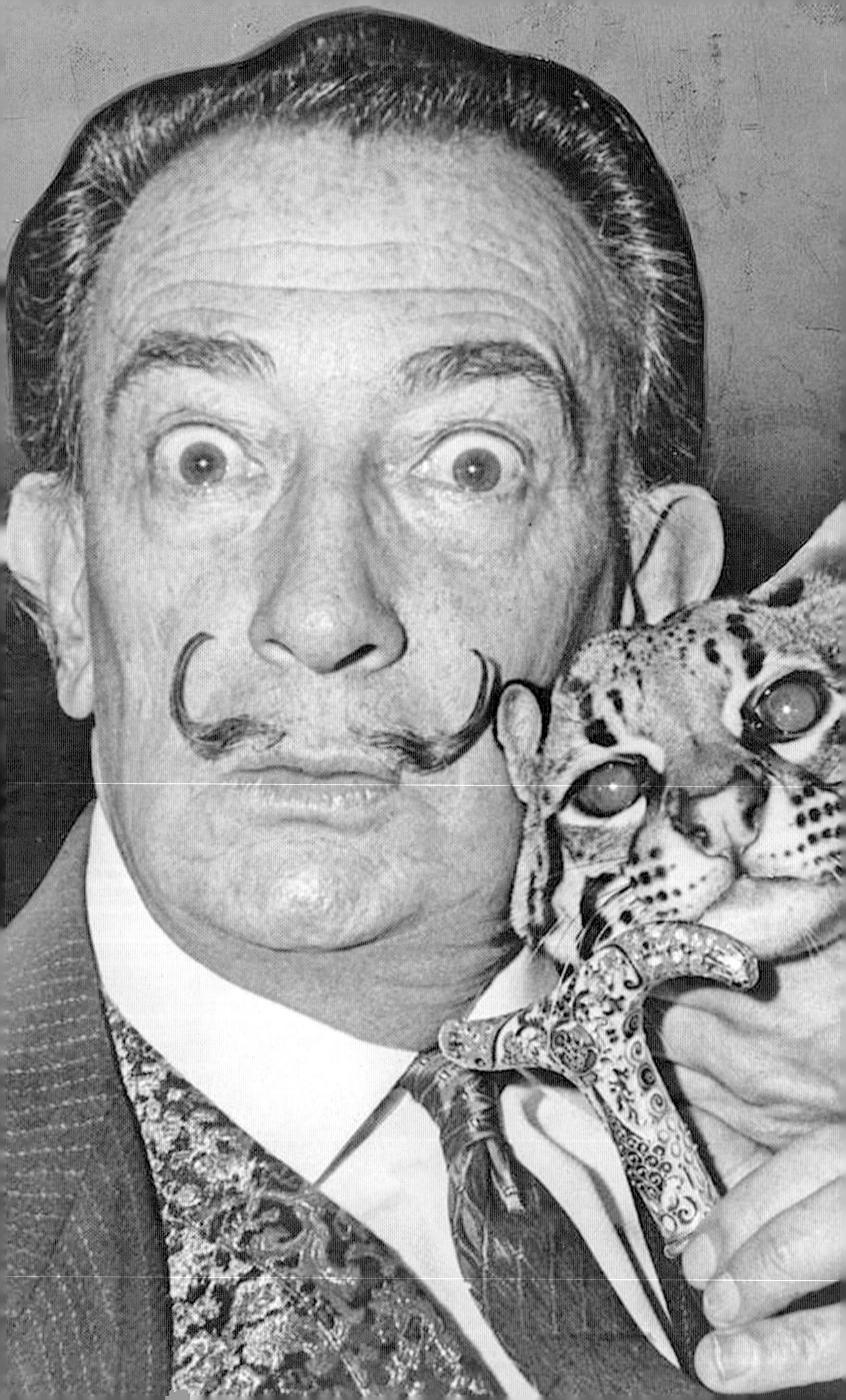

# Money, Art, and the Aura

Picasso and Dalí reached unprecedented fame in a world where the media rapidly marketed new icons for modern consumption. Jackson Pollock is another outstanding example of this new dynamic. He mostly owed his career to the diplomatic skills and wit of Lee Krasneer, a highly original Abstract Expressionist painter who married the artist and sacrificed her own career in order to launch his. It was through her that Pollock became involved with collector and modern art guru Peggy Guggenheim. Clement Greenberg, the most influential art historian of the last century, and Guggenheim's close collaborator transformed the movement of Abstract Expressionism from the laughingstock of popular culture to the white-hot artistic sensation of American modern art.

In August 1949, when Pollock's work graced the pages of *Life Magazine* along with a few pictures of him posing as a sexy, rugged, heroic man of action, the artist's canonization was complete. The behind-the-scenes support from the CIA sealed the deal.[27] In the early years of the Cold War, the CIA launched Operation Mockingbird: a large-scale program designed to more or less secretly manipulate news media organizations and cultural creators for propaganda purposes. In the Soviet Union, Socialist Realism—the official artistic style that dominated the Soviet Union between 1932 and 1988—effectively promoted a strong national identity and cultural pride. CIA officials swiftly cast their eyes on Abstract Expressionist artists such as Pollock, Rothko, and De Kooning. Their innovative abstract style stood in direct opposition to the rigid prescriptiveness of Socialist Realism, summoning the supposedly diametrically opposed essence of contemporary American identity. It is known that the CIA never financed Abstract Expressionist artists directly. They instead poured money into the staging and traveling of exhibitions across the world and media promotion, as well as financing the publication of catalogs. Sometimes, the power networks involved in the making of a successful career in the arts reach far deeper and get much darker than we can ever imagine.[28]

Would Abstract Expressionism have become such an influential movement without the support of the CIA? It is hard to say. But in a world where everything started to be mass-produced—a copy of a copy—a painting or a sculpture retained a magical aura of unique distinction. Abstract Expressionism certainly encapsulated a kind of primordial energy that veered toward the magical. Walter Benjamin's classic essay, "The Work of Art in the Age of Mechanical Reproduction" (1935), grappled with this very inescapable condition of experiencing art in the modern world.[29] His concern with the uniqueness of the work of art was linked to the shamanic origin of the artist and the ritual that cast the art object as an original and irreplaceable evidential trace of a supernatural encounter. The attractive power of the work of art as a relic of the past or a unique marker of the present transfers, to some degree, to the owner.

While the rules of the game had changed, the result had not. For all the rebelliousness and desire not to conform, modern artists were still, like their

Image 23 (facing page). Unknown. Salvador Dalí with his pet ocelot, Babou, and cane, 1965. Public Domain predecessors, producers of the most exclusive kind of luxury goods. It is essential to come to terms with this idea—not to justify the commercialization of art, but to understand that what hangs in museums and that we revere as "the greatest" twentieth-century art essentially is an exclusive commodity designed for the one percent. No other artist was ready to acknowledge this condition, and openly embrace it, as much as Andy Warhol.

Unlike many other Pop Art pioneers, Andy Warhol proudly hailed from the commercial world. He was the incredibly shy, gay son of poor Eastern European immigrants who settled in Pittsburgh. Once in New York, Warhol's career quickly skyrocketed from window dresser to designer for *Vogue* and other glossy fashion magazines. But what he really wanted was to become an artist.

He began experimenting with screen-printing and bold imagery appropriated from advertising and newspapers: Coca-Cola bottles, dollar bills, Marilyn Monroe, Elvis, car crashes, and electric chairs. Warhol extracted everyday images from popular culture and elevated them to iconic status: his obsessive repetition of objects and celebrities an emblem of fame and its existential hollowness. He understood that fame is a matter of branding, that branding is essential to the sale of commodities, and that repetition is the soul of fame itself.

Warhol's fixation with fame was the perfect answer to Walter Benjamin's idea that original and unique works of art have a special aura linked to the historical moment and context in which they were made—an attractive quality that reproductions cannot possess. Warhol's screen-printed multiplications replaced the uniqueness of the aura with a manufactured cult of the star as pure image, the superficial icon of the twentieth century. To those who did not personally know her, Marilyn Monroe was simply a commodity, just like a Coca-Cola bottle or a Brillo Box. In what essentially was the first truly successful marriage of painting and photography in the history of Western art, Warhol generated unprecedented financial opportunities for himself by multiplying one idea across many canvases before moving on to the next. In a pre-internet world, the multiplication allowed his Liz Taylor screen-prints to be simultaneously seen at galleries in Tokyo, Milan, London, and New York.

But perhaps even more importantly, Warhol turned networking into an art form. He was openly gay at a time in which artists like Jasper Johns and Robert Rauschenberg led closeted lives and avoided associations with Warhol to protect their careers. In 1962, he opened the Factory, his studio-cum-social club, which swiftly attracted a host of creative outsiders and mainstream celebrities such as Dalí, Mick Jagger, and Bob Dylan. Not only did the creative melting pot known as the Factory turn out to be of paramount importance to Warhol's creative potential, but it mainly generated a network of fans and collaborators that greatly amplified his relevance.[30]

Social networks, especially international ones, have been the recurring motif in the lives of famous artists.[31] A network linking art historians, critics, collectors, philanthropists, patrons, partners, and other fashionable artists became key—this is what art historian Arthur Danto called "the artworld" in 1964. He concluded that the art of the avant-garde needed to be explained as art by theories and discourses that were shared and understood by a close community of makers, professionals, writers, and institutions: the gatekeepers of modern art.[32] This matter of fact, which undeniably rules the contemporary art market, also shines a spotlight on the exclusionism that still defines the art world today.

Validation is the water of the art world ecosystem: the nourishment an artist's career needs to flourish. It can come in the form of a chapter in an art historian's new book; the review in a prestigious art magazine or on a website; a solo exhibition in a prestigious museum; a grant from a historical foundation; and so on. Validation is a process of confirmation that others in the art world agree your work is worthy of being seen and collected. It is the contemporary equivalent of the seal of approval that artists once received from the clergy, kings, the guilds, the academies, or the salons. Having freed themselves from the control of these institutional powers, artists also had to develop new validation systems, almost from scratch—art historians, patrons, and dealers were among the first in the game. Critics and journalists joined in during the nineteenth century and gained prominence as the glossy art magazine industry grew: *Art Forum, Parkett, Apollo, Art in America* . . . Auction houses, commercial art fairs, biennials and triennials, and curators followed.

By the mid-1970s, the rise of a new bohemian artist model inspired by the British punk revolution had revitalized the streets of the then-affordable East Village in New York. Jean-Michel Basquiat's tragic rise to stardom began here while tagging the walls of a gritty Lower Manhattan. In an ever-changing art world, fewer careers capture the "live fast, die young, leave a good-looking corpse" motto than his.[33] Art history often glosses over the artist's astute networking that helped him gain visibility in a bustling New York art scene of the late 1970s and early 80s, and what's more, critics and art historians rarely talk about how the art world killed him.

One of the most famous graffiti tags he left under the pseudonym SAMO (Same old shit) on the walls of a gritty Lower Manhattan tellingly read: "Playing Art with Daddy's Money."[34] Basquiat, a child prodigy from a disadvantaged Haitian/Puerto Rican home in Brooklyn, never went to art school. A high school drop-out at 17 and homeless, he sold postcards and t-shirts on New York City streets. Resourceful and determined, he hung out with the new generation of creative kids at the Mudd Club and Club 57. He was friends with Keith Haring and Kenny Scharf and soon became involved with Colab, an artists' collective supported by the National Endowment for the Arts founded in 1977. Promoting political art, the collaborative aimed at bypassing the official art world's hegemony by curating its own exhibitions and running art programs on cable TV.[35] Its epoch-defining 1980 exhibition known as the *Times Square Show* took place right in the heart of the city. It wasn't long before gallerists Annina Nosei and Larry Gagosian gave Basquiat his first show as well as their gallery basement as a studio. His 1982 solo show sold out on the opening night. Rave reviews followed. With his finger right on the pulse of the phenomenon, critic Rene Ricard penned an article titled "The Radiant Child," in which he noted: "We are no longer collecting art we are buying individuals"—he was spot on.[36] Buying Basquiat was an act of redemption for wealthy collectors living in a world where everything was commodified. Basquiat was raw, he was real, and his myth was on sale. Critic Jeffrey Deitch aptly summarized how the artist myth of Basquiat was spawned:

> Basquiat is likened to the wild boy raised by wolves, corralled into Annina's basement, and given nice clean canvases to work on instead of anonymous walls. A child of the streets gawked at by the intelligentsia. But Basquiat is hardly a primitive. He's more like a rock star, seemingly savage but completely in control; astonishingly prolific, but scornful of the tough discipline that normally begets such virtuosity. Basquiat reminds me of Lou Reed singing brilliantly about heroin to nice college boys.[37]

His friend, Keith Haring, cunningly identified authenticity as the true engine of Basquiat's artist myth—a symptom of the resilience of the romantic artist myth who suffers for his art, misunderstood by society and yet fetishized for transcending its trivial tribulations:

> Even in those early days he was doing collage drawings and color Xeroxes, his work had a kind of power which was unmistakably "real." The intensity and directness of his vision were intimidating. Jean-Michel was maybe a little bit too real for us. He was uncompromising, disobedient, and rude if the situation required it. Not malicious, but honest . . . When he began exhibiting his paintings, he remained true to his teachings and broke as many rules as possible.[38]

Haring's mythologization elevates Basquiat to messianic status and hints at the exploitation and speculation that surrounded him. In 1982 alone, Basquiat produced two hundred paintings. He was certainly burnt out by unscrupulous dealers determined to fetishize his blackness and capitalize on it. Cocaine and heroin killed him in 1988. He was 27 years old. He wasn't the first and certainly not the last artist to perish at the hands of the art world. BIPOC artists are especially vulnerable to the whims of a reckless and volatile art market that knows no loyalty.

Yayoi Kusama is today one of the most famous contemporary living artists but her rise to the pinnacle of the art world has been marred by discrimination and unbearable struggle. Dwelling on the periphery of normative experience, Kusama has developed a highly personal and recognizable aesthetic—a set of symbols, colors, and forms that she has used to make sense of an often hostile world. Intimidated by her womanizing father and terrified by her abusive mother—who wanted her to give up art—Kusama left Japan in 1958 and settled in New York. The relocation was suggested to her by none other than Georgia O'Keeffe. Three years earlier Kusama had summoned the courage to write to the living legend asking: "I'm only on the first step on the long and difficult life of being a painter. Will you kindly show me the way?"[39] O'Keeffe, who at the time lived in New Mexico, wrote letters to her contacts recommending Kusama. She started to exhibit work in New York almost immediately, attracting the attention of fellow artists Frank Stella and Donald Judd. During the 1960s, Kusama's work was exhibited alongside that of famous pop artists like Warhol, Oldenburg, Dine, Indiana, Lichtenstein, and Wesselmann. She will later complain that Warhol, Oldenburg, and Lucas Samaras stole her ideas. Exhausted by

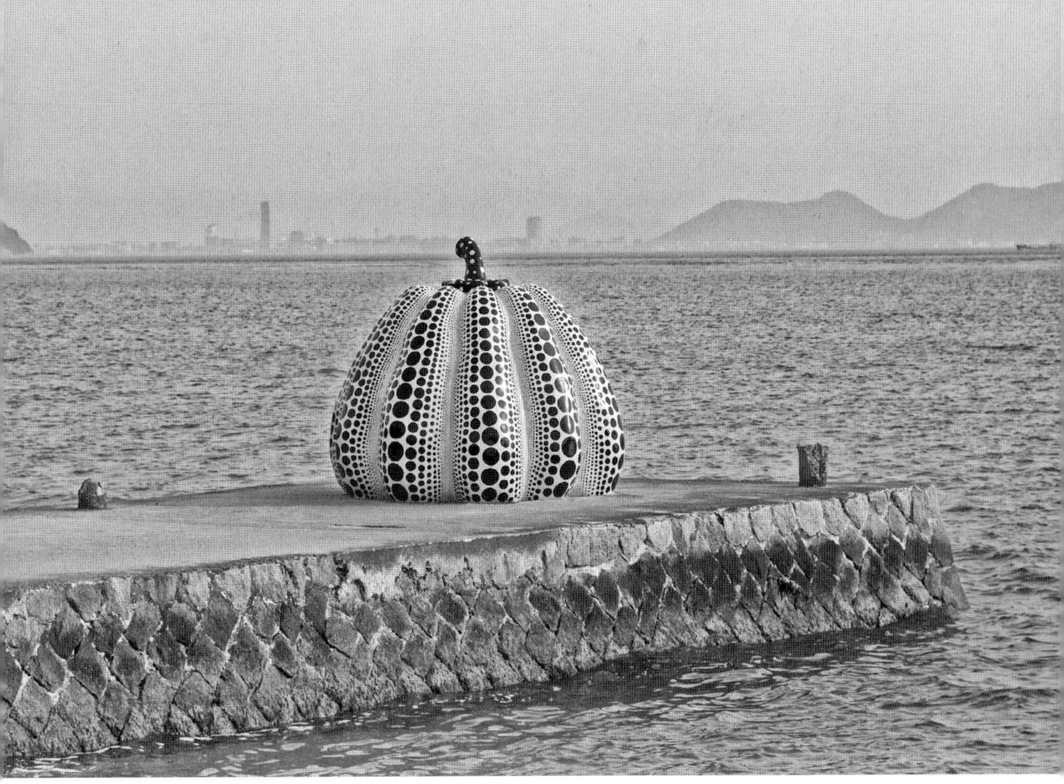

Image 24. Yayoi Kusama, *Yellow Pumpkin*, Naoshima, Kagawa Prefecture, Western Japan, 1994. CC BY 2.0 DEED

the sexism that pervaded the art world, Kusama returned to Japan where, in 1977, she entered a Tokyo sanatorium for treatment of her compulsions—she still lives and works there. Kusama went mainstream, breaking record sales and museum attendance in the 1990s as she represented Japan at the Venice Biennale (1993).[40] But this was not the first time the artist had exhibited there. In 1966, Kusama, with the support of artist Lucio Fontana and the permission of the Biennale's committee, installed 1,500 mass-produced plastic silver globes on the lawn near the entrance of the event during the first opening week. The conglomeration of convex reflective surfaces produced a grotesquely distorted multiplication of the surrounding space. The artist positioned two signs at the installation, one bearing the words "Narcissus Garden," the other "Your Narcissus for Sale." She then proceeded to sell the balls to passersby for $2 each. *Narcissus Garden* was a playful critique of the Biennale and the contemporary artist's condition: the artist willingly and knowingly stuck in the paradox of commercialization has to produce multiples and sell them to collectors who can only see themselves reflected in what they buy. The organizers of the Biennale attempted to dismantle it. But Kusama's work had already made headlines.[41]

The insidiousness of the artist myth lies in its art historical backbone. While the struggles these artists incurred are documented, museums and art history books have no interest in dwelling too long over the industriousness of artists, their self-promotion, and savvy steering of their careers. Nobody in art schools explains to students how these artists rose to fame as if the networking, strategizing, and savvy-steering were not essential skills in the making of artistic careers. The art world's foundations are still today built on the transcendental pretence that sheer genius is the only driving force that propels artists to stardom. It's what gives the artist the authenticity collectors want to buy. And yet, insiders know too well how the system works. When a glimpse of the pretence is caught by the public or critics, the bubble can burst unless, like Damien Hirst, Takashi Murakami, and Jeff Koons have done, artists boldly own their commercial strategization as an integral part of their conceptual process. They proudly identify as pop artists, the progeny of Warhol to whom "making money is art and working is art and good business is the best art."[42] The critics hate them. But they are among the wealthiest living artists.[43] Could it be that they are also among the most honest?

Tragically, during the nineteenth century, artists sought to liberate art from the grip of the state and bourgeois taste, only to discover that, a century later, art would be recommodified once more by dealers, collectors, and investors. The only truth: artistic rebellion had spawned a neoliberal art world.

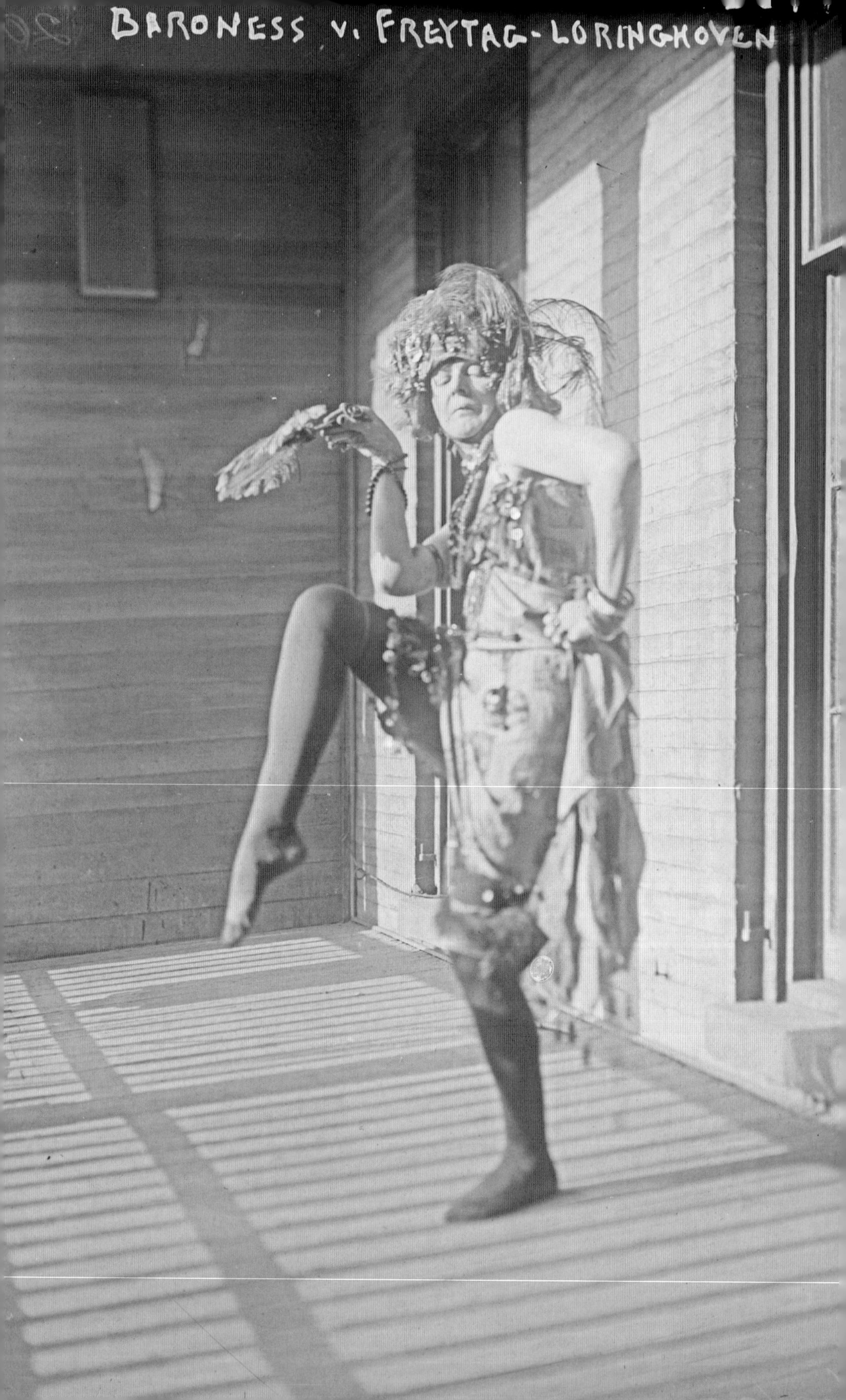
BARONESS V. FREYTAG-LORINGHOVEN

# 4 Responsibility: Art that Builds Better Worlds

Image 25 (facing page). Baroness von Freytag-Loringhoven. January 10, 1922. George Grantham Bain Collection (Library of Congress)

# The Renaissance Masterpiece that Gave Us Conceptual Art

On August 22, 1911, Prefect Louis Lépine, one of the most well-respected police superintendents in the world, was dragged out of bed by a phone call from the Louvre. At the other end of the line was acting deputy curator Georges Bénédite frantically reporting that Leonardo da Vinci's *Mona Lisa* had gone missing.[1] Lépine rushed to the museum with an army of gendarmes in tow—every door locked behind him.

It was too late. The painting's frame discarded in a corridor was all he found. The avant-garde writer Guillaume Apollinaire and Pablo Picasso were among the initial suspects—that lead only wasted his time.[2]

An international diplomatic scandal engulfed the Louvre. By the evening of August 23, alarming headlines accompanied by photographs of the Renaissance masterpiece traveled the world. But amid the raging controversy, a star was born: the magic of mechanical reproduction made *Mona Lisa* an overnight celebrity—a spell cast twice as the world's most famous enigmatic smile graced the front pages again in 1913, after its recovery. The thief turned out to be nothing like the crime-genius Lépine was hunting down—Vincenzo Peruggia, a near-illiterate Italian workman who built cabinets for the Louvre. It was a straightforward inside job. Peruggia spent the night in a broom cupboard before sneaking out of the building with *Mona Lisa* hidden under his coat.

Before returning to the Louvre, the painting was sent on a triumphant but swift tour of Italian museums. On January 4, 1914, Parisians lined the streets as *Mona Lisa* was paraded back to the Louvre. Over 120,000 visited the museum in the two days that followed, just to catch a glimpse of the true icon.[3] It rings odd, but it is true: it was *Mona Lisa* that launched conceptual art. The worldwide adulation for da Vinci's masterpiece quickly irked high-profile thinkers and artists. American art historian Bernard Berenson was "glad to be rid of her."[4] In 1919, Marcel Duchamp, nauseated by the unwarranted mass adulation made his views clear when he purchased a postcard of *Mona Lisa* and scribbled a mustache and goatee on her face. Adding the letters "L.H.O.O.Q." at the bottom—which, when pronounced in French phonetically, echo the phrase *elle a chaud au cul* or "she has a hot ass." Duchamp's message was clear: a slap in the face to classical art and the populist taste that blindly idolized the painting while knowing next to nothing about it. The conceptual pioneer disliked everything about the bourgeoisie—the hypocrisy, ignorance, intellectual conformity, and greed backed by colonialist and nationalist ideals that defined the comfort of their lives. By 1913, Duchamp had also lost faith in painting and its creative potential in a new age of mass communication. And perhaps more importantly, he had lost hope in the public and its willingness or ability to engage with cultural artifacts in deep and meaningful ways. In 1912, his painting *Nude Descending the Staircase (No. 2)* was rejected by the Salon des Indépendants in Paris. The organizers thought it wasn't cubist enough. Laughter greeted it once more in 1913, at the Armory Show in New York.[5] Today it is revered as a modern masterpiece inspired by chronophotography.

Scorned, Duchamp decided to tear the art world apart by producing objects that confronted the viewer that asked radical questions such as "What is art?", "What is art for?", and "What is the true, essential difference between art and craft?" Duchamp's questions reached beyond the politics of representation and taste. He believed the main purpose of art is to make people think rather than merely please or entertain. In 1913, he tested these ideas by purchasing ordinary, mass-produced objects, such as a shovel, a bicycle wheel, and a bottle rack.

The readymades, as he called them, the first manifestation of twentieth-century conceptual art, expressed one clear idea: paintings and sculptures belong to a very exclusive category of objects—they serve no practical function. Their artistic value is associated with the superiority of the mind over the skills and manual labor of functionality. Art is, he argued, first and foremost an idea. In the evidence of this, Duchamp postulated that an artist could, in theory, remove the function from a mass-produced object and thus instantly transform it into art. As it turned out, he was right.[6]

## Dada: The Artist as (Penniless) Provocateur

As the First World War raged, Duchamp and Dada artists tested their anti-establishment ideas in Zurich, Switzerland. They held dear the belief that the war—which had caused 40 million casualties and involved over thirty nations—was the natural outcome of capitalist greed and bourgeois hypocrisy. Night after night, at Cabaret Voltaire (the nightclub founded by the artist-performers Hugo Ball and Emmy Hennings), they dreamed up a new societal order, one that might counterbalance the madness that had swept the world over.[7]

Perhaps more than other new media for the time, photomontage captures the essence of Dadaist cultural iconoclasm. Unlike classical painting, which asked audiences to look away from the atrocity of an increasingly brutal world, photomontage dragged that very ugliness straight into the picture—fragments of truth juxtaposed to satirize and critique cultural and governmental corruption. Cutting and splicing from photographs, magazines, and newspapers, queer artist Hannah Höch denounced the persistent sexism that marred the lives of women artists even in the most experimental and open-minded movements. "Most of our male colleagues continued for a long while to look upon us as charming and gifted amateurs, denying us implicitly any real professional status," said the Dada pioneer as she reflected on her career later in the 1950s.[8]

It was also at the height of the Dada movement, in 1919, that artists Lucy Schwob and Suzanne Malherbe arrived in Paris. They soon changed their names to Claude Cahun and Marcel Moore—lovers for life, the two proceeded to explore identity and gender construction in unprecedentedly bold and sophisticated ways through photography, photomontage, and writing. Pushing against the gender binary, they advocated a new (for the West) and liberating conception of gender fluidity and multiplicity. Their introspective and existentialist work was mostly destroyed by the Nazis when the island of Jersey (where the two had relocated in 1937) was invaded. Not represented by dealers and no longer directly connected to her Parisian peers,

Cahun faded into obscurity until in the 1980s art historian François Leperlier resurfaced their work.[9]

Baroness Elsa von Freytag-Loringhoven, another important, and until recently mostly forgotten, female Dada pioneer and "proto-punk" artist, combined fashion, sculpture, performance, and poetry to embody an anti-bourgeois lifestyle. Some recently uncovered evidence points to the fact that she might be the true maker of *Fountain* (1917), a urinal tipped on its side and signed and dated "R. Mutt."[10] Usually attributed to Duchamp, *Fountain* is perhaps the most outrageous and influential work of art of the last century. Like other female pioneers, Freytag-Loringhoven's contribution to the field has been deliberately erased by art historians and curators. She is only now being reinstated as a protagonist of the early modern canon.

By the early 1920s, Freytag-Loringhoven had become well known in New York City's Greenwich Village as an avant-garde grand dame. The painter George Biddle wrote of a visit to her 14th Street studio: "It was crowded and reeking with strange relics, which she had purloined over a period of years from the New York gutters. Old bits of ironware, automobile tires, gilded vegetables, a dozen starved dogs, celluloid paintings, ashcans, every conceivable horror, which to her tortured yet highly sensitized perception, became objects of formal beauty."[11] Upon meeting her, Duchamp reportedly said, "She is not a futurist, she is the future."[12] But unfortunately, the future she embodied was not a financially sustainable one. A vituperative believer in anti-commercialism, Freytag-Loringhoven often found herself completely broke. She resorted to shoplifting and lost her home more than once. The art she made, as original and visionary as it was, had no market. Her nobiliary title came from her marriage to her third husband, Baron Leopold von Freytag-Loringhoven, who took his own life in 1918 and left her penniless. In 1923, she borrowed money to return to Germany, where she lived in abject poverty, selling newspapers on the street and living in a charity home.[13]

## Genealogies: Two Kinds of Artists?

Despite their disgust with everything bourgeois, many Dada artists came from upper-middle-class families. Their privileged backgrounds shaped their rebellious thinking and careers. The father and grandfather of Dada founder and performance artist Tristan Tzara were entrepreneurs in the forestry business. Tzara studied at a prestigious boarding school.[14] Man Ray's parents ran a small but successful tailoring business. Francis Picabia came from an affluent family. Duchamp's maternal grandfather, Émile Frédéric Nicolle, was a successful professional painter and his father a notary. Like Cézanne, Duchamp received a monthly stipend from his father until his death, in 1925, when the artist was 38 years old. The enfant terrible of modern art could have not plotted his artistic revolution if it hadn't been for this generous subvention.[15]

After the heartbreak caused by the reception of *Nude Descending the Staircase (No. 2)*, in 1913, Duchamp took a job as a librarian at the Bibliothèque Sainte-Geneviève in Paris, which gave him plenty of time to focus on his art. He realized that times had changed and that a new conception of the artist was needed. "There are two kinds of artists," he said. The artist that deals with society and is integrated into society and the other artist who is completely freelance and has no bonds with society . . . I did not want to depend on my painting for a living."[16] At this point, Duchamp openly stated that he no longer cared to paint for what he called the "immediate public" but that he would carry on for an "ideal public" who might understand his work fifty or one hundred years after his death.

Between the 1920s and the late 50s, the artist's role would change time and time again, and yet, Duchamp's distinction between the "professional artist" and the "freelance artist" has remained central to today's art world. That's the format implicitly taught at art schools, although professors often fail to tell students that they will also need to sustain themselves through another form of income or subsidy to continue making art.

Finally, an artist had provided a pragmatic alternative to the idea of the romantic bohemian. But little could Duchamp know that a much more dramatic fragmentation of the role of the artist was about to take place in response to the rapid growth of capitalism, pervasive social divide, sprawling urbanization, the automatization of life, and the rise of Nazism.

A new generation of modern artists began to see themselves as "social agents": activists whose voices could change society by spearheading political discussions instead of producing luxury goods for the rich. As new conceptions of artist identity rapidly expanded, the word "artist" increasingly turned strident, felt obsolete, and seemed inappropriate to describe the multifaceted nature of new creative makers.

Soviet critic Viktor Pertsov proposed a new idea of "artist as engineer"—the opposite of the emotionally fickle romantic myth. The new modern artist was a focused, sharp, and disciplined professional who carefully calculated every move.[17] These ideals were shared by Latvian-born artist Gustav Klutsis, according to whom the new artist of the postwar period should be a "public person, a specialist in political and cultural work with the masses, a constructor who has mastered photography, who can build a composition using entirely new principles."[18]

The new modern artist was a political agitator who instigated collective action and valued nontraditionally artistic activities as well as businesses like advertising. While both of Duchamp's artist-models were very much confined to the conceptualism of the gallery space, the new, interwar modern artist worked on the streets and produced works like posters or magazines, that could only exist there.

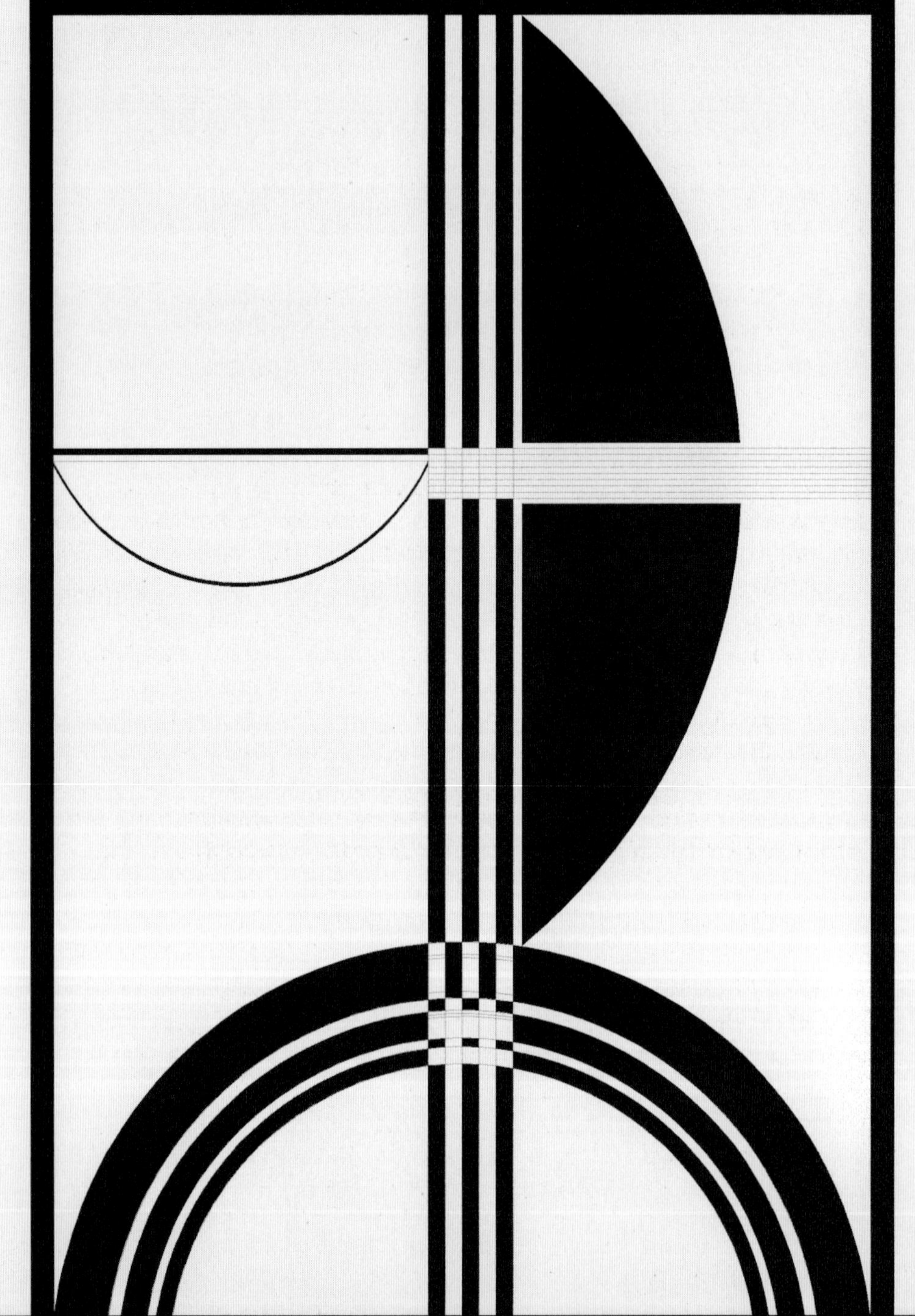

# Bauhaus: The Artist Diffracted

Not just painting, or sculpture—typography, printing, film, and photography became the new propagandistic weapons of new artists like Alexander Rodchenko and Lyubov Popova. Clear communication was paramount; effective design was essential. These artists found a new ally in the mass-produced image. They became editors and publishers. In 1924, Polish avant-garde artist Teresa Żarnower was appointed co-editor of the magazine *Blok*, the philosophical dissemination tool of an artist collective of cubists, constructivists, and suprematists. By 1927, she became editor-in-chief of the left-wing journal *Dźwignia*.[19]

The most meaningful and influential manifestation of this revolution in the conception of the artist was nowhere better exemplified than in Bauhaus—the German art school that, from 1919 to 1933, blurred the boundaries between architecture, typography, design, painting, performing arts, sculpture, and music. Bauhaus is still considered the most influential art school in modern history. It emerged at a time when Germany, wounded and exhausted after the First World War, suffered spiralling inflation, instability, and extremism that would ultimately pave the way for Adolf Hitler's appointment as chancellor of Germany. Bauhaus crafted modern aesthetics in which form followed function and ornamentation was superfluous. Traditional teaching was replaced by workshop-based, collaborative communities. Students learned from each other and from a stellar cast of artist-teachers, including Wassily Kandinsky, Paul Klee, László Moholy-Nagy, Marianne Brandt, Gunta Stölzl, Anni Albers, Lucia Moholy, and Ludwig Mies van der Rohe.[20]

The school's founder and first director, Walter Gropius, revolutionized the very idea of artistic training and thus, once more, reinvented the identity of the artist. No longer were students required to imitate the work of the old masters, as was the case in classical academies. Gropius believed: "False historical nostalgia can only blur modern artistic creation and impede artistic originality. [The teacher] has to direct the students to look ahead and strengthen their confidence in their own nature and in the power of time but without neglecting the legacy of the art of past ages with false pretentiousness."[21] To him there was no distinction between the craftsperson and the artist. And most importantly, he saw art as the seed of a brighter future where the atrocities of the First World War could not be repeated. "What we need," he said, "is the courage to accept inner experience, then suddenly a new path will open for the artist."[22] These ideals and approaches still today shape the philosophy of many art schools across the world.

Bauhaus was shut down by the Nazis in 1933. Many of its instructors migrated to Chicago (where the New Bauhaus was founded in 1937) and North Carolina (Black Mountain College, 1933). From this point onward, the identity of the artist was diffracted into a myriad professional realities. Bauhaus artists, like the Dadaists before them, had limited financial possibilities in an art world still characterized by classical

Image 26 (facing page). Teresa Żarnowerówna, *Untitled*, 1924 principles and an expanding art market that struggled to embrace new and divergent forms of expression as legitimate forms of art.

## Edmonia Lewis: Black Artists Matter

At the same time as the Bauhaus revolution gained momentum, in the United States the role of the artist was being radically redefined in an Upper Manhattan neighborhood called Harlem. The African and Native (Ojibwe) American trailblazer Edmonia Lewis accomplished the impossible during the second half of the nineteenth century by attending art school and developing substantial fame in the United States and Europe during her lifetime. Her representation of Native Americans, and the sophisticated nature of her neoclassical marbles, won her international acclaim.[23] A true advocate for social change, Lewis also made portraits of famous anti-slavery heroes, anticipating by more than a hundred years a practice of visual reclamation that is deemed of essential importance by contemporary artists today.

Lewis paved the way for other artists who saw an opportunity to heal and build a new African American identity through art. Poets, musicians, performers, and visual artists left the rural South and moved to Chicago, Detroit, and New York as the outbreak of the First World War increased demand for factory workers. They sought to advance the cause of human rights and social justice.

The artist model that emerged from Harlem combined Western and African heritages with the mediatic freedom of European avant-gardes. The neighbourhood bustled with African American-owned and -run publishing houses and newspapers, music companies, playhouses, nightclubs, and cabarets. Aaron Douglas, one of the most celebrated painters of the Harlem Renaissance (1918–37), equally drew from African art, cubism, and art deco. In 1935, Douglas founded the Harlem Artists Guild, with sculptor Augusta Savage, muralists Elba Lightfoot and Charles Henry Alston, and writer Arturo (Arthur) Schomburg. The guild aimed to support and promote young African American artists, with a special focus on politically grounded work centered around the "New Negro" movement.[24]

Art became the mortar in community-building and the shield against oppressive regimes. Augusta Savage founded the Savage Studio of Arts and Crafts in 1932, where the nascent talent of African American artists could be nurtured until ready to show in her gallery. Savage and her associates also understood the important role art plays in defining cultural identities. They harnessed the power of art to promote a renewed sense of racial pride and pursue artistic self-expression.[25] Savage saw teaching as her most important artistic practice: "I have created nothing really beautiful, really lasting, but if I can inspire one of these youngsters to develop their

Image 27 (facing page). Edmonia Lewis, *Indian Combat*, 1868. Marble; overall: 76.2 × 48.3 × 36.5 cm (30 × 19 × 14 3/8 in.). The Cleveland Museum of Art, American Painting and Sculpture Sundry Purchase Fund and Purchase from the J. H. Wade Fund. Public Domain

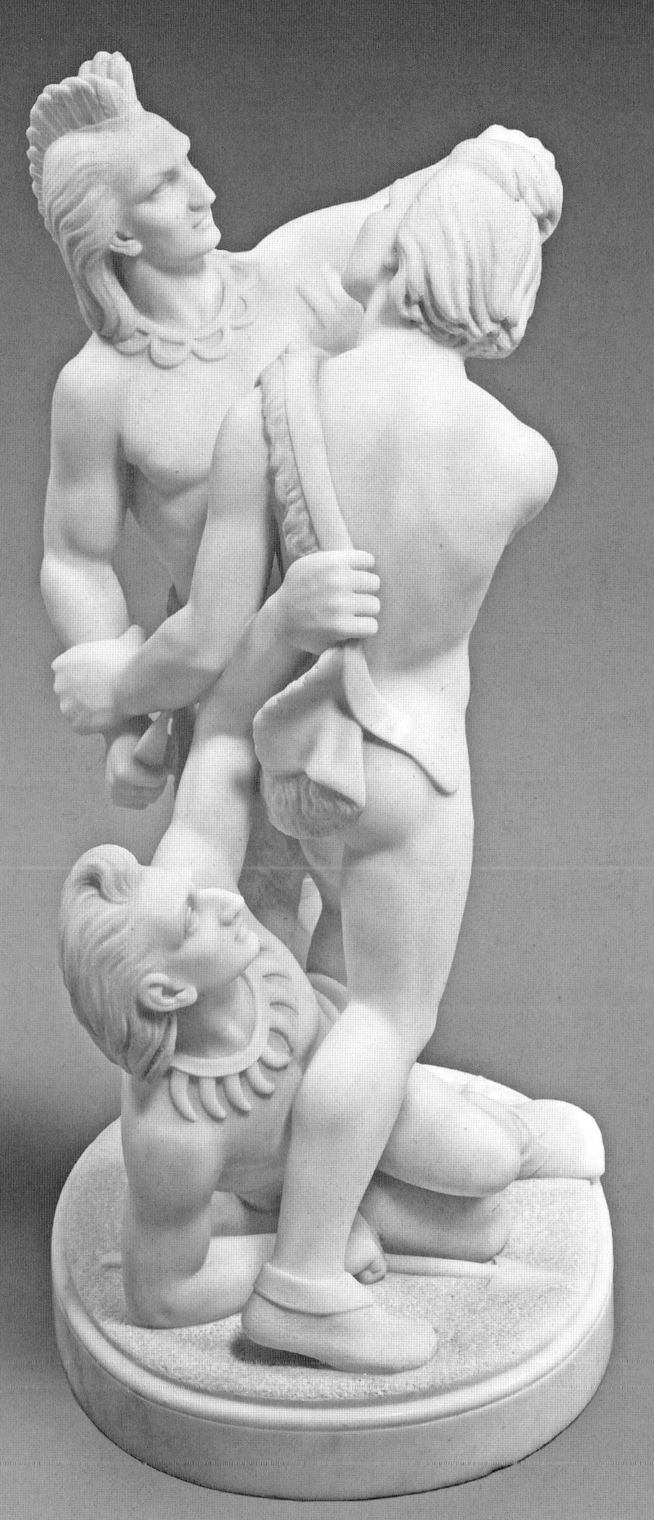

talent, I know they possess, then my monument will be in their work."[26] Just as talented as industrious, musician and photographer James Van Der Zee established a music conservatory with his sister, Jennie Louise, and a photo studio with his wife, Gaynella Greenlee. His photographs captured an intimate and introspective side of Harlem's vibrant social life. An accomplished portraitist, Van Der Zee also pioneered creative photomontage techniques that allowed him to superimpose poems to printed images.[27]

In Harlem, creativity and industriousness endlessly expanded the boundaries of what artistic expression might entail. An array of publications such as *Opportunities: A Journal of Negro Life*, *The Messenger: The Only Negro Magazine in America*, or *Fire!!*, which focused on young artists, enabled the dissemination of African American poetry, fiction, and academic essays across the country.[28] The powerful influence of the Harlem Renaissance quickly spread across the United States and beyond. Archibald Motley considered one of the great visual chroniclers of twentieth-century American life, often painted the buzzy nightlife of Chicago's Bronzeville neighborhood. His original and bold visual language captured a *joie de vivre* and creative energy of the African American community he knew but that was never shown in the press. Like many of his contemporaries, Motely believed that art could end racial prejudice. In 1918, he wrote "The Negro in Art," an essay on the limitations placed upon black artists, published in the influential *Chicago Defender*.[29]

The new radical Black pride promoted by these artists and thinkers laid the groundwork for the Civil Rights movement of the 1950s and 60s and continues to influence artists in America today.[30] Like no other art movement prior, the Harlem Renaissance had shown that the arts (in their expanded field incorporating performance, writing, and publishing) could change public opinion, define cultural identities, and promote societal bonding. The political stakes had never been higher than this for freedom, independence, and dignity—not the production of luxury goods. These were the true ideas that this new kind of artists fought for.

## WPA: Artists of the New Deal

While the Harlem Renaissance expanded the role of the artist as multimedia radical identity activist, the sociopolitical situation in the South of the United States rapidly changed. Between 1930 and 1936, from Texas to Nebraska, reckless farming practices, severe droughts, and high winds led to the so-called "Dust Bowl"—a series of sandstorms that devastated crops and killed livestock, bringing poverty and famine across the country. This ecological cataclysm—the culmination of centuries of exploitative, colonialist practices—coincided with the Great Depression (1929–39), the worst economic downturn in the history of the industrialized world.

In response to these dramatic events, in 1935, the US Government launched the Works Progress Administration (WPA), part of the New Deal Programs designed to kickstart the economy and provide work for millions of unemployed Americans. The WPA's Federal Art Program (FPA), which operated until 1943, recruited 5,300 artists with the goal of forging a new American identity in the midst of a historic catastrophe. In the process, it launched the careers of Dorothea Lange, Jackson Pollock, Walker Evans, Aaron Douglas, Mark Rothko, Lee Krasner, and Jacob Lawrence among others. For the first time in recent history, artists became full-time employees of the government. The program was structured around three participation tiers: the top-rank artists were paid $23.60 per week.[31] By comparison, an agricultural worker earned roughly 14 cents an hour, and $5–10 per week was the average wage. This financial support not only allowed artists to focus on research and develop their practices but also brought a sense of pride and validation that art mattered, at last; it was valued by the government, and it was a worthwhile investment.

The FAP applied no restriction to content, subject matter, or style; producing public sculptures and murals was encouraged. Over 8 million people benefited from new art centers.[32] While the experiment is today considered a great success, it was originally met with opposition from artists themselves. The American Federation of Artists claimed that the FAP would "in the long run substitute journeyman standards of art for truly artistic standards, mediocre common standards in the place of the highest individual standards." The editor of the *Art Digest* argued that "art is by nature free and ceases to be art the exact moment it is harnessed."[33]

Meanwhile, conservative outposts—perhaps predictably—condemned the initiative, labeling it a hotbed of subversive activity funded by taxpayers' money. Many of the works made under FAP were inspired by French Realism: the lives of the working classes, industrial realities, and societal problems. For the first time in the history of the United States, those living in rural towns, away from cosmopolitan big cities, saw art that not only celebrated but also critically questioned American history, culture, and values. In comparison, the art seen in major museums looked elitist, distant, and self-indulgent.

It is from this cultural climate that John Cotton Dana developed the idea of "the new museum" —which manifested in the 1926 opening of the Newark Museum—an institution that blurred the boundaries between art and design, prioritized accessibility, education, and underserved audiences.[34] Art by and for the common people, what back then (and often still today) went by the name of Folk Art, acquired more visibility and respect. The formation of the Harlem Artists Guild successfully pressured the program to welcome African American artists, too. Dox Thrash, an innovative and talented Black printmaker, supervised the FAP's graphics division in Philadelphia.

At this time, gay artists such as Paul Cadmus also enjoyed unprecedented exposure. His *The Fleet's In*, a satirical and undoubtedly homoerotic depiction of drunken sailors flirting with men and carousing with women, stirred up a national scandal.[35] Eventually, the program revolutionized the idea of American art. Indigenous American artists, such as Gerald Nailor and Julius Twohy, were employed by the FAP in more substantial numbers. The newly acquired visibility of their work led to the creation of the Indian Arts and Crafts Board in 1935, which promoted the development of markets for Indigenous American arts and crafts.[36]

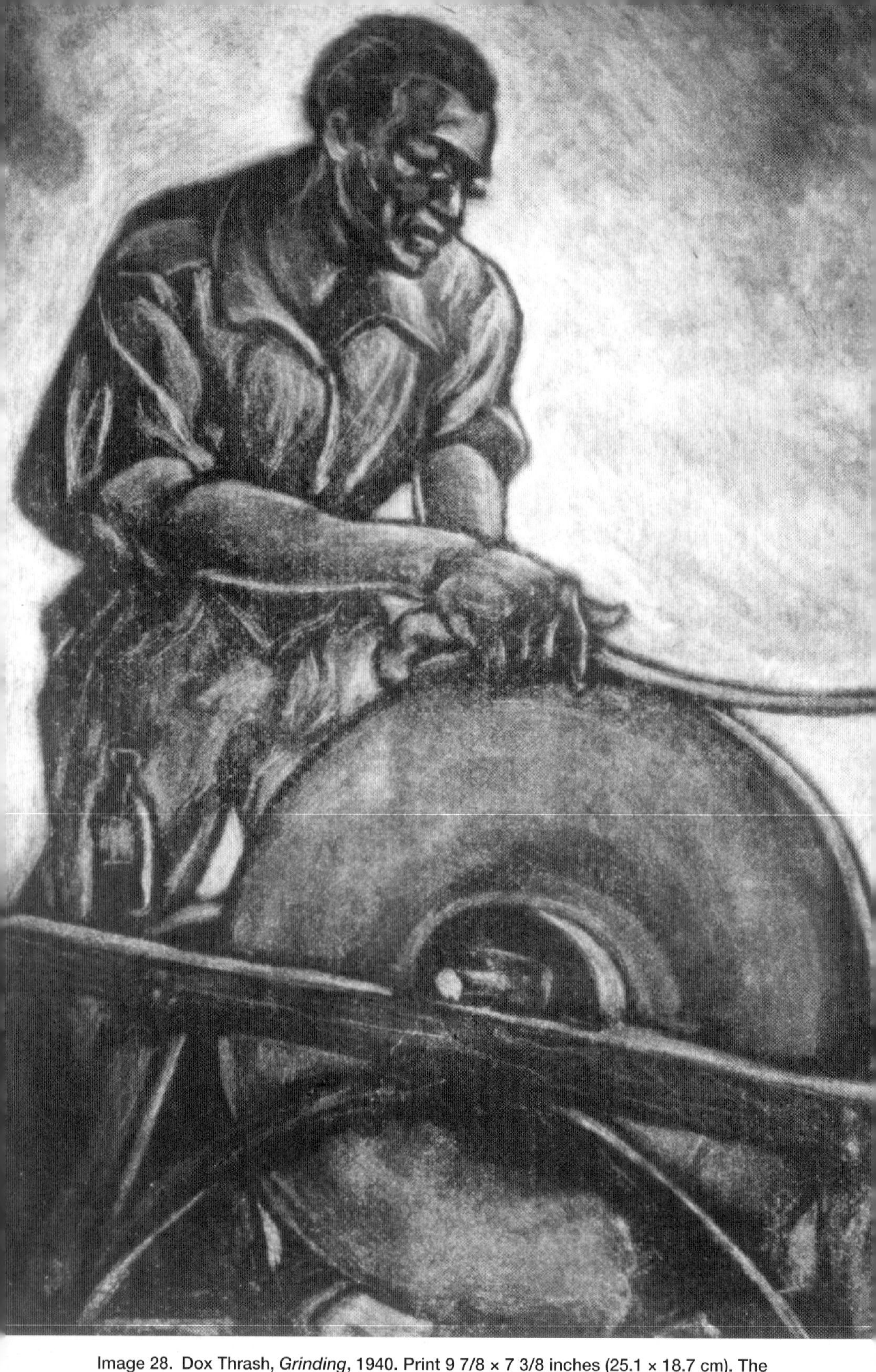

Image 28.  Dox Thrash, *Grinding*, 1940. Print 9 7/8 × 7 3/8 inches (25.1 × 18.7 cm). The Philadelphia Museum of Art / Art Resource, NY

For better or worse, the FAP democratized art and radicalized artists. It made them more than ever aware of the power of their voices. It also, to a degree, freed them from art historians, critics, and galleries—networks of validations essential to any artistic career until then. The generous weekly stipend often allowed freedom of speech to emerge and unbridled creativity to lead the way. These artists experienced an extraordinarily rare, and unfortunately short-lived, creative condition in which selling work no longer was a primary preoccupation. Above all, the FAP turned a generation of young American creatives into "career artists." "Even in that short time," de Kooning said of the project, "I changed my attitude toward being an artist. Instead of doing odd jobs and painting on the side, I painted and did odd jobs on the side. My life was the same, but I had a different view of it."[37] This sense of legitimization is still hard to negotiate for artists today.

## Artists of the Masses: A Double-Edged Sword

One of the most vivid manifestations of the political charge of FAP-sponsored art was the creation of 2,500 murals. By the end of the 1920s, the medium had gained popularity in Mexico as the government financially incentivized artists to produce murals celebrating Mexican values and immortalizing key moments in the Mexican Revolution (1910–20). Intentionally designed as Marxist-inspired tools for social change, murals were often large, colorful, realistic, and narrative-driven. With high illiteracy rates across the population, murals offered an invaluable opportunity to construct a new sense of national identity in the most practical and expedient of ways.

David Alfaro Siqueiros, José Clemente Orozco, and Diego Rivera set the aesthetic blueprints of subjects during the early part of the movement. Rivera thought that the "role of the artist is that of a soldier in a revolution." His portrayals of Emiliano Zapata and his followers were meant to make "the masses the hero of monumental art."[38] But by 1930, the Mexican government had started to breathe down the necks of artists, vetting themes and iconographies. As a result, many relocated to the United States.[39]

In the then Soviet Union, control over artists became even stricter. Russian premier Joseph Stalin despised the avant-garde for its inaccessibility and elitism. The new style of Socialist Realism quickly became a radical turn away from experimental and abstract art. It became the official Soviet artistic language utilized across various media, including posters, movies, architecture, theatre, and radio between the late 1920s and 60s. Stalin's regime went further, shutting down experimental art schools and removing early modern art from museums.[40] Those who did not flee were prosecuted, imprisoned, and often executed. Soviet artists were closely monitored and expected to paint social scenes that reflected communist values through clear and accessible compositions.[41]

Meanwhile, across Europe, new totalitarian regimes led by Benito Mussolini in Italy and Hitler in Germany began to impose similar restrictive measures on artistic expression. To repress the revolutionary fervor that pervaded the work of avant-garde artists, in 1937 the Nazi Party organized Munich's *Entartete Kunst* (Degenerate Art)

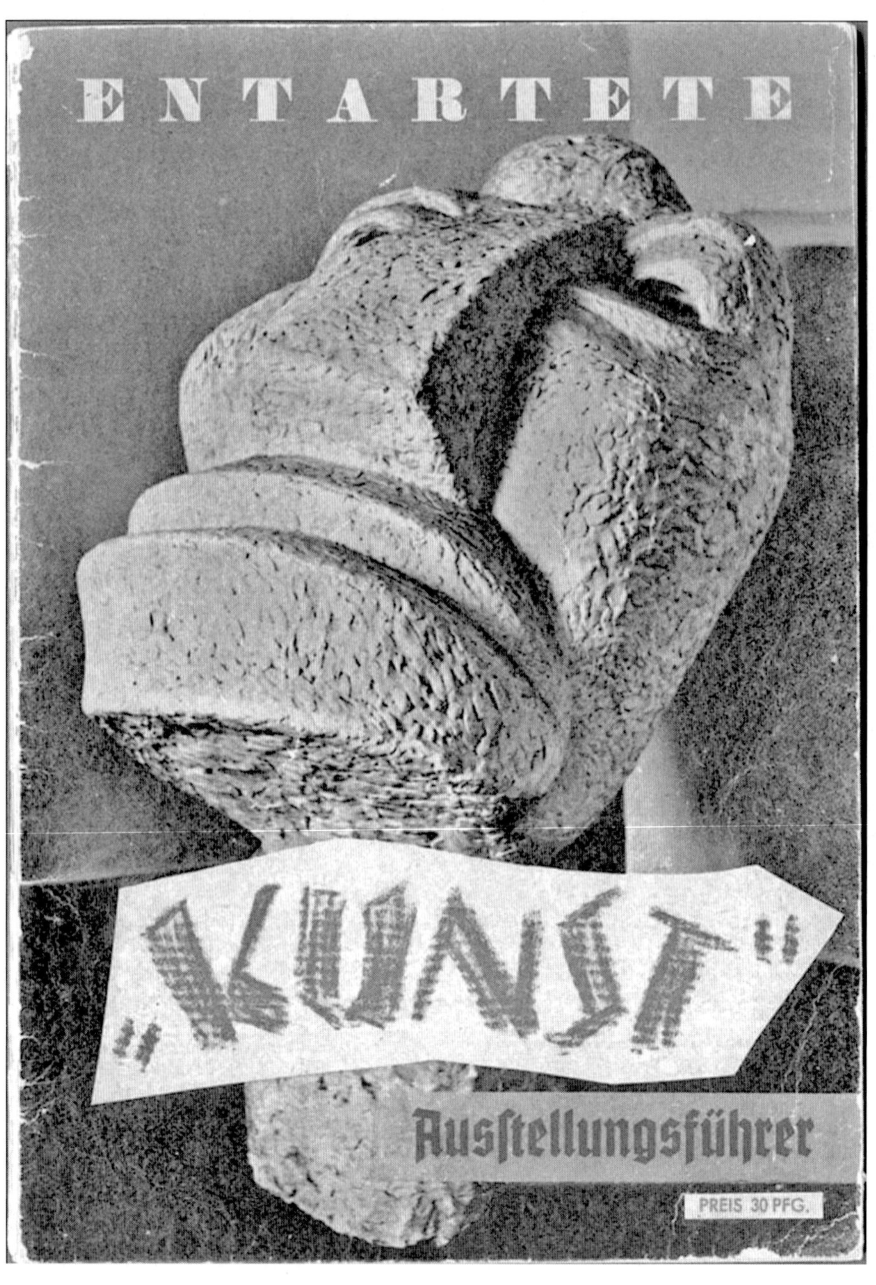


Image 29. *Entartete Kunst*, Degenerate Art Exhibition catalog, Front Cover, 1937, featuring Otto Freundlich's monumental sculpture, *Der neue Mensch* [The New Man], 1912. Ausstellungsführer, exhibition guide, published by the Reichspropagandaleitung, Amtsleitung Kultur. Public Domain

exhibition, gathering art that, in Hitler's words, "insulted German feelings, or destroyed or confused natural form or simply revealed an absence of adequate manual and artistic skill."[42]

The exhibition featured works by some of the best-regarded modern artists in the West, such as Paul Klee, Käthe Kollwitz, Oskar Kokoschka, and Wassily Kandinsky. The works were deliberately poorly hung and accompanied by derisive and biased wall labels. Hitler, himself an aspiring artist, was rejected from the Vienna Academy of Fine Arts twice because his realist paintings were deemed conservative. This was his revenge. "Works of art which cannot be understood in themselves but need some pretentious instruction book to justify their existence will never again find their way to the German people," said Hitler at the opening of the Haus der Deutschen Kunst (House of German Art) in the same year.[43] We still frequently hear that line repeated today, although those who parrot it don't seem to be aware of its origin.

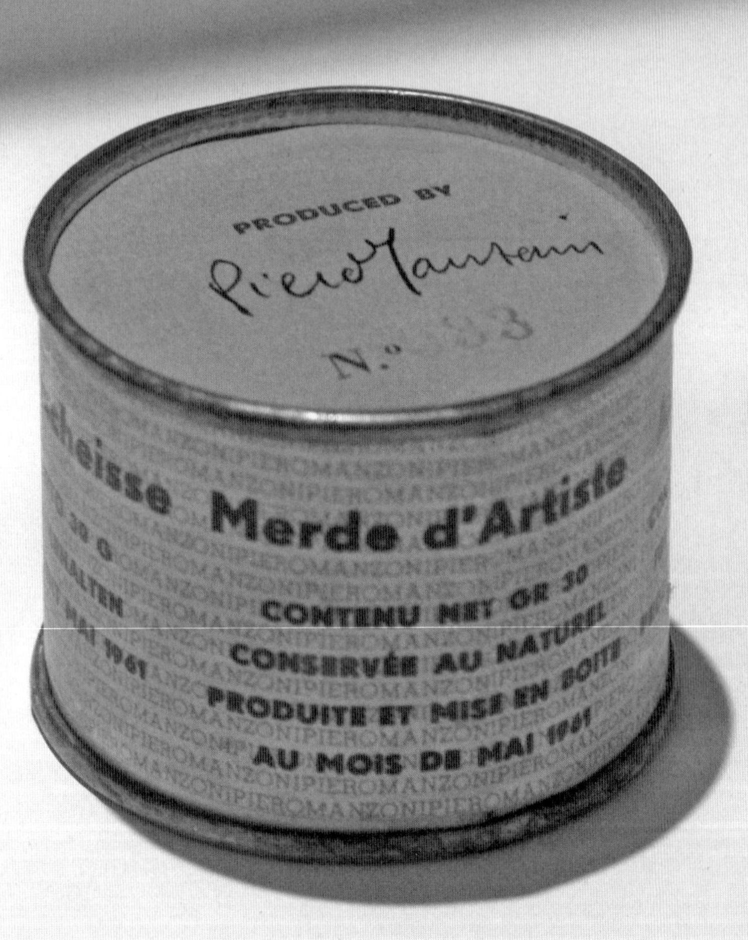


Image 30. Piero Manzoni, *Artist's Shit*, tin can, printed paper and excrement, 1961.
© 2024 Artists Rights Society (ARS), New York / SIAE, Rome

# 5  Art Capital:
# The Infinity of Currencies

## Worth Its Weight in Gold?

A little metal tin, like those found on supermarket shelves, sits on a pedestal covered by a glass case. But this one is special. It is reportedly filled with 30 grams (1 ounce) of freshly preserved artist's excrement. Yes, that's right.

The tin is the work of Piero Manzoni, a colossally irreverent conceptual artist whose unbridled creativity mocked the establishment and mercilessly exposed its flabby underbelly. Produced in 1961, in a limited edition of ninety signed tins, *Artist's Shit* has today won over the art world but remains mostly unknown to the general public.

*Artist's Shit,* like Duchamp's urinal, critiqued the commercialization of art and the fetishization of the contemporary artist by substituting mechanized manufacture for manual skill. In a letter to a friend, Manzoni wrote that "if collectors want something intimate, really personal to the artist, there's the artist's own shit, that is really his."[1] Point made: all ninety cans—price tagged at the same weight as gold—sold instantly. The joke has become funnier (or less so, depending on the point of view) over time. A tin sold at auction for $300,000 in 2016: much more than its gold equivalent value.[2]

So, what does Manzoni's tin and what we call "great art" have in common? The mystique. Did he, or didn't he? It's impossible to know for sure without destroying the work. This dogmatic paradigm is a critique of the art market and the collector's mindset. From a materialist standpoint, most art objects aren't worth much—any medium-sized painting by Picasso amounts to around $300 solely in terms of canvas and paint. But in 2016, *Femme Assise* (*Woman Sitting*), a relatively unremarkable, early cubist painting from 1909, fetched $63 million at auction. A larger canvas titled *Les Femmes d'Alger (Version 'O')*, 1955, broke previous records, netting $179.4 million.[3]

Manzoni's tin shamelessly points at the culturally inflated value of artworks. It exposes the true nature of art in the West: fetishization. It shows how artistic value is assigned by capitalist forces, not objective cultural consensus—such a thing does not exist. Manzoni's tin, like much of his body of work, which includes deflated balloons that once held his breath, gives the rules of the game away. There's the object, with its literal substance and genuine economic worth, and then there's the projection, the emotional investment that transforms it into currency as it passes from hand to hand. Each transaction writes its value into a validated history of art. Art can be a formidable financial asset. What involvement or control does the artist have in all this?

A rebel, social agitator, intellectual, propagandist, or provocateur? Works like Manzoni's *Artist's Shit* are symptoms of a modern crisis. Spread too thin across an ever-expanding range of media and disciplines, hollowed out by the growing impossibility of financial sustainability, in the 1960s, being an artist suddenly meant too much and nothing at the same time. What did it mean to be an artist in the aftermath of the Second World War's atrocities, after humanity had shown its ugliest face? What could be painted after the deafening silence that followed the detonation of atomic bombs and the utter desolation that followed the programmatic deployment of genocide? "To write poetry after Auschwitz is barbaric", wrote philosopher Theodor Adorno, in 1949.[4] What kind of artist could possibly emerge from the tragic failures of modernity?

The need to start from scratch became paramount. Radical, experimental, and anti-capitalist movements, such as the Gutai Group (1954–72) in Japan, focused on performance and happenings, which by nature eluded commodity fetishization. Founded by the visionary artist Yoshihara Jirō in 1954, the art collective focused on the relationship between the human body and matter. They believed art should be a direct manifestation of the human spirit, and this philosophy was reflected in their artistic techniques. For instance, Kazuo Shiraga, a prominent member of the group, was known for creating paintings with his feet, embodying the group's interest in the physical engagement of the body as a tool for art making.[5] Amid steady economic growth and a general positivist attitude, a number of artists based in northern Italian cities such as Milan and Turin began to make art that critically appraised the sociopolitical milieu of their time. The Arte Povera movement (1968–72), led by Giuseppe Penone and Janni Kounellis, emerged from a deep sense of existentialist crisis spilling from a fast-industrializing and ever more alienating world. It searched for a new kind of truth in the raw realism of poor, everyday materials. To make sense of this new world, they crafted new aesthetic gestures, syntaxes, and metaphors—new material languages that could reach deeper into the crevices of a nearly unrecognizable reality.[6] The 1960s also saw a significant shift in the production and consumption of information. More families than ever owned televisions, radios, and record players. Movies and magazines set new cultural trends, promoting glossy ways of living fueled by capitalist desire.

From the Vietnam War and the intensification of the Cold War to the assassinations of President John F. Kennedy and Martin Luther King, Jr., the 1968 riots, and the Stonewall Riots of 1969: led by the principle of human freedom and the political push of the Civil Rights movement, the 1960s were a tumultuous time of cultural change defined by the expansion of the middle classes in Europe and the United States and the simultaneous fragmentation of political perspectives.[7] The Black Power, Gay Liberation Front, and Women's Liberation movements that emerged from years of protesting and rioting radically changed the art world.

Like never before, artists felt a duty to process the traumatic and liberatory experiences of those years in ways that bypassed the politically biased and rhetorically loaded perspectives of official and institutional commentators. The body and the land became ideologically highly charged contested sites ripened with the promise of liberation. On the one hand, land artists sought to bypass the aesthetic, conceptual, and financial constriction of an increasingly unemphatic art world; on the other, minority groups found in artistic expression the possibility of finally becoming visible.

The feminist conceptual work of Niki de Saint Phalle, the performances by Yoko Ono and Carolee Schneemann, or the iconic installations of Judy Chicago openly addressed the marginalization of women in art. Deeply shifting the registers of visibility and invisibility in the context of cultural, general, and racial diversity were Gordon Parks and Roy De Carava's intense photographs, Faith Ringgold's haunting paintings, Warhol's drawings of gay encounters and silkscreens of drag queens, and Jasper Johns's collages mapping homosexual desire.

# Accessibility: Philosophy and the Taxi Driver

During the 1960s the art world also became further grounded in philosophical conceptions. While some artists challenged the power of oppressive institutions, others began to look inward, prodding the boundaries of art through ever more theoretically complex experiments.

Structuralist philosophy and the revisionist wave of post-structuralism that dominated the 1970s aimed at uncovering the ideologies that determine human thinking, along with cultural and social behavior. Structuralism is grounded in what the linguist Ferdinand de Saussure called "semiotics": the study of anything that can be read as a sign (an object or mark that means something). Thereafter, Claude Lévi-Strauss questioned the historical rigidity of structuralism, inviting more subjective interpretations and further valuing the experiences, beliefs, gender, race, and cultural upbringing of the interpreter as having an important role in the reading of images and texts.[8] The hypercritical approaches of structuralist and post-structuralist thinkers such as Jacques Derrida, Michel Foucault, Julia Kristeva, Frantz Fanon, Judith Butler, Gilles Deleuze, and Felix Guattari destabilized classical cultural pillars and paved the way for the challenging and speculative contemporary art of today. At the same time, their voices have led to the rise of an elitism that has made some art almost wholly unintelligible to wider audiences.[9]

An example: Carl Andre's *Equivalent* (1966) comprised rectangular compositions made with 120 construction bricks. Despite their different arrangement, each sculpture presented the same volume, height, and mass—hence equivalents. A textbook example of minimalism, the series caused major controversy when the Tate Gallery in London decided to purchase *Equivalent VIII* in 1970 for the sum of £2,297 (around £38,000 or $50,000 today). The museum was accused of wasting taxpayers' money on a pile of bricks.[10]

Minimalism and conceptual art have certainly delivered exceptional works of art, but others have flatlined to the point of alienating audiences who felt ridiculed and patronized. The frequently obscure and overcomplicated vocabulary of Western philosophy has at times transformed into equally cryptic aesthetics to the uninitiated (and many a professional).

Of course, it is true that a nuanced use of language can more aptly unravel the subtleties of the human experience. Yet, the choice of language and cultural posture predetermines the reach of an artwork's message. If it is too cryptic only a small audience will engage. While aspiring to reach vast audiences might not be the goal of many artists, it is also true that consensus can play an important role in assessing cultural value.

The new role that critical consensus seems to play in validating highly cryptic works of art led art historian Arthur Danto, in 1964, to declare the "end of art."[11] On viewing Warhol's *Brillo Boxes*, the art historian said that

> an era of imitation, followed by an era of ideology, followed by our post-historical
> era in which, with qualification, anything goes . . . In our narrative, at first, only

mimesis [imitation] was art, then several things were art but each tried to extinguish its competitors, and then, finally, it became apparent that there were no stylistic or philosophical constraints. There is no special way works of art have to be. And that is the present and, I should say, the final moment in the master narrative. It is the end of the story.[12]

So what comes after the end of the story? Critic Robert Hughes argued that a radical shift took place in 1962 as *Mona Lisa* traveled for the first time to New York upon the request of Jacqueline Kennedy. Amid unprecedented publicity, over a million people braved the cold to catch a glimpse of the Renaissance masterpiece. The first to have the honor was a taxi driver from Brooklyn who got up at 4:30 a.m. to arrive at the museum by 6:00 a.m., four hours before its scheduled opening time.[13] To Hughes, this new mass experience changed art forever. The fleeting encounter imposed by the enormous number of visitors and the security restrictions generated a new model: the celebrity artwork.[14] Astonishingly, twice in a century, *Mona Lisa* set the zeitgeist by polarizing opinions and casting her immense celebrity spell. One long genealogy of art might have come to an end, as Danto argued, but it was promptly replaced by another.

## Auctions Don't Make Artists Rich

The New York art dealer Leo Castelli preferred to be called a "gallerist"—a term that emphasized his knowledge of art and desire to promote new talent.[15] Ex-Office of Strategic Services (the precursor to the CIA), in the 1960s, and diplomat during the Second World War, Castelli invented the "warehouse gallery" format. Like Durand-Ruel a hundred years before, he also supported his artists with a regular stipend regardless of sales. The so-called Castelli Model carefully crafted the artist's brand by micro-managing their markets to avoid inflation, and actively promoting their profiles. He valued mutual trust and loyalty with his clients. His roster included some of the most important artists on the contemporary scene.[16]

By the beginning of the 1970s, the art world appeared more polarized than ever. Today, we have become accustomed to the exorbitant figures that works can fetch at auction. But don't be fooled: the millions hammered on the auction block don't go to the artist but travel straight into the collector's pockets and the auction house. This trend began in 1973 with a historical Sotheby's sale. On October 18, Robert C. Scull sold fifty important Abstract Expressionist and Pop Art works from his collection. He had bought many of these from Leo Castelli well before their value had become prohibitive. It is rumored that he paid just $1,000–2,000 for them.[17]

Scull (at birth Ruby Sokolnikoff) was the son of Russian-Jewish immigrants. His wife inherited a share in a taxi company that Scull turned into a New York household name through innovative marketing campaigns. Given his marketing expertise, it is not a surprise that the 1973 Sotheby's sale rapidly became a media circus. Scull hired a documentary crew to immortalize the event and called in CBS news reporters, then threw parties where celebrities and artists mingled. Scull knew that, in the art world, visibility is everything and that hype is the watchword. Crucially, he also understood the power of validation. A lavish catalog with the iconic *Ale Cans* (1964) bronze sculpture by Jasper Johns pictured on the front conferred an art historical gravitas that legitimized his collection.[18] The sale grossed $2.2 million (just under $12 million today). A Cy Twombly sold for $40,000, over fifty times the $750 Scull originally paid for it.[19] Sitting among the crowd, Robert Rauschenberg watched his *Thaw*, which Scull had bought from him in 1958 for $900, sell for $85,000. He famously confronted Scull after the sale telling him: "I've been working my ass off just for you to make that profit!"[20] Curiously, this is all that publications ever report about this exchange. However, Scull's comeback is equally important: "How about what you are going to make now? I have been working for you too. We work for each other!" Both were right.[21]

Rauschenberg had plenty of reasons to feel cheated by the system. Unlike film and music, which are covered by copyright, according to US law, art is a commodity bought and sold like many other mass-produced items. But Scull was right to point out that the sale would make Rauschenberg's future prices skyrocket. The collector had built an instant, new market for the artist. Thereafter, Rauschenberg became extremely rich as did almost all his contemporaries sold by Scull and represented by Castelli. And yet, the 1973 Scull sale is remembered by the same artists as a disaster for the art world. Rauschenberg himself told the *Art Newspaper* in 1997, from his 5,000 sq ft ocean-facing mansion in Captiva, Florida: "Business sure screwed up the art world universally, didn't it?"[22]

## Exposure Is Everything

Fast-forward twenty-four years to the autumn of 1997. In London, advertising guru Charles Saatchi opens the now legendary exhibition *Sensation* at the Royal Academy of Art. Shocking and irreverent, the show travels to New York where Rudy Giuliani, offended by Chris Ofili's painting of a black Madonna complete with elephant dung, tries to shut down the Brooklyn Museum of Art.[23]

*Sensation* was the final chapter of ten tumultuous years that had positioned London at the heart of the global art world. Many of the artists included were young and working class. They craved attention, fame, and money. To some, their art seemed brutal, vulgar, shallow, and even obscene. To others, it accurately reflected the times. Curator Gregor Muir recalled that, during the 1990s, "everyone from cab drivers to politicians was talking about a group of young artists. It felt like an opening up of art. Suddenly it wasn't elitist."[24] From Damien Hirst's sharks in formaldehyde to portraits of serial killers by Marcus Harvey and the occasional pornographic collage by Sarah Lucas, the Young British Artists (YBAs, as they came to be known) reinvented the Andy Warhol's pop-artist-entrepreneur model for the 1990s.[25]

The YBAs grew up in the 1980s, a decade defined by rapid economic expansion, alongside Margaret Thatcher's systematic dismantling of the welfare state—events that created an unprecedented disparity between the haves and have-nots and demonized those living in poverty. Largely critical of Thatcherism, the YBAs fostered a "can-do" approach and entrepreneurial spirit. Yes, the artists deliberately deployed shock tactics to attract attention (a strategy tried and tested by the likes of Michelangelo, Caravaggio, Bernini, and many more whom we revere today). But they did so in response to the glossy superficiality of the 1980s, its exuberant vacuousness, and capitalist optimism. The dramatic fall of communist totalitarianism and the end of the Cold War led to substantial cultural shifts. The 1980s had pushed the boundaries of taste and prudishness. Scandal after scandal, by the end of the decade, Madonna's music videos triggered media discussions on abortion, social justice, feminism, and LGBTQ rights. More extensive and graphic news coverage than ever bombarded viewers. Art had to change with the times. YBA art jolted viewers out of their comfort zone, then asked them why were they shocked?

The new entrepreneurial model they molded forever changed the artist's range of action and laid the foundations for the go-getter art world we live in today. It is not often remembered that Damien Hirst started it all. The son of a motor mechanic and a social worker, he was 12 years old when his father abandoned the family, leaving him to support his mother. He worked for two years on London building sites before applying to Goldsmiths College in 1986. Two years later, still a student, but having worked in some of the city's most prestigious commercial galleries, Hirst had come to believe that his work, and that of his peers, was just as good as what was sold on those white walls for hundreds of thousands of pounds. Like Courbet had done more than a hundred years before, he bypassed the validation of institutions by organizing and curating an independent exhibition for himself and his friends. With their help, he refurbished an abandoned warehouse in London's Surrey Docks, south of the river Thames, and produced a lavishly illustrated and extremely professional-looking catalog that was given away at London galleries and bookshops for free. He learned from Pop Art the importance of packaging. We do judge books by their covers. The exhibition was called *Freeze*, a snappy and memorable title. Supported by the successful pop artist and Goldsmiths faculty member Michael Craig-Martin, the exhibition attracted notable curators, journalists, and collectors such as Richard Shone, Nicholas Serota, Charles Saatchi, and Norman Rosenthal.[26] As the story goes, Hirst was so keen to have Rosenthal see the show that he offered to drive him to the exhibition and back.

It was an enormous hit. Many artists were signed up by galleries on the opening night, but Hirst himself failed to impress. To his dismay, his spot paintings—today a massive commercial success—went unnoticed. He had fallen victim to the power of labels. Since he organized the exhibition, everyone thought of him as a young and promising curator, not an artist. Undeterred, he took a second stab the following year with another self-organized and curated exhibition appropriately titled *Gamble.* By that point, he was certain of one thing: he needed to go bigger and bolder in order to be taken seriously as an artist. A 16-foot (5-meter) long glass cabinet featuring a rotting head of a cow and a swarm of flies destined to sizzle in a suspended bug-zapper did the trick. The exhibiting reeked of death laced with the noxious sweetness of the burnt sugar that fed the flies. Advertising millionaire Charles Saatchi loved it, purchased the piece, and offered to fund the artist's future work . . . his infamous "shark in a tank." Today, despite founded accusations of ripping off the work of other artists, with his net worth estimated at almost $400 million in 2022, Hirst is the world's richest living artist.[27] Though the press and young artists alike largely despise him, his influence and that of the YBAs have radically—for better or worse—transformed modern art and what it means to be an artist today.

Sarah Lucas and Tracy Emin, the rebellious girls of the YBA, nurtured a similar entrepreneurial flare. In 1992, they opened their own pop-up gallery space called *The Shop*, in London's East End, just off Brick Lane. In a dismal and scruffy storefront they crafted, signed, and sold all kinds of lo-fi trinkets. Obsolete, repurposed rubbish—it was a reaction to the world's tyrannies and hierarchies of unfairness. T-shirts, ashtrays, mugs, sculptures all laced in stoner-humor jokes—every object a conversation piece. *The Shop* was a mildly anarchic, punk, do-it-yourself, social melting pot. It desacralized art as a glossy institutionalized commodity. It mocked the hell out of the exhibiting space as a pure temple of transcendental contemplation and empowered women artists to set the rules of the game they wanted to play. *The Shop* attracted all kinds of people, from nearby residents to artists and influential curators. It closed with a bang on July 3, the same year, with Emin's birthday party called "Fuckin' Fantastic at 30 and Just About Old Enough to Do Whatever She Wants."[28]

YBA artists did not wait to be plucked from obscurity—they made themselves visible. They did not wait for opportunities to come their way—they created them. They didn't even wait for their school to validate their talent. Foolishness or pragmatism? Arrogance or genius? They all went to art school wanting to be professional artists who could support themselves making art, and that's exactly what they did . . . and then some.

# Part II

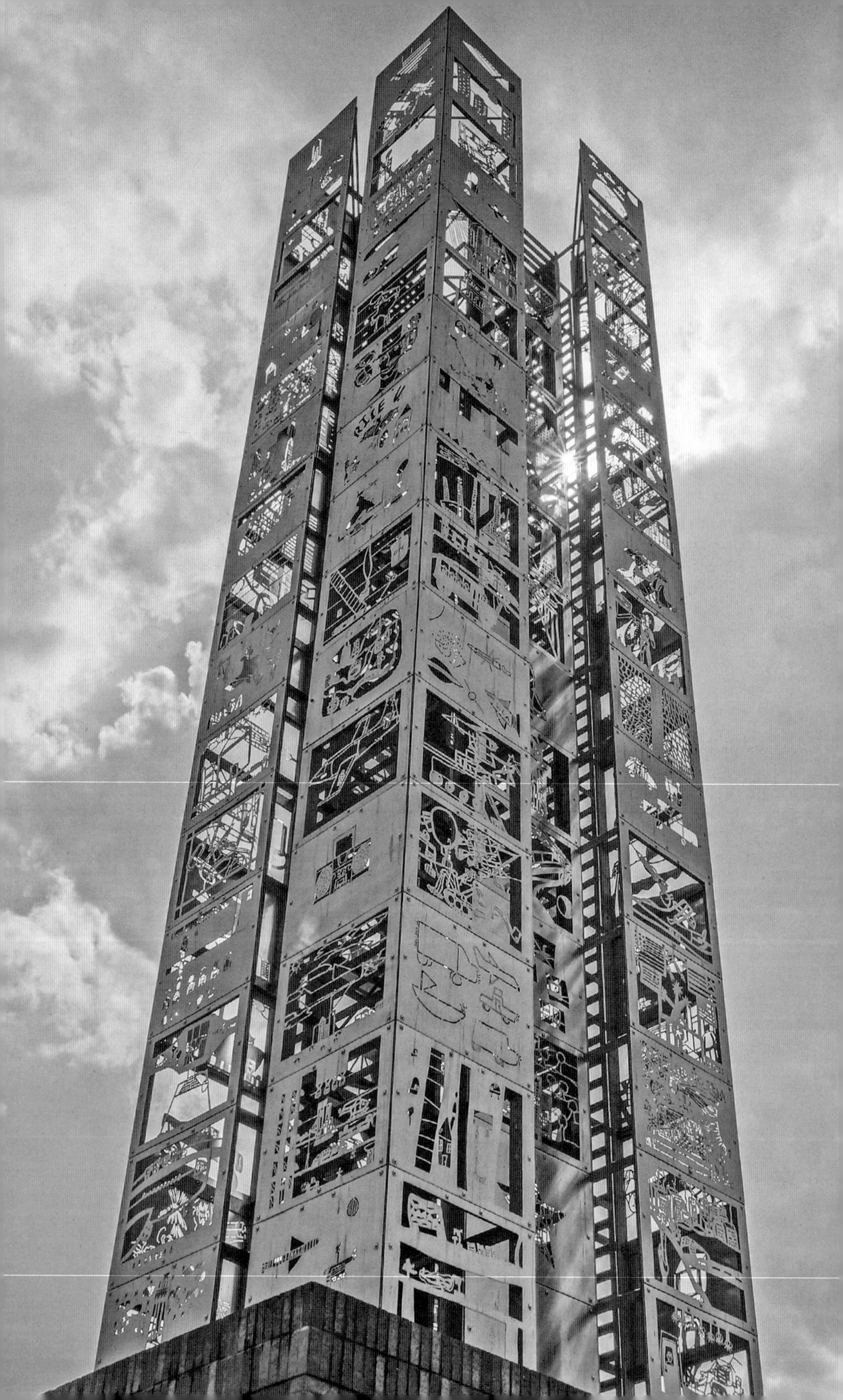

# 6 Institutional Dissociative Identity Disorders

Image 31 (facing page). Mel Chin, one of the Seven Wonders at Buffalo Bayou's Sesquicentennial Park, Houston, TX. Photographed in 2013 / Brando

# Capitalism as Cultural Disease

Media students are avid consumers of the industries they want to become part of. They are well versed in the communication systems of the ecosystemic reality they plan to inhabit. They are self-starters. They make demos, know labels and PR companies, and actively seek out opportunities to thrive. Nothing they do is a plan B because they understand the evolutional drive that shapes their professional field. They learn early on that one gig, regardless of how dismal it might seem, can lead to another and that commercial engagements can be great stepping stones. They are prepared to collaborate. They know it will not be easy, but they come to school with a pretty realistic idea of what their choice entails.

Instead, most art students tend to arrive at art school with little more than the artist myth already solidly planted in their minds. A monolith of unique genius singlehandedly withstanding a commoditized world populated by soulless replicants. They alone are alive and truly original. Lulled by patriarchal narratives of exceptionalism, they think their unique talent alone will lift them from obscurity. They know that most artists don't make much money, but somehow they'll surely be the exception. And they never think of art as an industry—this is a major (and often fatal) obstacle part of the artist myth that art schools perpetuate.

This conceptual framework is unsustainable. Oftentimes, after graduation, students abandon their aspirations and run to the stability of a full-time job in an unrelated profession, if only to pay back their art school loan. Others might choose to teach and continue to pursue their artistic career while earning a decent wage—it works for some. But often times teaching is not what they wanted to do. They were lured to art school by the myth of the artist: Picasso, Kahlo, Dali, Basquiat. That's what they dream of at least only because, unlike their peers in media studies, they won't have even encountered the art they will make. Most contemporary art is complex and intimidating to them. So, they just cannot know who they can be other than those monolithic icons from the past. Some will find out along the way, the majority will give up, disillusioned and heartbroken.

This level of disconnect between the reality of being an artist today and what is taught at art schools is not just the fault of faculties. The professional pathway we chose has changed dramatically during the past thirty years. We have not signed up for the type of job we are doing today. We feel betrayed by an ever-more corporatized higher education system outside of which we are unsure how to exist. Rampant neoliberalism has transformed higher education into a money-thirsty machine in which knowledge is a commodity and students customers. The education sector is damaged to its core.[1] The values we stood for are irremediably at odds with the terms in which our institutions are managed.

Most students are not willing to talk about their financial nightmares. But those who do talk leave no doubt about how grim matters are. In 2019, a 22-year-old student set himself on fire outside the Lumière University Lyon 2 in a bid to both protest and escape the dire situation he was experiencing. This is an extreme case, of course, but a 2018 study of 2,279 postgraduate students across twenty-six countries revealed that forty percent had suffered moderate to severe depression and anxiety, a rate six times higher than in the rest of the population.[2]

Faculties don't fare much better. Covid-19 evidenced the precarious state of employment in any public-facing industry, and higher education was no exception. A 2023 poll of 1,003 US faculty members led by Healthy Minds Network revealed:

> Overall, 64% of faculty reported "feeling burned out because of work" either somewhat (30%), to a high degree (19%), or to a very high degree (15%). Burnout was higher among women (69%) and gender minority faculty (71%) relative to men (57%). A higher proportion of faculty at 4-year institutions (68%) felt burned out than at community colleges (54%). Despite this, 67% of all faculty said they were satisfied with their job. Also on the positive side, 89% said they felt "competent and capable."[3]

In many countries, faculty have taken on significant administrative obligations, leaving little time for research and publication. Their productivity is measured through new metric systems that promote careerism, productivity, and enhance hyper-competitivity. Full-time positions are increasingly rare, while tenure (an indefinite academic appointment) has become the stuff of legends.

Perhaps surprisingly to some, to make ends meet, the most accomplished contemporary artists of our time, like Nick Cave, Dawoud Bey, Sophie Calle, Kara Walker, Eduardo Kac, Kerry James Marshall, Andrea Fraser, Gregg Bordowitz, Peter Doig, and even Ai Weiwei, teach.[4] Their work is in prestigious collections and their outstanding work has conquered a solid spot in the art history book. And yet, the sophisticated appeal of their art means that, in the case of most, a "day job" is still needed. Sometimes, institutional affiliations help them secure grants, residencies, and bigger opportunities. And of course, this day job is also where their research, thinking, and planning take place. Teaching is truly enriching. One is always exposed to the energy of the next generation. Innovation and criticality are the air we breathe. The derogatory statement "Those who can, do; those who can't, teach" doesn't hold water when it comes to art.[5] Still, the beneficial symbiosis between contemporary art and higher education is problematic in two ways, both of which negatively impact students: on the one hand, most of academia is pervaded by an aversion to capitalism and anything that is perceived as self-promotion; on the other, academia has turned into a neoliberal enterprise.

If capitalism is a cultural disease, then the dissociative identity disorders that pervade academia is among its most pronounced symptoms. Taken as a metaphor, dissociative identity disorder is a condition that afflicts all art institutions, faculty, and students alike. It is contagious. Contradicting ideological personalities inhabit the same institution or individual. It's not hypocrisy, it is now a congenital predisposition. The tail of the institution is convinced to be a charity while the head is well aware of being a corporation. Professors demonize capitalism in their lectures while they project slides from their MacBook Pro—the Apple logo covered by an Extinction Rebellion sticker. Despite the level of education and worldliness, academic life is often toxic, rife with envy, jealousy, dishonesty, greed, bullying, and harassment. Like in every other competitive profession, the truly generous and kind colleagues are rare. This is further aggravated by the fact that art schools love to portray themselves as ethical bastions of justice, fairness, and inclusion. The aftermath of George Floyd's murder, in May 2020, ignited a heightened scrutiny of institutional hypocrisy. Universities quickly shrouded themselves in BLM slogans while turning a blind eye to the systemic racism that has defined their pasts and still shapes their present.

Since the 1990s, academia has "addressed inequality" by conveniently keeping in place white privilege and hiring more white women rather than BIPOC professors.[6] According to Kalwant Bhopal, the author of *White Privilege: The Myth of a Post Racial Society*, "Universities' knee-jerk outpourings on racial equality are merely rhetoric. They are used as badges, showcasing inclusion, with no evidence in outcomes or practice."[7] How is this situation more equitable than any other institutional or corporate reality? And how can art schools continue to claim that art can build a better world when our art institutions can't set the example? The lack of diversity and tacit compliance with aesthetic paradigms known to exclude BIPOC and other minorities, as well as the perpetuation of the artist myth with its bohemian conceptions of creative purity, are part of the same toxic parcel.

## Skin-Deep Diversity

Large and irregular stitches. Ragged surfaces and smooth textures. Patches of denim juxtaposed to colorful swats of linen and cotton. Joyfully misaligned patterns. The quilts of the Gee's Bend artists who still work in a small rural community on a peninsula at a deep bend in the Alabama River are like no others. One of their most distinctive traits is "improvisational piecing." Unlike traditional quilting, which often follows a strict and preplanned pattern, Gee's Bend quilters freely piece together scraps of fabric, creating organic, unpredictable designs often suggested by the patterns and shapes of fabrics. This technique is a testament to the quilters' creativity, individuality, and resourcefulness. Their moment of fame came in the 1990s when curator and collector William Arnett noticed how their quilt patterns vividly, albeit incidentally, echo modernist painting. The Museum of Fine Arts in Houston, the Whitney Museum of American Art in New York City, the Philadelphia Museum of Art, and more—their rise to fame seemed unstoppable. Of course, this was a welcome turn of events for an African American community that for over sixty years had endured racial discrimination, land theft, and segregation.[8] But the topographies of the contemporary art market, and most of the art world alongside it, have been molded by colonialist logic—the mechanics, the blind spots, its classist, racial, and gender biases; the habit of privileging some styles and subjects over others; the exclusionary practices. For more than a hundred years, the art world has been unable to embrace diversity unless it saw a reflection of its own whiteness in who it perceived as the Other.[9]

Europe and the United States have dominated taste, markets, and ideologies until very recently.[10] Since the beginning of the new millennium, China's influence has started to reconfigure the colonialist blueprint of the art market while cementing the capitalist foundations of the art world.[11] Nonetheless, the art market remains far from the truly global entity celebrated in the media. Of the world's 195 countries, only roughly thirty-five have a foothold in the art market—and most of these barely account for two to four percent.[12] Even when seemingly more diverse today than fifty years ago, the global identity of the art market remains insidiously white or whitewashed at best. Diversity is only skin-deep. For example, many of today's well-known, BIPOC contemporary artists spent their formative years in the United States or Europe. Ai Weiwei moved from China to the United States in 1981. He studied in Philadelphia and San Francisco before relocating to New York a few years later.[13] Yayoi Kusama swapped Kyoto for New York in 1958.[14] Iranian visual artist Shirin Neshat also moved there in 1974.[15] Nigerian-born Njideka Akunyili Crosby relocated to Philadelphia in 1999.[16] And the list goes on. This is not a coincidence, but rather a strong indication that, even now, artists from all over the world must first become assimilated into Western culture and its creative languages in order to be acknowledged by the art market and other cultural institutions.

The power of context and cultural validation became central to the early stages of Theaster Gate's career, in 2007, before he became famous, the Chicago-based artist held a number of African-Japanese fusion-food dinners dedicated to his mentor, Shoji Yamaguchi, a Japanese potter who moved to Mississippi after the bombing of Hiroshima. As the story goes, Yamaguchi married a black civil rights activist with whom he started a commune where they combined Japanese pottery techniques with African American folk traditions. Gates's own pottery was deeply informed by his mentor's values, history, and progressive views . . . except that he never existed. Yamaguchi was an entirely fictional character created by Gates to gain visibility in the art world and expose the hypocritical racial/cultural connotations that validate an artist's work beyond its aesthetic or conceptual worth. As Gates explained,

> I'm a nobody, so the bowl is a nothing; the bowl looks like lots of other bowls that are mass produced you can buy for even cheaper than $25; the bowl has no magical context that would help get it valued in other ways. If I could be a somebody; if I could elevate [the bowl] beyond the everyday context, would people value it more? That became my social experiment.[17]

A performance? Cultural appropriation? A lie? Or plain truth? Regardless, it could have not worked better. Today Gates is one of the most in-demand artists on the contemporary scene.

The superficial diversity endorsed by the art world is mirrored by teaching institutions. Artists, art historians, and curators in the West, mostly unwittingly, promote cultural biases by perpetuating a specific brand of "conceptualism." Today, conceptualism has become the backbone of almost all contemporary art exhibited in art-world-connected galleries and museums.[18] A philosophically grounded concept is now essential to every artwork regardless of its medium. The concept is the "challenging part," the thought-engine that grants the work its artistic integrity, contemporaneity, and authenticity. It elevates the work beyond the mere ornamentation of craft.

Modern conceptualism, as it was founded by Dada in the 1920s, is a Western idea. It gained traction during the second decade of the twentieth century. The history of colonialism is grounded in the imposition of Western languages, beliefs, and ideals. Settlers and missionaries always believed their ideas to be superior to those of Indigenous cultures and accordingly proceeded to erase and hybridize as needed. In the history of colonialism, the colonizer has always been the modernizer and educator: the ameliorator, the redemptor. Political philosopher Franz Fanon argued that this paradigm led Africa to rampant cultural insecurity.[19] The artistic formation of Indo-Chinese and Indian artists was similarly conditioned by the idea that French painting was vastly superior to their traditional aesthetics. Artists in these cultures strove to overcome feelings of inferiority and failure by assimilating, imitating, and mastering Western approaches while, all along the way, forsaking their own.[20] I see this process of aesthetic colonization performed in art schools, over and over, as students from all over the world are implicitly taught to forsake their own aesthetic vocabulary to endorse the lingua franca of contemporary Western art instead. It is a quietly violent process: another manifestation of the dissociative identity disorder that pervades academia.

## The Art Market as Ecosystem

The art market is one of the many ecosystems contained in the bigger ecological reality of the art world; an interdependent and interconnected web of different entities. In 1935, botanist Sir Arthur George Tansley introduced the term "ecosystem" to describe a unified framework encompassing all the life-forms that together, as a community, support a site-specific reality.[21] As a metaphor, the term has widely been used in economics and management to designate complex social relations enmeshed in companies and institutions.[22] In most instances its use emphasizes the interdependency, symbiosis, and interconnectedness that shape relational politics and codependencies.

While economic and corporate ecosystems are often arranged in hierarchical ways, natural ones are not. In natural ecosystems, each participant is indispensable regardless of how small their contribution might seem at one moment in time. Natural ecosystems exist on multiple scales and time frames at once. Rethinking the art world as a true ecosystem entails giving up the hierarchical structures of capitalist and colonialist models in order to become part of a different interconnectedness in which power is decentered, distributed, and fragmented.

In an ecosystem, trees are not more important than grasses or frogs, fungi, or dragonflies. Anthropocentric hierarchical structures typical of capitalist thinking distract us from what is essential. The award, the solo show, the prestigious grant, the power branding . . . Instead, the concept of ecosystem foregrounds reciprocal and sustainable networks of generative interactions devised to benefit multiple parties. It dissolves the egocentric myth of the artist to reveal the networks that define the artworld—not as a lie or a sham—but as the true ecological system one has to engage with. But ecosystems are not safe environments—none can be. Ecosystems are by nature unbalanced and the ability to adapt quickly to changes is critical to one's survival. Accepting and embracing the elemental forces that will shape one's journey and understanding that these, and not talent alone, will define the trajectory of one's flight, is absolutely essential.

For better or worse, the art market is alive—a concatenation of vast geographies, individuals, colonies, tribes, and hives. In this ecosystem, there are too many stars and not enough sky. Fame and success often result from unpredictable astral alignments and environmental conditions. Colossal forces such as technology, politics, and the global economy define the art market seasons. Gravitational pulls are determined by the ever-shifting polarities of supply and demand. This ecosystem is now kept alive by the power of neoliberal capitalism: a long-term unsustainable model that incentivizes growth and accumulation. But as an ecosystem, the art market is also marred by extractive practices, and its biodiversity is constantly at risk. Like the greenhouses in a botanic garden, its survival is artificially engineered and carefully fine-tuned. Museums, galleries, auction houses, art fairs, art schools, universities, the publishing industry, banks, art material suppliers, art historians, curators, collectors, and critics are only some of the territories and organisms that in one way or another financially and conceptually make it what it is.

Ecosystemic conceptions of the art world thus invite us to become and remain aware of the geology of this landscape. How can one find the right place wherein to thrive, even if temporarily. Who will prove a symbiotic ally and who a parasite? What kind of fertile or poisoned ground are we sinking our roots into? Can we develop alliances that might neutralize toxicity?

## No Natural Evolution

Say, for example, I discover a brilliant young artist on Facebook. After a crazy week at my house in the Hamptons, he has made 30 abstract paintings for me, which I've bought for a total of $90,000. Having posted examples on Instagram, I enter one of these paintings into a contemporary day sale and ask two business associates, who are cut in on the deal, to bid it up to $150,000. After the sale, a benchmark auction price posted on *Artnet*, and news of the artist's inclusion in a forthcoming museum show—which happens to be curated by a friend of mine—establishes my new acquaintance as a hot young artist. Over the next six months, we discreetly sell 20 more paintings at auction and privately for an average price of $70,000 each.[23]

Does this sound cynical? Well, it is the blunt truth behind the making of the most successful artists today as lucidly sketched out by art journalist Scott Reyburn in a 2015 article for the *New York Times*. None of this is taught at art schools.

The alternative history of Western art that I have presented in the previous chapters strips bare the traditional art historical rhetoric that has perpetuated the artist myth and that continues to conceal the socioeconomic forces that drive the successful careers of celebrated artists. This is not to say that successful contemporary artists are frauds, or that art history is a sham. It is just how the system has worked for well over a century. It is what art history books omit in favour of the heroic rhetoric that positions art as a transcendental and pure expression of human unparalleled greatness.

Western culture has been shaped by a sense of protagonism and hubris of which colonialism is the ultimate outcome. Centuries of conquest and subjugation, endorsed and often promoted by religious authorities, have idolized personal success. The pioneer, the conqueror: a mythology of the hero (doused in patriarchal fumes) that plays out in the cultural and personal sphere with equal intensity. A confirmation, a mission, a manifest destiny—the hero is divine. In popular culture, the trope of the hero is still the only one worth living. It is better to live one day as a lion than a hundred years as a sheep, they say. But is it? How about living fifty years as an earthworm? Or a thousand as a lichen?

Even after the millions of deaths caused by Covid-19 our perception has not shifted one bit. The hero most people aspire to be is still the rock star or the Hollywood actor, not the nurse, the doctor, the teacher, or the bus driver who made personal sacrifices to keep the world ticking through some hefty dark times. Capitalism blinds us with glittery promises of social exceptionalism that we promptly buy as lifelong happiness models. Terribly insecure and fragile, we need to be constantly reassured that our lives have meaning and that our actions and thoughts matter.

Membership to nobility is a birthright: a matter of blood. But societal elevation from common mortality can be earned otherwise. Becoming a successful artist is one way. To appear veritable, the divine ascension of the artist must, at least from the outside, seem spontaneously natural—an evolutional process. A metamorphosis from caterpillar to butterfly. The myth of the artist relies upon an absurdly intense fetishization of genius devoted to the erasure of its own genesis. Art historians have often acted like natural historians—pretending to discover, pin down, archive, and objectively describe a newly discovered animal or plant when, in truth, the fictitious metanarrative of art's evolution has been entirely masterminded by them.

As I've demonstrated, brilliant artists whose work we see in museums and publications have always been clever entrepreneurs, their creativity evident in both their art and their ability to self-promote. Nineteenth-century artists had to forge these skills (which art schools still ignore) from scratch, but today enlisting the assistance of market gurus, agents, spin doctors, promoters, and other online hype generators helps artists to create markets, persuade collectors, lobby museums, and broker deals with galleries. Once operating discreetly, in the undergrowth and at the fringes, you can now find them all online—just google "art agent" or "artist representative." Enough money will get you an art career of some kind. Fake it until you make it?[24]

A multitude of PR firms, agents, career counselors, and managers lurk behind the meritocratic facade that the cultural industry strives to uphold. This subject is taboo for art history and academicians alike. If the success of the art we choose to write about is not genuinely spontaneous, then what does that say about the credibility of what we wright? But today, the whole culture-production ecosystem is commercialized to the bone. A string of financial crises and the pandemic have made the old "pay to play" models (aka vanity projects) become the norm. Some galleries now charge artists substantial fees to produce solo or group exhibitions. This supports their business models at the expense of creative individuals desperate to launch their careers.[25] To many, from the outside, it will look like you've made it. But what would it mean to you?

## Muddy Waters

The art world, in each and all of its many parts . . . is corrupt in the following ways:

a) It's managed completely by the rich as a plaything.

b) It likes to appear concerned with the poor, social problems, etc., but is not and usually acts against social interests.

c) Many "prestige" institutions, museums, galleries, etc., are really around in order to increase the value of paintings for the private gain of collectors, investors, and sometimes, artists.

d) Many of the rich, society people who control things have no real background in art or anything else, the picture of superficiality and "good" manners.

e) The "auction houses," again run by the banks, really, and staffed by wise-ass society girls, otherwise unemployable, overeducated, and flunkie art historians.[26]

This was the assessment of artist-cum-art critic Gregory Battcock in 1978. In 2016, *ArtNews* critic Andrew Russeth pointed out that Battcock's diagnosis is still valid.[27] I can confirm that nothing much has changed since. Should this, too, be taught at art school? It's brutal, but why ignore all this as if it did not bear any relevance to our creative journeys? What is the point of talking about art in a vacuum, or as a transcendental icon of which we can't openly consider the true matrix?

From the outside, for instance, it might seem that auctions are part of a wholly separate reality from the art we see in museums. But, in truth, they are the bedrock of the art world. They define taste, hierarchies of influence, and set up stratigraphies of power. They are part of what is technically called the "secondary market": the resales of artworks from collector to collector. The "primary market" is where artworks are sold for the first time, directly from the artist's studio—which is where the artists make their money. Subsequent resales on the secondary market almost always bring no revenue to the artist but can substantially increase the value of their future works (see the Scull/Rauschenberg example in Chapter 5), so this can be another form of long-term, productive exposure. In the United States, a resale royalty rights bill aims to establish a modest, five-percent payment to artists based on the purchase price of work sold at auction. However, the maximum payable is capped at $35,000—at the time of writing this proposal has yet to move forward.[28] More than seventy countries, including the United Kingdom and member states of the European Union, provide some resale royalties to visual artists.[29] But unless art sells for millions, very little revenue can be raised.

Furthermore, the art market is a wilderness that remains thoroughly unregulated and intricately nontransparent.[30] For this reason, its higher peaks (auction houses included) have become a haven for financial speculation and money laundering. Up until the Second World War, dealers would buy art cheaply at auction for collectors. But more recently, auctions have become alternative and unmissable investment opportunities for the hyper-rich. Some investors are genuine art lovers, others are speculators who solely buy art for profit, while others are essentially interested in buying a status-symbol trophy. These three personalities often overlap to some degree. Turning cash into art is a kind of "safer banking." Monet and Picasso are stable investments in which financial growth is certain. Many firms specialize in managing financial portfolios in which an art collection is nothing more than assets. Art by some of the greatest names in the history of art function perfectly as collateral for loans. Though the art market represents a small part of the global economy, the international art trade in 2022 was valued at $67.8 billion.[31] And with fewer old masters (the safest investment) available on the market, museum-caliber contemporary artists have begun to work just as well. Much of the attention contemporary art now gets on the international stage is down to this.

A professional artistic career of the kind that might have attracted a student to art school is substantially based on this type of marketing and "marketeering" rather than originality and talent alone, or the simple and honest pursuit of one's personal expression. At the top level of the art market, it is no longer the voice of the muses one hears but that of investment companies serenading the super-rich. Sometimes a work of art acquired at auction for investment never leaves the crate in which it is packaged. It travels straight from the auction house to a free-port tax haven in Geneva, Beijing, or Singapore. There it will wait in climate-controlled darkness, like a luxury wine or a gold Rolex watch, until it is sold at auction, again, a few years later.[32] It's true: art can be pure—pure currency.

## Echoes in the Valleys

One of the major obstacles between us and an ecological conception of the art world is posed by institutions, how we have let them shape our minds, expectations, and conceptions of value and worth. Artists obsess about museums—secretly or less so, they all aspire to get their work one day. The bigger the better: the Met, Tate, MoMA, NAMOC, Guggenheim . . . The museum is the top validation layer in the art world. It has been historically so for over two hundred years. The museum is not a lowly commercial gallery, it's divine—as the name implies. Deriving from the Greek *mouseion* meaning the "seat of the muses," the museum is a place of transcendental inspiration in which the human and supernatural merge.

However, as we now know, museums are not immaculate beacons of culture devoted to education. For decades they have been founded by oil, weaponry, or big pharma money, they have participated in artifact theft, and their trustees have been involved in unethical financial practices.[33] They, too, look for redemption (and hefty tax breaks) among the divine ranks of the museum.

In 2015, the art press revealed what those working in the field already knew: five major commercial art galleries determine what we see in museums. Artists represented by David Werner, Hauser & Wirth, Marian Goodman Gallery, Pace, and Gagosian Gallery accounted for thirty percent of the contemporary art exhibitions staged in US museums between 2007 and 2013. This is the senior league of art from which top curators and institutions broker the terms under which successful artists might be given the museum's ultimate stamp of approval in the form of a solo show—a move that will increase the value of their work, past and future. Museums are generally cash-strapped and commercial galleries have been known to provide financial help essential to the successful staging of important shows that feature their artists. This form of symbiosis has more recently caused a major shift: the kind of art sold at the high end of the art market is more than ever aesthetically aligned with what we see in museums.[34] This is now the art that defines taste across the world. This has now become the art students often wish to make.

It's true, great art museums (for better or worse) are still relevant. But the heavy hitters are devoted to historic, not contemporary, art. More than 7.5 million visitors walk through the Louvre's doors every year (to see the *Mona Lisa*). A notable exception is Tate Modern, with nearly 4 million visitors per year, but it is a free museum in a world-class capital city that attracts millions of tourists every year. Despite appearances, contemporary art audiences are very small in comparison to other industries like film and music. In most countries, admission tickets to art exhibitions at major museums are expensive.[35] Blockbuster art shows barely attract more than 500,000 visitors. The most attended exhibitions of all time are group shows or those that feature the work of such sacred monsters as Picasso, Basquiat, and Ai Weiwei.[36] In contrast, TV series and films on streaming platforms such as Netflix attract millions of viewers, while music videos are today watched for free on YouTube by billions.[37] Measuring cultural impact is difficult, but streaming figures provide a good indication of the reach and impact of ideas and values that are more likely to define the cultural climate. And of course, TV and online adverts continue to set life-aspirational gold standards. Like a drop of water carving stone, manipulative representational strategies and stereotypical characterizations define our perception of race, gender, age, and ableism more than anything else. What has more impact on society today, an advert or a painting?

In the nineteenth century, when it temporarily wriggled itself out of the stronghold of the aristocracy and the church, art played a much more powerful societal role. The nineteenth century was the age of the gaze. The Salon and its scandals attracted roughly a million people over six weeks (twice as many as blockbuster exhibitions do over three to four months today). It is against the interest of any art school to point this out to students, especially in light of the exorbitant fees they charge (in the United States, especially). Some art forms still have the ability to change the world; others, I am afraid to say, no longer do. But the idea that art can build a better world is a slogan that inevitably appeals to young aspiring artists, so art schools spread the message—a hollow mantra that amounts to little more than a great marketing ploy facilitating the making of luxury goods/investments for the very rich.

Is our work meant to change people's minds or perpetuate the echo chamber in which we already live? Who is it for? Too frequently, art schools lead students down a path of self-indulgence and introspection. Too much emphasis is placed on guiding students to find their artistic voices. Worrying about who might or might not be listening is not deemed important. Is it a surprise then that so many fail to be heard by the art world after they graduate?

Communication is central to any ecosystemic reality. Some modes of communication are tried and tested. Others are experimental and constantly evolving. What one writes, paints, composes, and where one decides to share it changes enormously in relation to these questions: Who is my art for? Who am I speaking to? It is never too early to ask. From Alice Patrick, Banksy, JR, Naoufal "Rocko" Alaoui, To'Ree'Nee' Keiser, Mona Caron, and Shepard Fairey to Tavar Zawacki, since the beginning of the new millennium, street artists have reinvigorated and bolstered the political power of muralist art. Their work attracts substantial attention in the media. This kind of art is truly accessible, and it inspires and motivates people. Land artists Raven Chacon (Navajo), Cristóbal Martínez (Mestizo), and Kade L. Twist (Cherokee)—members of the collective known as Postcommodity—have generated substantial public discussion with their *The Repellent Fence* (2015), a project that comprised a 2-mile-long row of twenty-eight giant inflatable balloons that over the length of four days straddled the US–Mexico border.[38] The artwork's temporary but striking presence, which echoed the duration of Indigenous rituals, engaged local communities, questioned conceptions of social visibility, and challenged the power of borders as quintessential symbols of political, cultural, and physical separation.

Community-based artists like Cannupa Hanska Luger, Zuo Jing and Ou Ning, Susan Rodgerson, Barnaby Evans, and Robert Karimi, or collectives like Edible Hut (Detroit), Huston Community Artists, the Artists Co-op (New York City), Chicago Public Art Group, B人BEL (China), Paper Moon Puppet Theatre (Indonesia), and many more, prioritize community engagement, generating collective benefits that are often measurable and quantifiable. However, these artists do not get wealthy from their important and engaged work, nor do they attract the attention of mainstream institutions. Most students find their work interesting on a theoretical level—good material for classroom discussions and assigned readings. But most of them inevitably value more the work that ends up in the prestigious museums, mostly because the artist myth is still alive and kicking in their minds.


## The M-Word: Exposure Doesn't Pay Bills?

Money is dirty—the backbone of the artist myth; the most unnecessary and damaging trope in the history of the art world. This concept gained strength in the nineteenth century, from the rise of the artist as an independent (upper-middle-class) hero and the idea of art as a pure form of personal expression. Money pollutes true creativity, end of story—so it is still claimed. But how can we claim so when in the United States students pay up to $200,000 for their BAs or $150,000 for their MFAs (Europe is still competitively cheaper at this point) to learn how to make art.[39]

The "corporatization of higher education" is very real and, whether we like it or not, all faculty are implicated, those who pose as revolutionaries and outsiders included. Across workshops and classrooms, art schools and universities are extremely politicized, and yet, the critique seems to conveniently stop at the "m-word." The money students pay; the money part-time professors won't earn; the money students will, most likely, never recuperate after graduating.

Oscar Wilde said, "When bankers get together, they talk about art. When artists get together, they talk about money."[40] Artists are more likely to complain about the money they don't make, and for some, it feels like a badge of honor. It perpetuates the myth of the artist as a martyr/survivor of a reckless capitalist world. It harnesses a sense of presumed authenticity and heroism,—a highly dysfunctional identity complex that students inherit from their professors, institutions, and bad art history books that have romanticized the artist to death. This "money-taboo" syndrome manifests in the general inadequacy of many young artists to manage projects, deadlines, budgets, and other economic aspects in their lives. According to the myth, the true artist is volatile, messy, scatterbrained, unreliable, capricious . . . Successful artists learn at their own expense that today's world requires them to be industrious, proactive, very present, and focused in order to succeed. Art schools insistently ignore the other sides of the artist's identity: the entrepreneur who must generate opportunities and the administrator who needs to balance the books. The time has come for schools to take responsibility (mostly because of the fees they charge) and deliver serious and up-to-date programs on finance, project/time management, and the art market (for artists, not art administrators) so that these important conversations can move from corridor rants to professional growth.

In 2015, American actor and blogger Wil Wheaton sparked outrage on social media when he revealed that the *Huffington Post* would not pay him a penny to republish one of his blog pieces. In response, he penned the tongue-in-cheek article, "You Can't Pay Your Rent with 'The Unique Platform and Reach Our Site Provides'."[41] In March 2016, the makers of the reality-TV show *The Bachelor Australia* approached students from the Australian Institute of Music and the Sydney Conservatorium of Music offering the opportunity to play live in an episode. The compensation was offered in "exposure." To provide some perspective, the show was produced by Warner Bros International Television Production, a subsidiary of WarnerMedia, the same multinational that earned $30.4 billion in 2020. The request prompted a director of the Australian trade union, Media Entertainment and Arts Alliance, to state: "Artists are not there to be taken advantage of. Exposure does not pay the bills."[42] For months thereafter, the mantra "Exposure does not pay bills" swept the music and film industries like wildfire. The art world quickly joined in.

We now live in the Age of Free Content (soon to be the Age of Artificial Intelligence). We are surrounded by more free art than ever before, and we live in a world where

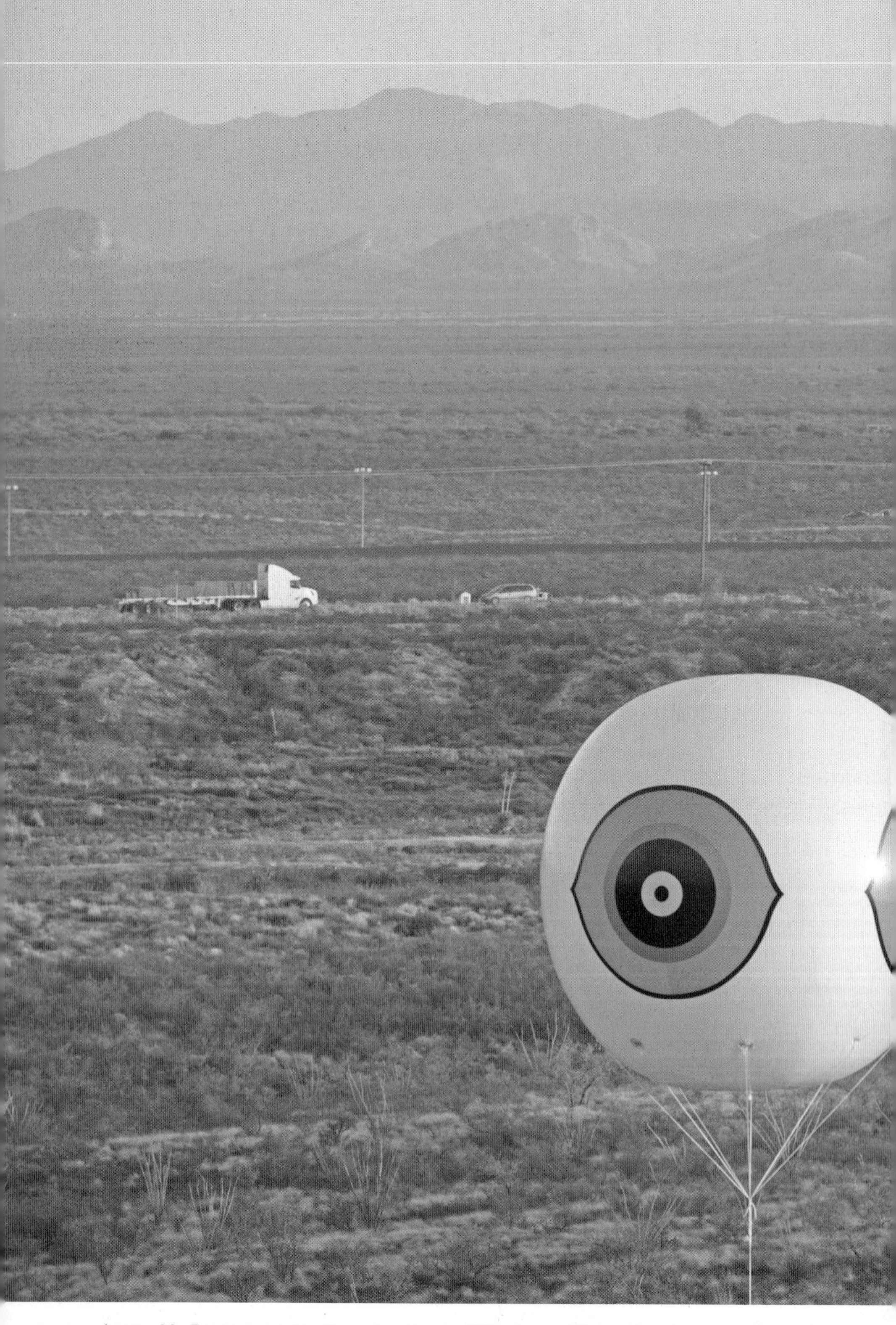

Image 32. Postcommodity, *Repellent Fence*, 2015. Image Michael Lundgren, courtesy of Postcommodity

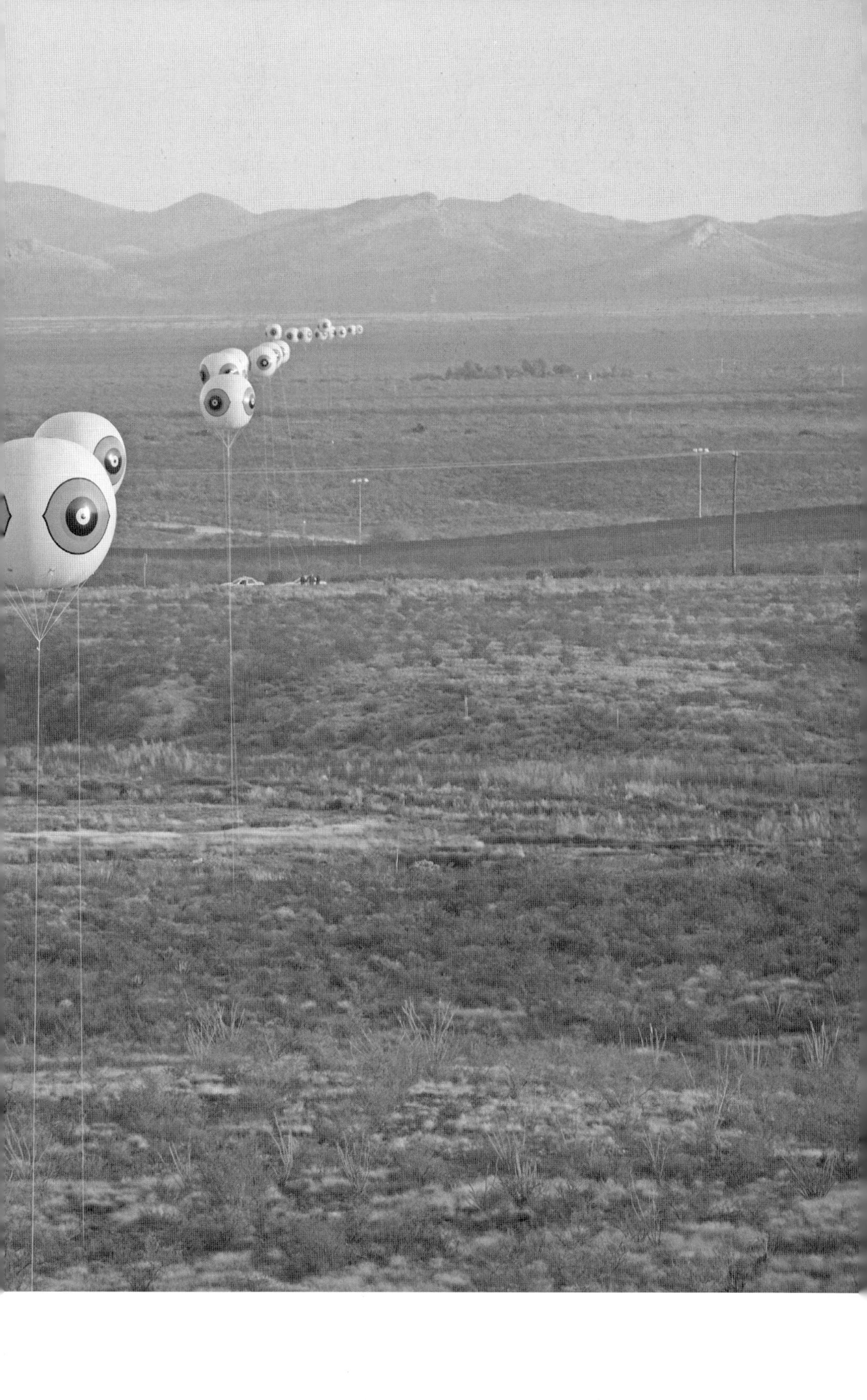

media digitization has dramatically altered the terms of production and consumption. One might well ask why so many artists are making their work available for free on multiple media platforms if exposure truly does not pay bills? It is because, as it turns out . . . it *does*. Or rather, it will not pay today's bills, but it might pay tomorrow's. It's a gamble.

This situation has further exposed the serious lack of understanding young artists have of the art world and its financial dimensions. The art world is a complex ecosystem and one has to take time to study its topographies, climates, and seasons in order to flourish. No gallery or museum is alike—independent, supported by grants and endowments, philanthropists, nonprofits, charities, corporate, blue chips . . . Some institutions have money, others really don't.

It is, however, true that institutions tend to develop parasitic relationships with artists and curators. They smell desperation and take advantage of it. This tendency has naturalized itself because the field is hyper-competitive. But in general, independent art galleries are rarely owned by billion-dollar multinationals as is the case for film and music. Thirty percent of all art galleries run at a loss, even in a buoyant market. The remainder barely scrape by, with only eighteen percent claiming a profit margin over twenty percent.[43] And, unsurprisingly, the 2020/1 global pandemic has made the financial picture look a lot bleaker. Being an artist entails taking risks and evaluating monetary currencies in the context of opportunity costs—and yes, exposure. Every institution is different and working with them is a two-way engagement—it's a symbiosis. Unless one decides that staying in the cool shades of the undergrowth is what works for them, in an oversaturated ecosystem visibility is everything. Art schools don't prepare students to professionally navigate these arduous territories—this is a serious problem.

So, while it is true that artists are often exploited, it is also true that this happens because for decades art schools have miseducated students about the financial side of art and the art market. Making money into a subject of shame has led to an obscurantist regime that ultimately only penalizes lower class artists. The superficial social media conversations around the "exposure does not pay bills" refrain ultimately harmed students and young artists the most while unveiling a disproportionate sense of arrogance and entitlement. Where does this attitude come from? The artist myth . . .

Before the birth of photography, film, and TV, talent seemed rare and exceptional. That's no longer the case. Today countless talent contests—whether spotlighting singers, dancers, or cakemakers—have revealed the sheer amount of gifted people out there. There's so much new music, film, and art to hear and see every day. The avalanche of content simultaneously exhilarates and daunts. The internet gives everyone a chance to shine but often only for those fifteen minutes Warhol predicted in the 1960s; now perhaps even less . . . So much "talent" available at the swipe of a thumb can only mean one thing: while almost anyone can share their music online or post their short films, photographs, and designs, competition in all fields is fiercer than ever before. The market is flooded. This saturation has the same consequences in the art world as in any other market: if supply exceeds demand, the price drops. Regardless of how long and hard one has worked to gain their skills, if there's no, or little, demand for one's work then it is very likely that no money will be involved.

## NFT and AI: Is the Future Online (Is There Any Future Left)?

Since the beginning of the new millennium, from Frieze to Art Basel, Art Dubai, and the Beijing Art Expo, the new supermarkets of art have largely contributed to a growing interest in "affordable art collecting." As of 2023, over 260 art fairs have become part of the art world ecosystem. The success of the art fair in recent times is intimately linked to a change in the art-buying demographic that has occurred since the 1970s and its consumption habits. Art fairs appeal to high-income professionals who prefer a one-stop-shop buying experience over the traditional "travel and scout" model of the eighteenth-century Grand Tour. I want it all and I want it now. Art fairs are fast, competitive, and ultra-contemporary. In a sense, they are the new Parisian Salon: a mostly superficial visual gorging where quality is a rarity. But this is the way we experience most art today—by the bucketload. A Chubb survey found that over fifty percent of collectors are most likely to purchase art seen on social media than elsewhere.[44] The internet has had a profound impact on the art market, too. But it hasn't just changed how collectors buy. It is changing how artists think, make, and exhibit work. The "Instagram state of mind" is a double-edged sword. Artists are less concerned about how good their work may look on a wall than how it will look under a thumb that scrolls through hundreds of thousands of images each hour. But social media does not aim to replace the gallery or the museum. It is instead once more expanding our conception of what art is, how it is made, and how it is accessed. It is democratizing art like never before. It is allowing artists to bypass galleries and even reinvent the validation symbiosis. In the "Instagram art world," being endorsed by a celebrity is much more prestigious than receiving a good review from an art critic published in a prestigious magazine.

In art terms, 2021 will be remembered as the year of the "non-fungible token," or NFT. NFTs are unique and certified digital artworks—images, film clips, animations, and even poems can be sold online. Like a painting or a sculpture, they are unique, but unlike a painting or a sculpture they come with an embedded digital provenance that assures authenticity and value. NFTs essentially are unique digital files that live on a blockchain—a digitally distributed, decentralized, public ledger across a network—and can be displayed on TV and computer screens.

In February 2021, Beeple (born Mike Winkelmann) sent shockwaves across the art world when he snatched a whopping $69 million for *Everydays: the First 5000 Days*, a composite NFT comprising 5,000 of his works.[45] While many heralded the new dawn of a fairer market where digital artists will finally make money, it is worth noting that Beeple was already a well-known graphic designer and animator working with the likes of Ariana Grande, Justin Bieber, Childish Gambino, Nicki Minaj, and Apple as clients.[46] The sale was orchestrated and promoted by Christie's. Relatively unknown artists are welcome to try their hand at selling NFTs (and many have tried . . .), but the results will be likely far less impressive without the backing of such a colossal validation network. New format, same old story? The NFT boom ended in September 2022 as trading volumes fell by a catastrophic ninety-seven percent, which generated an astonishing $2 trillion loss of value.[47]

Questions about quality, authorship, and creativity have also been more recently raised by the rapid emergence of Artificial Intelligence (AI) and its extremely versatile applications across the fields of photography, illustration, film, and sound. It was a Hungarian artist, Vera Molnár, today remembered as the "grand dame of generative art," who began to produce computer-drawn patters in the late 1950s.[48] Since then, computer applications across the artistic spectrum have mushroomed. Animation, photo- and film-editing—computers have become indispensable in many forms of art making, but AI will most likely also change the world, not just art, similarly to how the internet and other colossal inventions, like the telephone and TV, did before it. The implications for aspiring artists are many and, at the outset, not very positive. Some applications of AI essentially expand existing digital media into new and fascinating territories that mostly reconfigure the dynamic between work and artist. In Refik Anadol's enormous "data painting", for instance, AI interpretations of millions of data produce spectacular and ever-evolving imageries. Where does the artist begin and the technological mind end? Was there ever a clear-cut distinction? Digital artist John Gerard has also harnessed the creative potential of AI in monumental video works that focus on climate change. In AI, artificial neural networks mimic the network of neurons in the brain, enabling computers to "learn" from data used to identify more similar data. Artist Anna Ridler generates her own data in order to retain creative control over her projects but others simply rely on AI's ability to draw from online archives in order to produce images, texts, footage, and sound from brief, and often rather vague, verbal prompts. The result can be striking, at times so very convincing that differentiating a common digital photograph from an AI-generated one can be hard if not impossible at first glance.

In April 2023, artist Boris Eldagsen won the World Photography Organization's Sony World Photography Awards for a piece titled *The Electrician*. An uncanny and sleek black-and-white photograph in the style of 1930s masters shows two women, one behind the other, hugging in a tense and pensive way. The jury's feathers were ruffled when the artist revealed the AI-generated nature of the image.[49] AI's creative opportunities are endless, and artists of all kinds will certainly use it to expand once more the very idea of what art can be.

But on a more mundane level, AI will spell the end of freelance work for many photographers and illustrators working in the commercial field. Film, fashion, advertising, textile, game design, architecture, and other fields have already been hit hard. AI will enable many sectors already dealing with increased production costs to generate the graphics and text they require for free. However, AI freely scrapes from online archives of billions of artworks produced by artists while obviously giving no credit or royalties back since, in the process, works of art are deconstructed, processed, reconstructed, and assimilated to the point of unrecognizability. It's as if millions of artists' works have been pillaged and compressed to produce a hyper-artwork without author. To make matters worse, AI generators can accurately reproduce the styles of established artists, thus raising urgent copyright and authorship questions. Lawsuits against major AI providers like stability.ai and Midjourney have been filed.[50]

Will AI kill human creativity? Most likely not, but it will motivate artists to reinvent their identities once more in order to survive.[51]

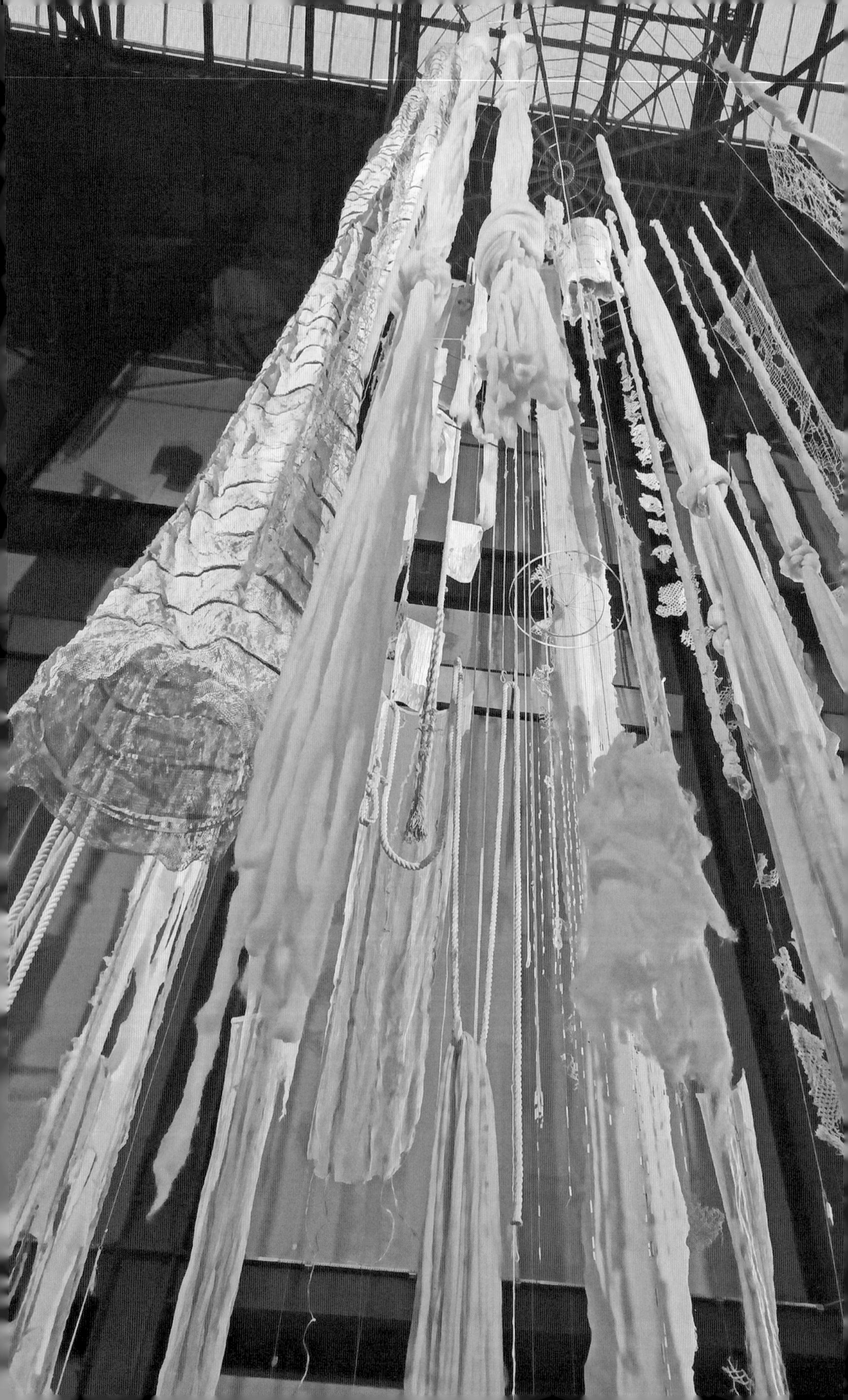

# 7 Outsiders and Professional Amateurs

Image 33 (facing page). Cecilia Vicuña, *Brain Forest Quipu*, 2022. Installation view, Tate Modern, London. Photo: Dominic Alves. Public Domain CC BY 2.0 DEED

# The Artist's Voice: Canonical Deconstructions in the Age of Hypercriticality

Unidentified, unmarked, anonymous—the large black-and-white photographs in Dawoud Bey's series "Night Coming Tenderly, Black" stare back at the viewer—stern, uncompromisingly silent. The rich and nuanced tonality of the gelatin silver print invites close inspection—these black-and-white enigmas seem simultaneously familiar and hauntingly distant. Unguided by labels on the wall or introductory text by the door, this journey quickly becomes uneasy. At last, after so much blind navigation, a wall text at the heart of the exhibiting space sheds some light. Each image captures a landmark of the "Underground Railroad," a network of safe houses and sheltered locations that slaves might have come upon while on their journey to freedom. In place of the alluring dawns or golden sunsets of eighteenth-century painting, Bey presents an often eerie American landscape at twilight.

In the artist's words, the series—inspired by the work of African American photographer Roy DeCarava and the poetry of Langston Hughes—is "a visual reimagining of the movement of [early nineteenth-century] fugitive slaves through the Cleveland and Hudson, Ohio landscape as they approached Lake Erie and the final passage to freedom in Canada."[1] Bey's visual journey reaches deep into the history of Western landscape painting, its aesthetic ambitions, psychological depths, and elitist biases. Expansive stretches of peaceful countryside or breathtaking mountaintop vistas are absent simply because they would be life-threatening to a fugitive: depending on the color of one's skin, visibility is vulnerability. In their place, seemingly impenetrable thickets of trees, ominous lake waters, and vividly white picket fences loosely contextualize a first-person encounter with an unwelcoming landscape that, through the photographic lens, we experience from the point of view of the freedom-seeking slave. "Night Coming Tenderly, Black" is a powerful, and rare, example of art that can have a positive impact on society. The photographs invite viewers to stand in someone else's shoes, see with their eyes, and feel with their hearts. They show how we, people of different colors and races, can inhabit the same landscape while existing in thoroughly different worlds.

Should art be political? Art for art's sake: in the 1830s, writer Théophile Gautier argued that art needs no moral justification, that it should not educate or serve a social purpose.[2] Painter and artist provocateur James McNeill Whistler agreed: "Art should be independent of all claptrap – should stand alone . . . and appeal to the artistic sense of eye or ear, without confounding this with emotions entirely foreign to it, as devotion, pity, love, patriotism and the like."[3] Frederic Nietzsche, however, could see right through the inherent contradiction: "When the purpose of moral preaching and of improving man has been excluded from art, it still does not follow by any means that art is altogether purposeless, aimless, senseless."[4] Nietzsche understood that the very act of representation is inescapably political. It is a biased, selective, and always ideologically driven negotiation with reality. What is chosen as subject, what is left out of the frame, the mood instilled by lighting, what occupies the

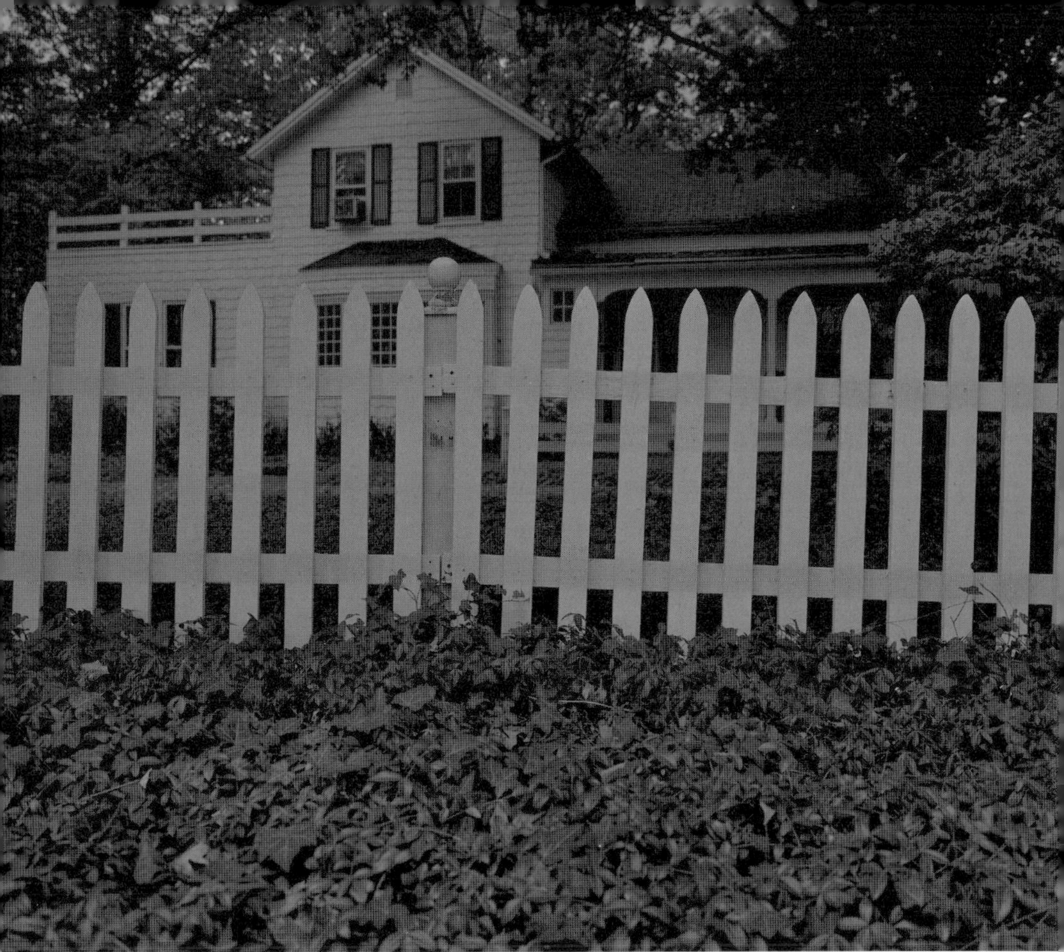

Image 34. Dawoud Bey, *Night Coming Tenderly, Black: Untitled #1* (Picket Fence and Farmhouse) 2017, gelatin silver print. Courtesy of the Art Institute of Chicago. Purchased with funds provided by the Rennie Collection. © Dawoud Bey

foreground . . . even the most seemingly innocent bunch of flowers is wrapped in political, social, and ecological questions.

Today, following Covid-19, the rise of social justice, the controversies resulting from global conflicts, and the growing urgency of the climate crisis, art's purpose is being again brought into question. Contemporary artists may not intend to be propagandists or politicians but, at every step, they are always intellectually and critically engaged with their identities, gender politics, cultural backgrounds, and societal positionings. More than anything, that's what seems to matter right now, in the age of hypercriticality—the artist's voice, its legitimacy, credibility, truthfulness, and integrity. Contemporary art is an amplifier; an interface through which we encounter and decode the complexities and nuances of the world. It connects time and space, reconfigures past histories, and offers endless opportunities to envision new features. Today artists are expected to give talks, write essays, curate exhibitions, and rally communities—in many different ways they are expected to be activists.

Some have made the balancing act between politics and aesthetics an art form in its own right.

Apsáalooke/Crow artist Wendy Red Star's installations and photographic work critically addresses the cultural constructs that define the lives of Indigenous people in the United States. In the series "Four Seasons," which references a famous natural history diorama made by taxidermy pioneer Carl Akeley for the Field Museum in Chicago, Red Star sits on Astroturf, wearing traditional clothing, surrounded by inflatable wild animals and plastic plants. Huge photographs of majestic American landscapes have replaced the meticulously painted landscapes of natural history dioramas—the folds in the paper deliberately reveal the fictitious cheapness of this modern, critical *trompe l'oeil*. The series reminds us that nature is a cultural construct, that white Western males have had a privileged role in shaping it, and that within it, Indigenous people only exist in a romantically remote mythology that ultimately lessens their humanness.

For decades Mel Chin has produced category-defying, thought-provoking works that constantly expand and reconfigure the role of the artist. His now-iconic *Revival Field* project, for example, showed how art may help with environmental remediation by harnessing the capacity of plants to extract harmful metals from polluted soil. Keen to enrich our conception of ecological complexity, his *Seven Wonders* sculpture is a monumental and profound exploration of the intersection between nature and human civilization. The seven pillars, each standing 70 feet tall and made from stainless steel, are etched with drawings of native plants from the Houston area that often go ignored but upon which the well-being of a vast ecosystem depends.

The work of The Propeller Group, a collective based in Ho Chi Minh City (formerly Saigon), has challenged political power structures and identarian notions through multiple media. Their *Viet Nam The World Tour* (2010–), a "rogue nation rebranding project," employed the aesthetics of viral video and graffiti to subvert, in collaboration

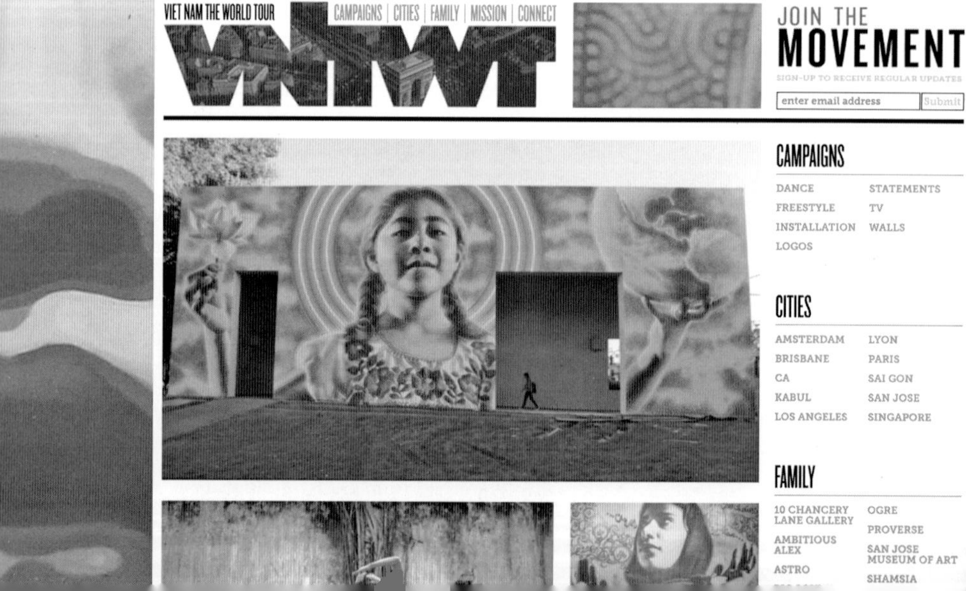

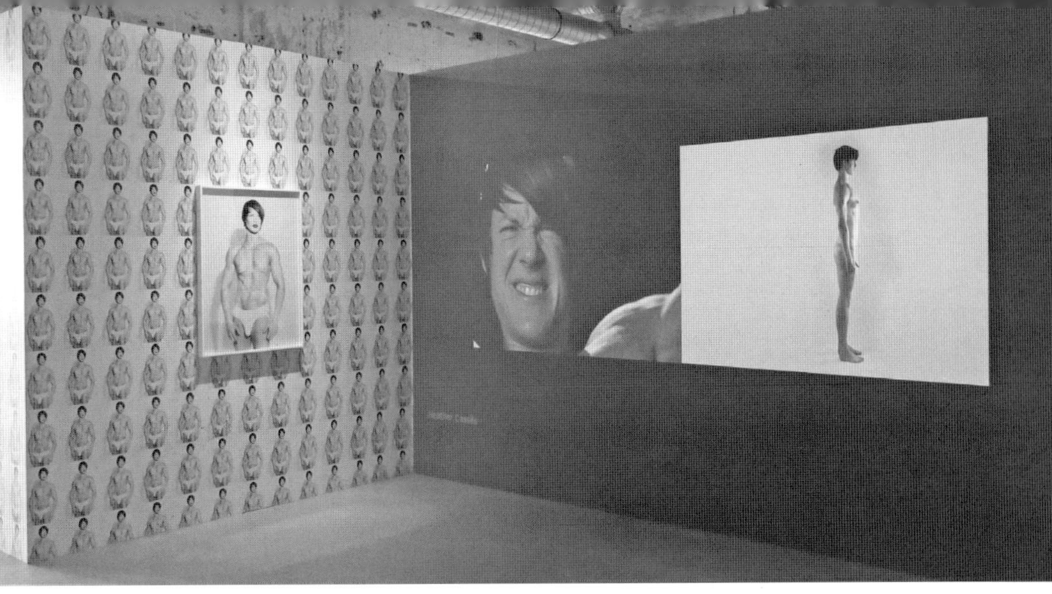

Image 35. Cassils, exhibition shot from *GenderBender* exhibition at MU Hybrid Art House, in Eindhoven, 2014. Photo: Rene Passet. CC BY-NC-ND 2.0 DEED

with many creative partners and performers, the nationalistic representations that the West has imposed upon Vietnam. Their *Television Commercial for Communism* (*TVCC*) (2011–12) invited the advertising company TBWA Vietnam to pitch a rebranding of the communist post-Cold War era. Exploring the historical relationship between capitalism and communism, the video project foregrounds the contemporary importance of equality, cooperation, and sharing. A shift toward local politics, more especially, has also impacted Chinese art. Independent curator, art critic, and gallery director Johnson Chang Tsong-zung has noticed that in recent years "the cultural tide has gradually been changing. Increasingly, non-Western new-wave artists have tended to return to Indigenous experience and local history for inspiration."[5]

As part of her research-based art practice, Chicago-based artist Nia Easley has led guided tours of the city's Avondale neighborhood to trace back the erased histories of nineteenth-century black settlers. Focusing on segregation, displacement, and gentrification, Easley examines the cultural, economic, and political sedimentations that reshaped the area over time, challenging stereotypes and common assumptions about urban cultural blueprints and ownership. Her ephemeral interventions reinvent the purpose and function of the artistic process from research and studio practice to live collaborative and empowering socio-cultural encounters.

Chilean artist Cecilia Vicuña has worked in a variety of media, including poetry, documentary films, objects, performances, and aural installations. Her work, which draws from Indigenous traditions and customs, encompasses political activism, environmental advocacy, human rights, and cultural homogenization.

Image 36 (facing page). Propeller Group, *www.VietNamTheWorldTour.com*, 2010.

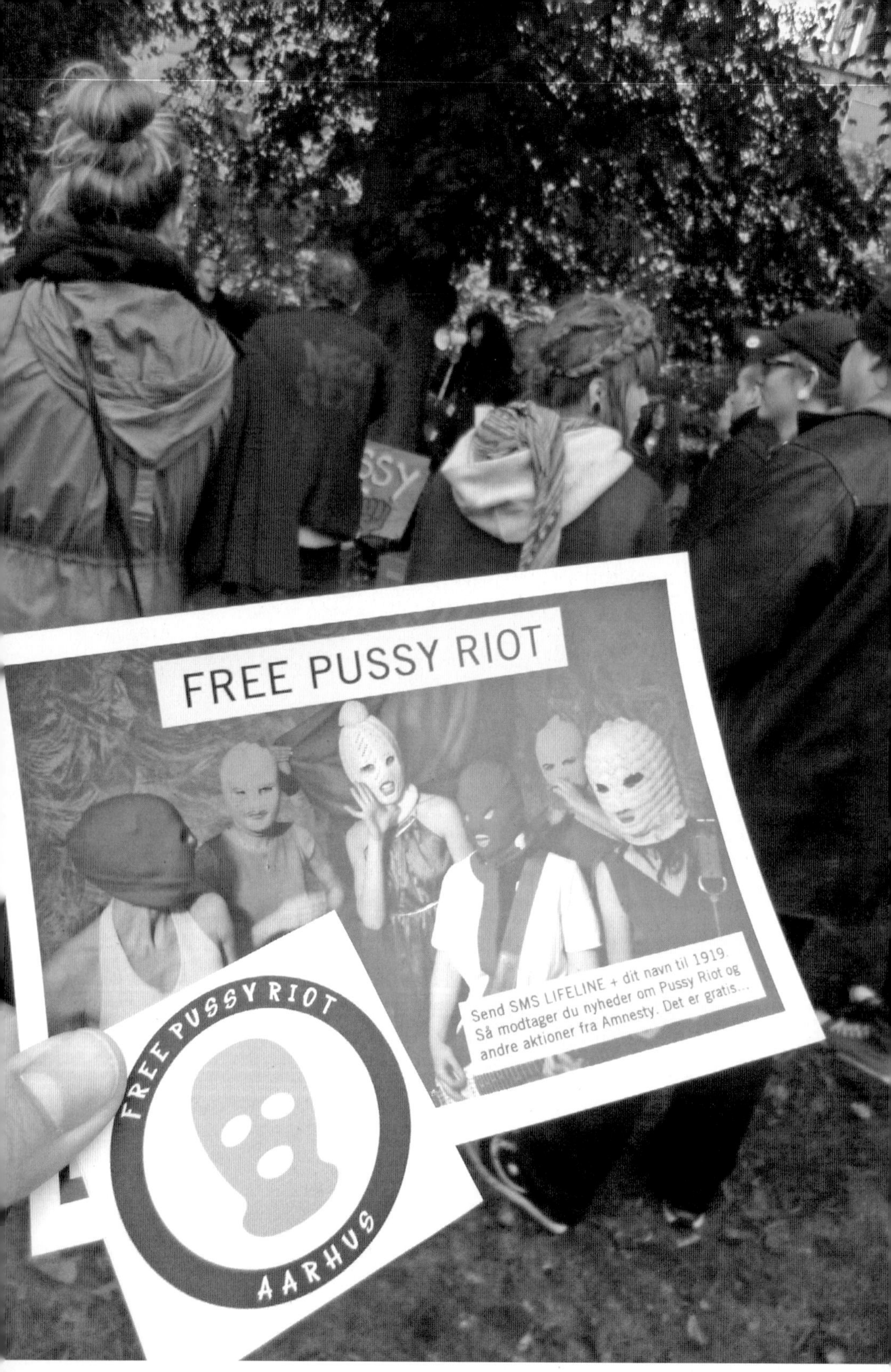


Image 37. *Free Pussy Riot*, 2012. Photo: Prachatai. CC BY-NC-ND 2.0 DEED

Oftentimes, as in the case of Vivien Sansour's humanitarian art projects like *The Palestine Heirloom Seed Library* and the *Traveling Kitchen*, artists engage with national identity politics while also reclaiming agricultural biodiversity to feed communities.

Sometimes artists also play important roles as highly political proponents of underrepresented and oppressed minorities. Through a range of highly imaginative and creative durational performances and using their own body as a site of biopolitical resistance, Cassils have highlighted the struggles and triumphs of the trans experience, making it a central theme of their art. This has not only helped to embolden trans identities on the art scene, but also sparked conversation about the misrepresentation of trans culture in the mainstream media.

Gaining global notoriety in 2012, after images of them staging a guerrilla performance inside Moscow's Cathedral of Christ the Saviour, the all-female collective Pussy Riot forever redefined the boundaries of artistic practices, demonstrating that art's ability to impact political conversations is still alive and kicking, especially when it engages outside the gallery space and away from market forces.

And more recently photographer pioneer Nan Goldin has been instrumental in exposing museum corruption, particularly in relation to the Sackler family's funding of art institutions. Goldin led a demonstration at the British Museum, the Louvre, the Met, and the Guggenheim, protesting the family's implication in the opioid crisis sweeping the United States. The Sacklers, who made their fortune from Purdue Pharma, the company that developed and marketed OxyContin, had been major donors to the museum. Goldin's numerous "die-in" protests highlighted the ethical issues surrounding the implicit compliance of the art world.[6]

These are only a few examples of the many ways the political voices of artists are getting louder. While the media coverage they receive is in some cases substantial, the art world is still struggling to fairly incorporate their voices beyond dangerous objectifying tropes. Oftentimes, institutions are keen to obfuscate their glaring white privilege by showing the work of BIPOC and LGBTQIA+ artists. Trapped in oppressive identity politics, these artists are only heard if their minority status becomes the subject matter of their work. Canonical deconstruction is possible, but it must be handled carefully. Trailblazing curator Okwui Enwezor not only called for a question of artistic personality (as discussed in the Introduction) but also advocated for a thorough restructuring of our conceptions of history and culture. Enwezor argued for a move beyond the notion of inclusion, which underlines the primacy of the white, Western canon, to actively expand our conceptions of what art can be, what conceptual and aesthetic languages it can speak, and what art can ultimately say and do. His objective was to destabilize the foundations of naturalized hierarchies to radically enrich artistic expression with increasing social, political, and psychic liberties.[7]

# Feedback Loops: Death by Referencing

Art history is inbred. An obsession with referencing has turned academic essays into exclusionist traps that categorically repel nonacademic knowledges from different cultures. The structure of the "good academic essay," how it should be built, its constricted expressive and tonal ranges, its first-person phobia, along with the predetermined conception of what makes a valuable academic contribution . . . the issues are endless.

The purpose of the humanities is to produce innovative thinking, but as soon as that emerges, scholars smother it. Institutionalized structures and processes ensure this happens with impeccable precision and timeliness. Peer-reviewing can squeeze the life out of an original manuscript.

Scholars often still reference the same small pool of white, male authors—the ones in fashion, their friends, the clique clutching to the status quo who always cite each other because citation is a form of exposure linked to validation. Few other things in academia are more tragic than a professor inciting a cultural revolution while obsessively footnoting every sentence. We have grown hyper-critical of content but take form for granted, as if form did not ultimately define content. It is so that, bit by bit, our scope of vision has narrowed. The essay has become a trap. We hear the voices of the canon speaking through the work of a younger artist, so we warm up to them because in the fresh originality of their work we catch a glimpse of Duchamp's urinal or see the reflection of Lichtenstein's stenciled neatness. This is the game art history has always played: echoes and feedback loops. It was no coincidence that Indigenous artist Cannupa Hanska Luger gained notoriety in the art world when one of the world's most influential curators, Hans Ulrich Obrist, noted that his *Mirror Shield Project* (2016) employed a similar tactic to that used a hundred years prior by Duchamp.[8]

Essay referencing mirrors this approach. Line by line, we build an echo chamber that confirms, at least on paper, that we are right. A referencing game of affirmation we call Western knowledge. Other cultures play it, too, of course. In Chinese, Japanese, Indian, and Southeast Asian art, for a very long time, accurate referencing was the only model available to art making—a kind of referencing so close to the source that one could hardly tell the voices of each artist apart. In these cultures, closely referencing, or accurately copying, was a virtue.

On the other hand, Western art, and Western culture with it, has lulled itself into a state of self-deceit wherein it has reduced expressive freedom to a veneer. Classical art had no problem with openly owning this condition. So many Renaissance paintings of the Madonna and Child endlessly echo the same iconographical solution invented by someone else. But art history, we are told, champions innovation—and incremental innovation, in the history of Western art, has almost always been driven by commercial interest. Artists innovated to compete with rivals and gain patronage. The history of Western art is grounded in what, in truth, is an incremental modularity. One step back two steps forward—adding something new to something old, artists have allowed art historians to confidently say something original while safely clinging to tradition. This is how the metanarrative of art history—the influential sequence of styles and movements that has been sold to us as a natural evolution through time—has calcified. But nothing about its chemistry or atomic structure is natural apart from, perhaps, its capitalist root.

All the artworks we learn about in art history books were validated by a critic, purchased, positioned in someone's collection, and eventually gifted to a museum. That's truly how they got there. This is precisely why "museum art" can never equate to true freedom beyond what it represents. This art comes to life already a prisoner of mediation, compromise, privilege, and exclusivity. The homogeneity and coherence of the Western canon are founded upon this premise. In response, Asian and African art have been relegated to the "ancient times" chapters of the art history book, implicitly cast as retrograde, labelled primitive. Many art history texts today still fail to appropriately acknowledge the massive debt that Modernism owes to African art. And those that do, tend to recount visits to the Parisian Musée d'Ethnographie as inspiration rather than appropriation.[9]

In 2020, leading cultural economist Clare McAndrew acknowledged: "We're still faced with a stark picture of underrepresentation and lower success for female artists and minorities." At the same time art market specialist Charlotte Burns noted that a rise in sales of women artists reflects a "top-heavy" market rather than systemic change: "The majority of growth is driven by five artists, who represent 40% of global sales. That's also something we see with the market for African American artists where it's also not a big change: 7.7% of all exhibitions and only 2.37% of acquisitions."[10]

These figures point to a problem that's bigger than the art world but that nonetheless is grounded in its self-referential obsession. If we are not prepared to change the art world's structure, any kind of course correction the gatekeepers apply is only ever going to be cosmetic.

There has been no such thing as an organic growth of diversity in the art world and across institutions over the past fifty years. The commonly used phrase "injecting diversity" speaks volumes.[11] On this account, the art world has failed, terribly. But the world has grown rightfully impatient and wants to see diverse institutions right now, so diversity is "injected", quickly, like a vaccine. Unfortunately, this has proved not to be a real cure for institutional racism.

Returning to Enwezor's argument, the concept of inclusivity might not be the right place to start. Inclusion entails letting or inviting someone *in*. But where to? Granted access to a system designed solely to benefit those who built it—new arrivals will likely perish. This is why our very notion of art, how we talk about it and exchange it, needs to change from the ground up as well as the top down, along with the notion of what an artist is, of course. To begin to see a real, radical change, we must also give up this idea of the inside and outside. A process that begins with the reconsideration of the "outsider artist."

## Who's Left Outside and Why?

Who is an outsider artist? Fundamentally, to be an outsider artist means to be unaccepted by the official art world. It means to be excluded and to have one's creative expression sidelined and delegitimized. It means to be irremediably overlooked—systematically and forever banished from the art historical accounts that matter. From the "inside" of the official art world of galleries, museums, art magazines, and auction houses, the term designates a creative individual who is usually self-taught. As a result, their work is called naive in the sense that it betrays a lack of training and competence; it is not founded upon the "incremental notion" of art historical referencing, it does not add something new to an old discourse, and as such it is deemed irrelevant. The mere existence of outsider art as a category is the tangible sign of the cultural bankruptcy that defines the official art world.

The concept is fairly recent—mid-twentieth century—and was originally placed on the map by French artist Jean Dubuffet (1949) with the phrase *Art Brut* (raw art). Dubuffet stated:

> We understand by this term works produced by persons unscathed by artistic culture, where mimicry plays little or no part (contrary to the activities of intellectuals). These artists derive everything . . . from their own depths, and not from the conventions of classical or fashionable art.[12]

In 1972, art critic Roger Cardinal coined the more commonly used English translation "outsider art."[13] Cardinal emphasized that a lack of art historical knowledge and professional supervision were essential traits in outsider artists.

The website of the Outsider Art Fair now suggests a sense of unease with Dubuffet's and Cardinal's original conception: "Over the years, the parameters of Outsider Art have expanded dramatically to include art made by a wide variety of art-makers who share this common denominator of raw creativity. Outsiders come from all walks of life, from all cultures, from all age groups."[14]

But it would be naive to assume that *Art Brut*, despite its connotation, at any rate, still completely lay outside today's art world. Dubuffet studied at the private Académie Julian where he became friends with artists Juan Gris and Fernand Léger. Six months later, he left. He kept in touch with Gris and Léger and continued to make art, but his practice was intermittent until 1942 as he focused on his family's wine business at Bercy.[15] Although drawn to Expressionist art of the kind that still perplexes mainstream audiences, Dubuffet's own thick impasto works could never truly be "outside." His gesturalism and composition embodied elements derived from Fauvist and Expressionist artists like Matisse and Munch. His art was exhibited in popular Parisian galleries. He eventually gained the endorsement of the most influential art critic of the last century, Clement Greenberg, who went so far as to claim: "Dubuffet is perhaps the one new painter of real importance to have appeared on the scene in Paris in the last decade."[16]

But it was this intimate involvement with the art world and the art historical discourses of the time that allowed Dubuffet to see value in the work of true outsider artists. Joaquín

Torres-García (Uruguay), Tarsila do Amaral (Brazil), and Diego Rivera (Mexico) had found inspiration in Indigenous Central American art. And Fauvist, Dadaist, and Surrealist artists more especially had all, in different ways, relished the "untrained artist" as a modern purity-myth drenched in primitivist clichés—a new kind of noble savage amid the hyper-industrialization and growing moral corruption of the early twentieth century.

The rise of the "professional amateur" in Western modern art, as seen in the "childlike" work of Paul Klee, Matisse, and Picasso, was yet another act of defiance against Classicism. It did not come from not having studied art, but from knowing it far too well. Picasso reportedly said: "It took me four years to paint like Raphael, but a lifetime to paint like a child."[17] But the protagonists of modern art never really got even close to the unbridled creative freedom of true outsider artists. In truth, the difference lies in the fact that outsider artists never had the privilege to opt in or out of their outsider status at will. Even at the height of their "naive phases," Picasso and Matisse made work with audiences, galleries, and collectors in mind.

Outsider artists often make art as part of a survival mechanism that gives meaning to their lives—they primarily seem to do it for themselves. Japanese outsider artist Akane Kimura "enjoys the sound of her marker pen moving quickly and continuously up and down when drawing as well as the sound when the pen comes off the paper and hits the drawing board. For her, it is a kind of exhilaration," says the Japanese curator Seina Kimoto.[18]

Outsider artists tend to be wildly different from each other. They are not a movement, not only in the way that they approach expression and materiality but also in their conception of what being an artist actually means. Leonhard Fink, who draws large-scale, hyper-detailed birds'-eye-view maps from memory, does not hesitate to call himself a "super-genius."[19] Others, such as George Widener, are mathematical prodigies with incredible memorization skills. Sometimes, as in the case of postman Joseph Ferdinand Cheval, they spend decades clustering thousands of pebbles with mortar to build an impossibly fantastical castle.[20]

The more one studies outsider artists, the more the idea of "authenticity" so central to the tortured artist myth of Romanticism looks feeble at best or downright fraudulent at worst. Outsider artists don't happen to be privileged upper-middle-class individuals. Their struggle is wholly different; it is visceral, individual, self-absorbed, and often self-consuming. This does not necessarily make their art "better," but it often makes it more original.

Western art history is a narrative of "trophyism": a cultural safari that champions, validates, and perpetuates the taste of a white economic and cultural elite that has commissioned and acquired art to aggrandize themselves. This art historical narrative has shaped our taste and cultural conception of the artist. This is not to say that there is no value in art history—the opposite is true. But a more socially just art world and the emergence of new artistic forms depend on an understanding and acknowledgment of these significant structural constraints through the way they have conceptualized and treated outsider artists—along with other forms of othering.

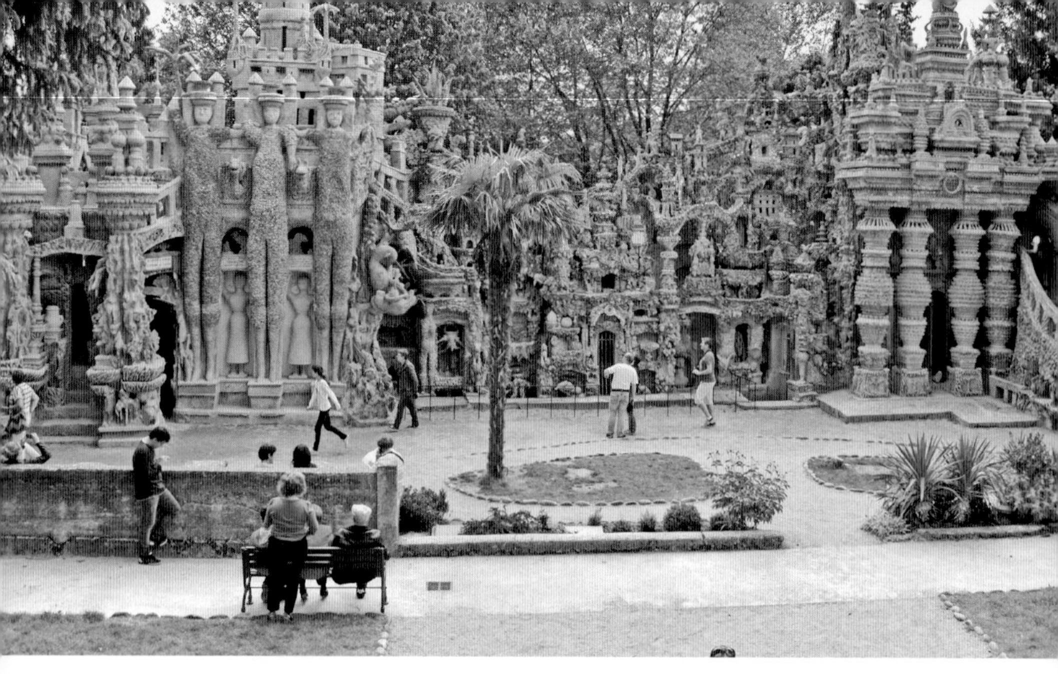

Image 38. Joseph Ferdinand Cheval, *Palais idéal du facteur Cheval, côté Est*, 1879–1923. Photo: Benoît Prieur. CC-BY-SA

## Decolonizing Art?

The production of knowledge has often entailed extracting, archiving, categorizing, institutionalizing, and inevitably objectifying. Dubuffet's appreciation of outsider art led him to salvage the work of artists from the disinterest of psychiatric hospitals. Nonetheless, this well-meaning gesture ended up inadvertently into an institutionalization of outsider art. In 1976, he gifted more than 5,000 works to the city of Lausanne in Switzerland. Since 1976, they have been part of the Collection de l'Art Brut. Can it still be called "outsider" when in a museum and featured on the pages of art catalogs or when it has begun to exert its own aesthetic influence?

There is a chance that the institutionalization of outsider art might represent the breaking point of increasingly palpable tiredness with the "death by referencing" syndrome that has characterized Western art. Since 2015, the Met, the Brooklyn Museum, and the Smithsonian have exhibited outsider art. This has led to the rise of a market roughly worth $40–50 million.[21] Interest began with a groundbreaking exhibition held in 1979 at the Hayward Gallery in London curated by filmmaker—and collaborator of Dubuffet—Victor Musgrove, with Roger Cardinal. Titled *Outsiders: An Art Without Precedent or Tradition*, it gathered the work of forty-two artists from Europe and the United States. As the catalog shows, Musgrove and Cardinal were determined to expand the notion of outsider art beyond Dubuffet's original conception: "[Outsider artists] are not naive or Sunday Painters . . . Nor do they produce 'psychiatric' art via the intermediaryship of art as therapist."[22] By 1989, outsider art had its dedicated magazine: *Raw Vision*.[23]

In 2006, the *Inner Worlds Outside* exhibition at the Whitechapel Art Gallery juxtaposed insider and outsider art.[24] Three years later, a nonprofit organization named the Museum of Everything launched a program of ambitious exhibitions held in venues as prestigious as London's Tate Modern. In 2013, they were invited to participate in the 55th Venice Biennale curated by Massimiliano Gioni. Inspired by the self-taught Italian-American artist Marino Auriti who filed a design with the US Patent office for his *Palazzo Enciclopedico* (*The Encyclopedic Palace*)—an imaginary museum housing all the key inventions in the world—the exhibition displayed outsider and mainstream art in the same galleries. This growing trend highlights a shift in the conception of the artist and also in the way we make and write about art.

Gioni brought works by Carl Andre, Tacita Dean, Walter De Maria, and Marisa Merz in conversation with drawings from Shaker communities transcribing divine messages, and those of shamans from the Solomon Islands peopled by deities and demons. Loosely organized around the idiosyncratic display principle of the cabinet of curiosities, the curatorial selection exposed the aesthetic and conceptual cultural biases and reductionism that have characterized Western art over the past one hundred years.

Foregrounding the obscure, the occult, sidelined knowledges, and the personal, Gioni also radically questioned the role of the artist. One of his objectives was "to look at the relationship between knowledge and information, and the idea that knowledge can be revealed and can come in the form of epiphany rather than a conquest of studies."[25]

Although Gioni did not contextualize his biennale in these terms, it seems obvious that in many ways his approach was at least in part aligned to what we today call the "decolonization of art history."[26] Reassessing and questioning the prevailing Eurocentric stories that have historically molded the international art scene is a difficult part of decolonizing the art world. In a contemporary context, decolonizing the art world is about creating a more inclusive and diverse art scene, although it could really mean reinventing it from scratch, taking cues from ecosystemic realities. The will to upturn categories, hierarchies, and concepts mostly predefined by white, cis, male, Western artists and art historians is a way to free art from the exclusionism of the canon and the colonialist forces that idolized it. It is an opportunity to rethink our starting points, methodologies, and perspectives beyond the colonialist tropes that still haunts the art world today.

While outsider art has been for a long while associated with psychiatric hospitals and disabilities, more recently the term has also come to designate cultural minorities who have been deliberately sidelined. In her exceptionally powerful book *Art on My Mind*, feminist critic and social activist Bell Hooks clearly spells out the problem: "The politics of racism and sexism create a cultural context wherein white male artists work within an art world that is predisposed to accord them recognition and visibility."[27] Hooks evidenced how the power of white-supremacist capitalist patriarchy in the art world produces images that implicitly position the white male as subject and BIPOC as object. To challenge this power relation is to threaten the art world's status quo and unspoken biases. Right now, outsider art of any kind is a disruptive force that challenges the institutional order governing our thinking and naturalizing power structures along the way. No surprise that outsider art has been all along kept outside . . .

Outsider artists remind us that art could always be altogether different, that it needn't be grounded in references, history, and cultural conventions agreed upon by the dominant majority; that its originality may know no precedents, and that it might even speak a language we still have to learn. Outsider art is not the outside, it's the art that artists concerned with galleries, sales, and museums will never make. If there's any freedom in making art, that's where it can perhaps be found: in those untrained, creative individuals who pursue their drives and impulses without fearing critics or selling their souls to dealers.

It's often said, in a pejorative way, that outsider artists are obsessed. But isn't obsession the only true form of freedom to which we humans can aspire? Captivated by our own creative instincts; busying ourselves to forget momentarily, or otherwise exorcise and embrace, the ineluctability of death. The outsider artist is utterly engrossed in their endeavors for years—sometimes a lifetime—driven by a sheer sense of wholesomely intimate joy, focused presence, or trance-like frenzy simply derived from the process of the creative act.

At the bottom of the artist's myth lies a fraudulent appropriation of what rightfully and all along belonged to those who have been called "outsider artist" and to everyone else who has never considered turning their creativity into a paid profession and their art into a commodity. The matter is not one of commercialism, but honesty; a matter of not shrouding oneself in someone else's cape to conceal the power relations and networks of interest that define one's creative output, ethics, and values. It is a matter of no longer co-opting someone else's identity to perpetuate a myth designed to sell more art.

It is through the figure of the outsider artist, the paradoxes it entails and the absurdity of its condition, that we can begin to envision a way out of the art world's entrapments. This way out, however, requires a level of responsibility on behalf of the artist. The boldest moves of all. Instead of blaming the market, the schools, the galleries, and the museums for today's inequitable art world, artists might want to begin to carefully consider how they also perpetuate an inequitable art world. And art historians, critics, and curators are not off the hook either . . .

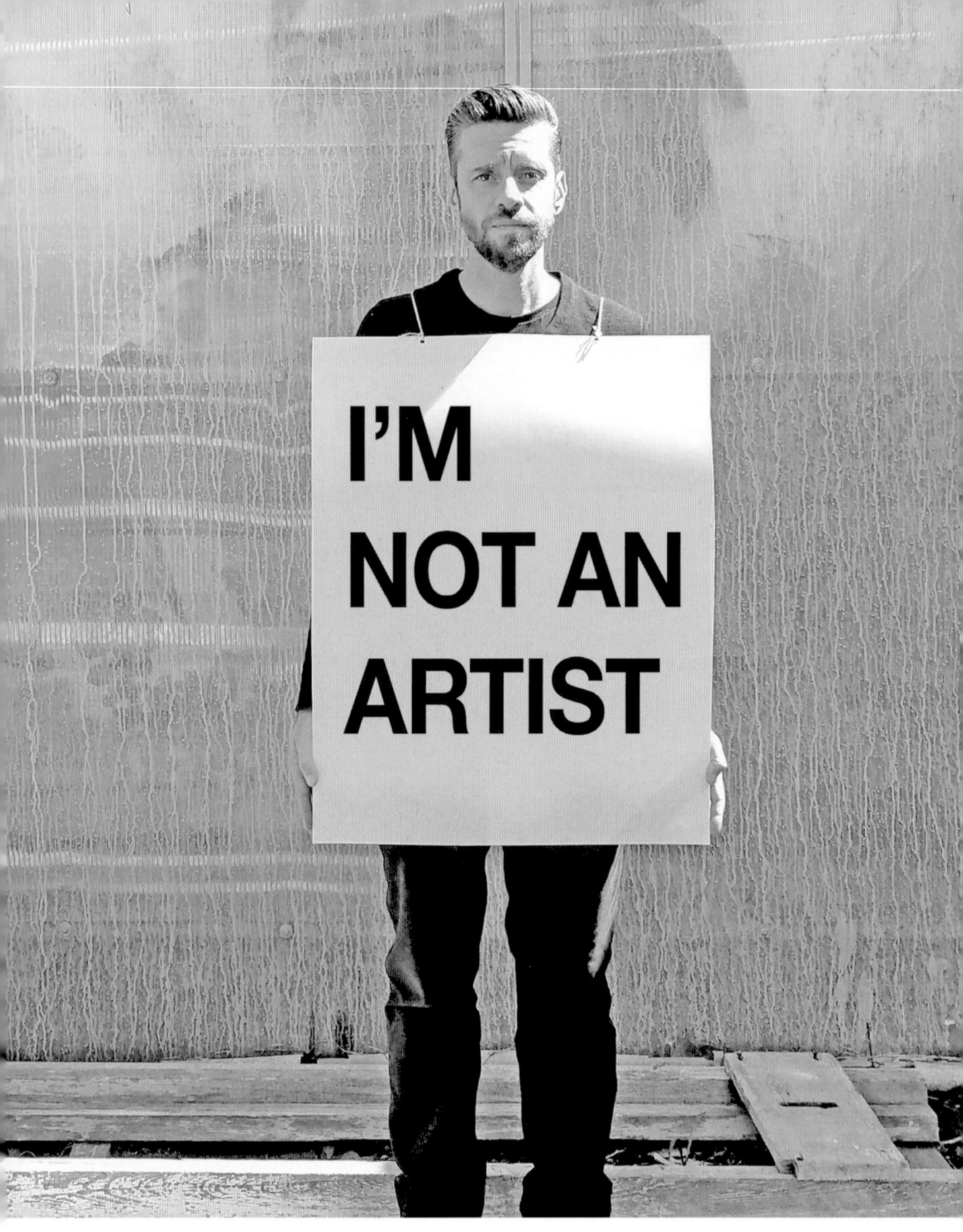


Image 39.  Giovanni Aloi, *I'm Not an Artist II*, 2019, photo concept Giovanni Aloi, photography Chris Hunter. © Giovanni Aloi

# 8  I'm Not an Artist

# What's in a Word: The Capitalist Realist Matrix

The matter is not purely linguistic, nor is it one of political correctness, or language policing. Words *are* powerful. They are world-forming. They are the true backbone of the human condition. Words define the scope and depth of our thoughts. They outline the borders of our individual and shared cultural identities. They hierarchize societal structures. They can deceive, erase, and obscure—their material weightlessness is never equivalent to the burden they bestow upon others. Much of the meaning of words is inscribed in their intonation and the silent expanses that unravel among them; the phonetic soaring flight of those that enliven as they intersect with the sharp edges of the ones that cut deep.

Dubuffet knew that language shapes our creativity, but he also knew that it could entrap it: "Art does not lie down on the bed that is made for it; it runs away as soon as one says its name; it loves to be incognito. Its best moments are when it forgets what it is called."[1]

Over the past 150 years, globalization, technological innovations, and collective traumatic events have redefined not only our conception of what art can be but also our expectations of the cultural roles it might play. It is perhaps no surprise that, today, the word "art" means next to nothing, or indeed anything.[2] Perhaps, Piero Manzoni's 1961 iron and bronze pedestal inscribed "The Base of The World, Homage to Galileo" placed upside down in a field in Herning, Denmark, said it all. Taking Dada readymade notions to their logical conclusion, Manzoni cut to the chase humorously turning the whole world into a self-authoring, colossal artwork—as big as the planet. Neither inside nor outside, no more creator and created, no artist or audience, nor reality or fiction.

While his gesture might seem preposterous to some, Manzoni pointed at a very true conception of what we call the art world today: an endlessly evolving, uncontainable, self-perpetuating, and unjust, technocratic ecosystem. Signs of this future to come were already visible at the end of the nineteenth century with the rise of the modern "-isms," all of which simultaneously demonized and fetishized the gallery space and the collector, while still craving the validation only institutional prestige can bestow. This contradictory model has in different capacities been addressed by critics of capitalism including Frantz Fanon, Gilles Deleuze and Félix Guattari, Sylvia Wynter, Fredric Jameson, Slavoj Žižek, Cedric Robinson, and Mark Fisher.[3] Among others, these philosophers have critiqued the naturalization and internalization of capitalistic forces, demonstrating how they permeate everything we think and do, leading our every step to misplace our life goals often in the pursuit of an abstract ideal of freedom that simply cannot exist.

Fischer argued that "capitalism is a monstrous, infinitely plastic entity, capable of metabolizing and absorbing anything with which it comes into contact."[4] According to him, since the end of the 1980s, and in part as a result of the collapse of the Soviet Union, capitalism has become a collective psychological condition defining the essence of our subjectivity through a "pre-emptive formatting and shaping of desires, aspirations, and hopes."[5] Evidence of our inability to escape the naturalization of capitalism, Fischer observed, is that inevitable paradoxical commodification, the inevitable merchandizing of artistic gestures of rebellion such as punk or grunge (think about the tragic dissonance a Nirvana t-shirt so aptly captures). Is it surprising that artists whose practice openly challenges the capitalist system also continue to display their art in prestigious galleries, sell their works to collectors, and issue limited editions? Is it at all possible to be truly radical and still be part of the art world?

It is easy to demonize neoliberalism as a life-defining (or denying) force. But the metrics by which we measure our professional success or compare ourselves to colleagues are not only defined by neoliberalism; *they* define neoliberalism. Late-stage capitalism thrives on disorienting and deceitful feedback loops. Academia exclusivity and the art world have always been held together by superficial notions of prestige, brands, and affiliations. Capitalist-defined forms of elitism are imbedded in their hierarchical structures. They don't have to be. We have made them so and it is us, with our incessant fragility and addiction to personal validation, who continue to give them the power that, in return, they use against us.

## Validation: Success as Existentialism

Designer Charles Eames said, "Artist is a title that you earn, and it's a little embarrassing to hear people refer to themselves as an artist . . . it's like referring to themselves as a genius."[6] When can one truly say, "I am an artist?" Upon graduation, or after obtaining a postgraduate qualification? When one rents a studio? Or when does one become a good enough artist? How do we measure success and accomplishment across such a diverse and challenging ecosystem where art simultaneously means anything and nothing?

Artists of all colors and stripes—including those who openly abhor capitalism—proudly gloat on social media when they sell work. The likes and congratulations pour in. All of a sudden, money and institutional validation matters a great deal. Forget the freedom, the rebelliousness, the anti-comformism, the fight against the system—when the institution rings and the money sings, most artists will answer, quickly. The exceptions are rare.

Were they not artists enough before, while they humbly toiled away in the studio, relishing every moment of their creative journeys? Does it matter if their work remains unseen or unsold? Why is money always the ultimate validator? Success is affirming. At least temporarily, it keeps at bay our inborn existentialist void: that sense of meaninglessness that haunts our every action and decision in life. I matter. Success validates our life—journeys in our eyes and in those of others. It's a confirmation that, ultimately, in this live performance without rehearsals called life, we have managed to get at least something right.

Today, the metrics by which we measure our worth are deeply skewed. They are always external—relentlessly so. Narcissistic mirrors—social media thrive on our addiction to affirmation. Corporations make billions out of it. We are hooked to the game, artists included. Of course, true success lies elsewhere, away from institutional validation bestowed upon us by others. But it is often elusive or even invisible, sometimes not just to others but to us, too. Oftentimes, success only flickers as we glance at the rear-view mirror. Some artists know it, others don't; some young artists will never stick around long enough to find out.

Ultimately, all the works of art we study in Western art history books, regardless of style and medium, have one thing in common: they have been purchased by someone. Money, a transaction—not just their quality or unreserved public admiration—secured their spot on the museum wall. Transaction after transaction, the more we see them reproduced in books, films, and posters, the more we like them. Familiarity is reassuring but it is not the same as greatness.

In the first part of the book, I have traced lineages of validation to expose the networking and marketing strategies that have enshrined modern and contemporary art masters. Validation results from a type of symbiosis necessary for professional development and success. It establishes and inflates the status of an artist and the value of their work. Validation is a social process—it is consensus as assessed by influential gatekeepers.

Curators, art critics, and art historians have been traditionally in charge of validation—their job is not to serve artists, as some seem to believe. They are the trendsetters, storytellers, and talent scouts. Most importantly, they are symbiotic collaborators. Curators need to see art. They might decide to exhibit it in galleries. As a result, critics will review exhibitions and give artists—yes—exposure. In vegetal terms, exposure is the sunlight an artist needs to grow. For an artistic career to flourish, it is important that exposure steadily increases over a relatively short season. Think of it in mathematical terms:

(exhibition + reviews) × frequency = validating prestige

Artists who understand the value of exposure also understand that exhibiting work is only half of the picture. They know that attracting critics, curators, and art historians to exhibitions is important—it's a way to establish delicate symbiotic relationships in which people know other people you need to know. Complex, often grotesque, courtship rituals are central to forging long-lasting alliances in the art world. Networking is central to one's first steps and is essential to keeping a career alive when/if it takes off. Art professionals swarm around art fairs, biennials, triennials, and award ceremonies. Being there at the right time and mingling with the right network is essential.

At the beginning of their careers, young artists are more likely to receive reviews by critics who write for online zines, local newspapers, or blogs. From an ecosystemic perspective, none are ever too small to matter. They all count. Validation is a geological process. It takes time. Like soil sedimentation, one review lays over another, then another, and one more until the artist's rock-solid profile emerges from the swamp of art school mediocrity. A review in an influential art magazine such as *Art Forum*, *ArtNews*, and *Art in America*, or newspapers like the *Guardian* or the *New York Times* means major exposure. At the beginning of a career, garnering reviews requires initiative. One has to identify and reach out to other ecosystemic partners and attract them to the exhibition. Invite art historians and critics for a coffee followed by a private tour. Research who they are and what they have written. Mention that you are familiar with their work and that you like what they write. Being part of the art world is all about building relationships and reciprocal networks of support. Exposure = more opportunities since the more influential people become aware of an artist's work, the more likely they are to be offered more interesting opportunities. And, exhibition after exhibition, the opportunities to sell work to collectors also multiply.

Experts carefully evaluate many factors as they price works of art. It is not a science, but it is not magic either. Like pheromone, prestigious collectors rub off their kudos on an artist when they purchase their work. Acquisition by a prestigious collector adds value to the work. Serious collectors are often guided by advisors who are very well-networked—they are the art world's pollinators. Buyers trust them to build power-statement collections.[7] Wealthy people have wealthy friends. If an artist's work hangs in their living room, it will be seen by others who can pay for it—we are back to the value of exposure . . .

Galleries in New York's Chelsea district, London's Mayfair, or central Hong Kong engage in careful career-topiaries. They won't sell to just anyone with money. Their call is only audible to those who are tuned to certain frequencies of prestige. Some parts of the art world ecosystem are off-limits to most. Top-end galleries groom the markets of lucrative artists to avoid sudden inflation and subsequent catastrophic crashes—long careers are essentially based on these careful, and often invisible to most, financial manipulations. So what is success, then?

We are again caught up in the feedback loops of the art world ecosystem. One either sells work for good money or the professional "artist" label remains elusive. You'll die a Sunday painter—forever haunted by impostor syndrome. Does it matter if one enjoys the journey? If money is an issue, making anonymous-looking, mass-produced art for corporate offices and hotels is also an option. Ever considered that? Some of those artists earn very good money. Do they love what they make? They don't need to be validated by critics, art historians, and curators. Their work is valued by interior designers and corporate art buyers. Maybe *they* are the only truly *free* artists? They flourish across the grasslands of the art market ecosystem—anonymous—away from the official art world. Certainly a less glamorous option. Those artworks will never end up in art history books or on museum walls. They won't receive awards.

Art historians write about art that says something new, political, challenging, and urgent. By intention, corporate art often says next to nothing. It's *meant* to graciously fill space and politely disappear into the background. Yet, there are thousands of artists out there making a good living with that type of work. Have they gone to art school? Some have and some haven't. Are they professional artists? They certainly are as far as the tax office is concerned. But none of my art students want to be that type of artist, despite the income stability that can bring. There are green pastures at this end of the art ecosystem. And yet, it's the other side, the sublime and dramatic landscape of artistic peaks, waterfalls, and valleys they are drawn to . . .

## The Professional, the Hobbyist, and the Impostor

While the origin of capitalism in the West as an economic system can be traced back to the colonialist roots of the sixteenth century, some of its components are undeniably part of older social structures. Like many other social animals, humans live in hierarchies. This is not to say that capitalism is an inborn, uncontrollable human tendency; rather, the rigid hierarchies of ancient China and Japan, the caste systems of Africa and India, and the feudal systems of Europe have been defined by our obsession with hierarchizing and our tendency to fetishize power and the exclusive objects that represent it.[8] Today's professional labels are modern vestiges of past hierarchical structures. The doctor, lawyer, chef, stylist, and artist are more than jobs—always intended for life—they are modern "nobiliary titles." These labels define us for ourselves and for those around us. They instantly box us into pre-digested cultural contexts. We are hardwired to ask about a new acquaintance's profession at the earliest opportunity. It reassures us. It helps us to quickly fill in the blanks—perhaps too quickly. The label inevitably says something about one's income or lifestyle. Maybe it's our animal instincts? Dogs smell each other's bits when they meet—which probably tells them more than an hour of human small talk can reveal. For better or worse, our species has evolved differently.

Identifying with one professional activity can be dangerous. This approach harnesses us to a capitalist system we cannot escape without losing ourselves. It flattens our complex and multifaceted human identities down to a fictitious and stereotyped single one that is relentlessly external. Professional identification can lead to an unpleasant entanglement with sheer careerism. The art world is a case in point. The art historian, the curator, the critic, the art dealer—not just the artist—the network of power relations that hold these professional labels in place can quickly become suffocating, even toxic. Labels restrict our creative range of action. Despite the relentless claims that art equates to freedom, the art world is still highly suspicious of individuals who switch creative personas at will or embody more than one at once.

As a label, the term "artist" inscribes antiquated ideals of specialization that are much harder to sustain in our current economic context. This is not to say that we should not specialize, but in a financial world where the part-time condition is the new normal, is it fair to train artists as if a full-time job awaited after qualification?

Over the past twenty years, teaching institutions and corporations have capitalized on the rise of part-time positions. This is a double-edged sword for workers as well as employers. Part-time workers are always cheaper. They are easier to exploit since they have next to no contractual rights, often work with no pension or health benefits, and can be let go, like ballast, when the institutions struggle to stay afloat. On paper, it sounds bad. But there's more to working part-time than playing the game capitalism wants us to play—it can be a form of resistance. The flexibility that often comes with part-time employment can adequately support the pursuit of other creative endeavors. Actors and musicians are culturally more prepared to take on part-time work as a normal condition of their chosen career. But while musicians and actors gain authenticity from juggling different jobs as they work to hit the proverbial big time, contemporary artists often feel implicitly undermined by the same predicament.

The romantic myth of the artist is uncompromising: its unbridled and uncontainable passions are all-consuming and cannot be put on pause to work a shift at Walgreens. Holding down a day job tarnishes the aura of mythical authenticity. However, that's what being an artist today, more often than not, means and that's what it has entailed for over most of the past century. But, perpetuating the myth, art history books and museums have always omitted that crucial bit of information. Of course, when a dealer tries to sell a painting for more than a few thousand dollars, prospective buyers want to be reassured they are purchasing the work of an expert, not a dabbler. However, in truth, the list of creative individuals who supported their creative careers with part-time employment is endless.

Poet and essayist T. S. Eliot worked full-time as a banker and then as an editor throughout his career.[9] After becoming a successful writer, Bram Stoker kept his job as a theatre manager for twenty-seven years.[10] Philip Glass worked as a plumber and cab driver well into his successful years as a minimalist composer. In 2001, Glass recalled:

> While working, I suddenly heard a noise and looked up to find Robert Hughes, the art critic of *TIME* magazine, staring at me in disbelief. "But you're Philip Glass! What are you doing here?" It was obvious that I was installing his dishwasher, and I told him I would soon be finished. "But you are an artist," he protested. I explained that I was an artist but that I was sometimes a plumber as well and that he should go away and let me finish.[11]

Chicago-based artist Ivan Albright worked as a carpenter all his life while he painted excruciatingly detailed works that each took a decade to complete.[12] Barbara Kruger subbed as a graphic designer for *Mademoiselle* magazine.[13] Thanks to his cousin who worked in the MoMA's publicity department, in 1960, artist Sol LeWitt ended up manning the museum's book counter while Robert Ryman and Gene Berry served there as security guards.[14] Neon artist Dan Flavin worked as a guard at the American Museum of Natural History in New York.[15] Painter Luchita Hurtado held a job as fashion illustrator.[16] For years, Julie Mehretu waitressed by day and painted at night.[17] Photographer pioneer Gordon Parks worked as semi-pro basketball player, busboy, and waiter.[18] The part-time condition has kept the creative hearts of many artists pulsing throughout the decades. Creatively managing time, organizing, prioritizing, and juggling occupations can help developing key skills, foster motivation as well as nurturing the desire to keep plowing through. Finding the right combination can be rewarding and fulfilling. Getting good at it is an art form.

In 1968, artist Charles Henry Alston recommended finding a job that has nothing to do with one's practice: "maybe a nightwatchman or something like that; or be a mathematics teacher where two and two is four and no argument and no discussion."[19] This model might still work for some. But, today, seeking part-time work closely related to one's creative field and building a portfolio of creatively aligned or intersecting occupations can lead to a successful and rewarding long-term career encompassing multiple employers, media, and industries. Working for multiple employers enhances skill development, and unlike the loss of one full-time job (a catastrophic financial event for many), a network of two or three part-time occupations will most likely never fall through at once. Full-time job security is an illusion, a capitalist trap that keeps people shackled to one employer just as long as they are needed.

William Carlos Williams understood how the synergy between poetry and medicine augmented his creative life. "They are two parts of a whole," he contended in his 1967 autobiography. "It is not two jobs at all . . . one rests the man when the other fatigues him." The prime minister of Albania, Edi Rama, draws while making important political decisions: "I began to understand that my subconscious was being helped . . . by my hand to stay calm while my conscious had to focus on demanding topics."[20] He exhibits in galleries worldwide. Betye Saar describes how, inspired by Joseph Cornell's boxes, she felt compelled to build her own following the killing of Martin Luther King, Jr., despite needing to continue working numerous day jobs.:

> I was an artist, but I still needed a job so I could pay my mortgage and put my girls through college. I worked as a social worker, designed enamelware and jewelry with Curtis Tann, and did some costume designs for the Inner City Cultural Center. I taught and lectured and traveled, but I always still made my art. I've never been an artist for the sake of making art to sell. I just like to do what I want and if it sells, fine.[21]

The shadows of the artist myth stand between us and a fulfilling career: the Sunday painter, the amateur, the hobbyist. A dreadful lack of credibility has for over a hundred years haunted the part-time condition. The root of this bias is inherently sexist. It was mainly women who dabbled in pocket-money jobs; assumed to lack natural commitment and stamina while their husbands—confident and reliable—led prestigious managerial roles.

The hobby is a manipulative capitalist invention. The etymology of the word derives from hobbyhorse, a child's toy, recreational, a nonprofessional endeavor, an innocuous pastime.[22] Capitalism has deceived us into thinking that our paid job is fundamental to our identity and that nonmonetizable activities that fill our time in constructive ways are petty and insignificant. By the early twentieth century, the hobby had been marketed as a solution to the growing alienation generated by the fast rhythms of modern life. In its circular twistedness, capitalism has always imparted the affliction and administered the cure while monetizing both. Artists are particularly sensitive to the judgment of those who don't take their creative endeavors seriously. No artist wants to ever be considered a hobbyist. This psychological vulnerability has singlehandedly supported the recent success of graduate qualifications—an indelible initiation, a true validation of one's professional commitment.

Postmodernism relished the amateur approach as an opportunity to explore the creative potential of chance, deskilling, imperfection, fallibility, and failure. To experiment means to embrace the flickering of the professional in charge and the fumbling amateur who intentionally takes foolish risks.[23] But like in a badly structured "choose your own adventure book", the myth of the full-time professional artist keeps us stuck in capitalist feedback loops. The time has come to truly, and not just performatively, embrace the "professional amateur."

## Shooting Stars

What is longevity in the context of the art world's ecosystemic seasons? Any career is subject to unpredictable external forces, ebbs, and flows. Any sense of security is the symptom of a temporary state of delusion. Whether artworks sell at the local art market, or an artist is picked by an internationally acclaimed gallery, everything can instantly vanish. In this sense, the art market is as volatile as the fashion or music industries. Style and genres come and go, taste changes quickly, with the seasons. Only a minute proportion emerges from the undergrowth of the art world and an even smaller fraction flourish for longer than a decade. Rirkrit Tiravanija, Kara Walker, Cindy Sherman, Yoko Ono, Jeff Koons, Marina Abramović, Anish Kapoor, and Chris Ofili are not the norm; they are the exception.

The art market knows no loyalty. Most galleries follow trends and switch artists as needed. They have no obligation to develop someone's career or promote it beyond the immediacy of commercial interest. Under the pressure of contracts commissions and production schedules artists on gallery rosters often end up making work they don't care about.

Peter Doig recalls a time when he experienced artist's block. Chris Ofili then told him, "You have to remember, it's not a job."[24] In more than one way, Ofili was right. Making art is not a job if one especially understands art as a journey of creative expression, inquiry, communication, activism, and self-discovery. While the proverbial "big time" will elude most, everyone can be on the journey: a steadily creative life filled with meaningful moments of personal success and accomplishment.

What is success? How long can it last? Metrics and scales—the ones imposed on us by others, the ones we impose on ourselves. Proportions and relativities. In this situation, too, an ecosystemic perspective that focuses on our immediate reach, impact, and influence might substantially assist us in making smart decisions. Art schools and universities could at least guarantee this level of success if only they committed to teaching financial planning, time and project management, as well as sharing honest insights into sustainability as integral and compulsory parts of their programs. Failing to provide students with the essential knowledge and skills they need only damages them. A symptom of this is the incessant stream of online articles discussing the reality of "artist's burnout."

Let's be clear: being an artist has always been a privilege. Nobody ever said it was going to be easy. Being creative entails negotiating constant personal confrontation, devastating self-doubt, and endless vulnerability. Today, students seem to be less and less prone to put up with stress, pressure, or any kind of suffering the world throws at them. Like many other things, being an artist simply isn't for everyone. The general cultural assumption among the young seems to be that, if it hurts, then something must be wrong with the system. A self-absolvist maneuver that unfortunately leads, in many cases, to failure.

A colleague once said over coffee, "Sometimes, I feel like I'm working at a dream factory." In a sense they were right. I don't think many students would be thrilled to hear that they are putting themselves in debt for life (in some cases) so that they can have the pleasure of juggling multiple freelance and part-time jobs while rejection letters from galleries rain on them. They have come to art school lured by the full-time artist myth and their hearts are bound to be broken because of it.

## The F-Word

Admittedly, I do not have much interest in what art critic Jerry Saltz has to say, but the title of an article he penned in the summer of 2020 caught my eye: "My Life as a Failed Artist." There Saltz confesses:

> It pains me to say it, but I am a failed artist. "Pains me" because nothing in my life has given me the boundless psychic bliss of making art for tens of hours at a stretch for a decade in my 20s and 30s, doing it every day and always thinking about it, looking for a voice to fit my own time, imagining scenarios of success and failure, feeling my imagined world and the external one merging in things that I was actually making. Now I live on the other side of the critical screen, and all that language beyond words, all that doctor-shamanism of color, structure, and the mysteries of beauty—is gone.[25]

Saltz describes his bohemian life in a rough-and-tumble 1973 Chicago where he ended up opening a successful, independent gallery with a few artist friends. According to his cinematically nostalgic account, in the ten years that followed, he sold his work and lived in a nonheated loft with little furniture—"I was an artist," he proudly proclaimed. Clearly, not even the best-known critics are immune to the pitfalls of the romantic artist's myth . . .

Seemingly happy to work for hours on end each day, he embarked on—of all things—a massive series of altarpieces based on Dante's *Divine Comedy*. He continues:

> But then I looked back, into the abyss of self-doubt. I erupted with fear, self-loathing, dark thoughts about how bad my work was, how pointless, unoriginal, ridiculous. "You don't know how to draw," I told myself. "You never went to school. Your work has nothing to do with anything. You're not a real artist. Your art is irrelevant. You don't know art history. You can't paint. You aren't a good schmoozer. You're too poor. You don't have enough time to make your work. No one cares about you. You're a fake. You only draw and work small because you're too afraid to paint and work big.[26]

It is impossible to know what was really happening in Saltz's mind, and it would be wrong to judge, but self-doubt is an essential part of the creative process. It can be productive, or it can kill if someone believes in the genius-monolith model. The narcissistic root that supports the romantic myth of the artist can bear catastrophic consequences and lead to everyone's nightmare: *failure.* Failure is hard. Creative individuals put themselves on the line on a daily basis. In time we learn to confidently tiptoe on the edge of absurdity. Being creative is very risky—financially and mentally. Failure is good friends with absence and loss. It can be dreadfully hollowing. Failing is unquestionably personal. It always hurts. Deeply. But failure can also be a clearing: an open swathe in the forest canopy through which light can come through; a space where new growth can come to life. It is the root of the new. Failure is the decay that turns rubble into fertile humus. Yes, it stinks, it is riddled with bacteria and other microbes. It is always messy. Perhaps most importantly, failure has to do its thing: ferment, fester, and stink. The process takes time. From failure we learn to resist like a weed, or to bud again after the storm. Not talent, but resilience is the only thing that all accomplished creative people have in common. They just never give up.

Perhaps, Saltz could have persevered regardless? Only a few can sustain an unbroken string of successes in the arts or any other career. How much success is enough? Finding the courage to carry on, and summoning the strength to see past failure, depends on how we frame ourselves. Events are events—between the event and our response lies freedom.

Saltz is only a failed artist in his mind and in relation to the benchmarks set by the romantic artist myth. Isn't ten years of artistic accomplishment enough? Toward the end of his article, Saltz proudly affirms that those "artist years" gave him the essential tools he needed to become the successful art critic he is today. That sounds like success to me. This is the damage the artist's myth causes to all kinds of talented, creative individuals—it clouds the horizon with impossible benchmarks that distract from the real point: *inner growth.*

Whether it culminates in substantial public recognition or not, each creative activity we undertake plays a fundamentally important role in our personal fulfillment and that of others around us. In a poignant essay titled, "If at First, You Don't Succeed, Celebrate," art critic and curator Lisa Le Feuvre exhorts: "Perfection is satisfying, but failure is engaging, venturing into the unknown. After all, if an artist were to make the perfect work, there would be no need to make another. To cite Samuel Beckett: 'Ever tried. Ever failed. No matter. Try again. Fail again. Fail better'."[27] John Baldessari advised his students: "Art comes out of failure. You have to try things out. You can't sit around, terrified of being incorrect, saying, 'I won't do anything until I do a masterpiece'."[28]

But how can art students learn from their failures when the word itself was banned from education in the early 2000s? A pedagogical catastrophe. Students are no longer allowed to fail. They just "don't gain credit." Or in the worst-case scenario, they "haven't passed *yet*." Of course, customers can never be wrong, so how can they possibly fail? Are we still looking for confirmation that the professor–institution–student relation has been seriously corrupted? Today's students are infantilized and de-responsibilized. Educational institutions have endowed them with a "shopping mall mindset." Everything is a transaction. Professors sell goods and services. The experience must always be comforting and pleasant, just like in mass retailing. The reward that only prolonged discomfort generated by challenging texts brings is seen as utterly unnecessary. The syllabus is a shopping list. At the end of each class, some students check how many items are in their "tote bag." They expect immediate results, measurable and tangible weekly growth. This model might work for the sciences or finance, but not for the arts.

Akin to Yelp reviews, the course evaluations students are invited to fill out at the end of the semester further strengthen the "shopping mall mindset." Shielded by anonymity, they unleash their sadistic selves and punish professors often punish professors for not being lenient. Negative student evaluations are in turn used by the institution to penalize instructors by refusing pay raises and denying promotions. Studies have over and over shown that, in this context, women and BIPOC instructors are penalized more than other groups and yet, once again, art schools are not doing enough to build a fairer and more equitable reality. This system girdles the social structure of the art school; stunting innovation and creativity, it fosters a regime of fear where risk-taking is implicitly discouraged and in which professors choose the easy route to avoid problems. Failing a paper will only lead to a series of hearings and contestations that will absorb hours and hours. This, too, is a major blow to true pedagogical growth and it thoroughly devalues the art school experience.[29]

The demoralization that comes with failure is the seed of a new beginning. We cancel that word, and with that, we take away the students' right to real personal and professional growth. Learning to internalize failure makes future failures more manageable, less painful, and more productive—it is edifying. Erasing the word sets them up to fail badly rather than better.

Ultimately, as experts know, the art world is one of the toughest and harshest professional environments. Failure is its main currency. Countless rejection letters from curators, galleries, and institutions are the only post-graduation guarantee. Those who have learned to survive the heartbreak might stand a chance to carry on, but what will the rest do?

## Blooming Narcissus

Narcissism manifests on a broad spectrum that ranges from what is considered normal to an unhealthily self-absorbed personality disorder.[30] Narcissists don't know failure because, in their own view, they never fail, so they never learn from their mistakes. By removing failure from art education, institutions foster narcissistic inclinations. However, narcissism and creativity share something important—a sense of personal centrality and relevance crucial to the myth of the artist. Narcissism became topical in 2016 as the media rushed to pseudo-psychoanalyze Donald Trump at the dawn of his infamous presidency. That year, I asked an MFA cohort if they thought narcissism played any role, at all, in what they do as artists. The most awkward "don't look at me" kind of silence was eventually broken by a dismissive collective "naaah!"

Nonetheless, most creative people seek attention—it confirms our existence. Novelist Milan Kundera understood the importance of this existentialist basis and was driven to create four categories into which people fit based on their relationship with attention:

> We all need someone to look at us. We can be divided into four categories according to the kind of look we wish to live under. The first category longs for the look of an infinite number of anonymous eyes, in other words, for the look of the public. The second category is made up of people who have a vital need to be looked at by many known eyes. They are the tireless hosts of cocktail parties and dinners. They are happier than the people in the first category, who, when they lose their public, have the feeling that the lights have gone out in the room of their lives. This happens to nearly all of them sooner or later. People in the second category, on the other hand, can always come up with the eyes they need. Then there is the third category, the category of people who need to be constantly before the eyes of the person they love. Their situation is as dangerous as the situation of people in the first category. One day the eyes of their beloved will close, and the room will go dark. And finally there is the fourth category, the rarest, the category of people who live in the imaginary eyes of those who are not present. They are the dreamers.[31]

The need for attention is a necessary condition of narcissism. But it's not easy and takes humility to cultivate confidence in one's abilities without succumbing to narcissism. Everything is a matter of shades and degrees . . . Current cultural discourses have overmined fragility as the anti-patriarchal *passe-partout* to authenticity. Balancing confidence and fragility in the face of inevitable failures and rejection is key. Those who get it right become the rare "dreamers" that Kundera speaks of.

The artist's myth is intrinsically and deeply narcissistic. The sense of protagonism, superiority, and arrogance are all engrained into narcissistic exceptionalism. From Gauguin to Picasso, Pollock, and Dalí, the giants of modern art have often set a bad example for today's aspiring artists—their attitude towards the women in their lives is only the tip of a colossal narcissistic iceberg. Picasso is quoted to have said, "God is really an artist, like me . . . I am God, I am God, I am God."[32] To Sigmund Freud the artist was

> . . . one who is urged on by instinctive needs which are too clamorous; he longs to attain to honor, power, riches, fame, and the love of women; but he lacks the means of achieving these gratifications. So, like any other with an unsatisfied longing, he turns away from reality and transfers all his interest, and all his Libido, too, onto the creation of his wishes in life.[33]

Owning the artist label in ways that are visible to others instantly fulfills narcissistic instincts, at least temporarily. In this sense, Keith Arnatt's famous black-and-white photograph in which he holds a sign stating, "I'm a real artist" remains one of the most provoking, tongue-in-cheek works of art about the "artist's status" and its existential meaning. *Trouser-Word Piece* (1972) was originally disseminated as a double-sided card, a provocation directed at "those colleagues in the conceptual art world who wanted to become famous and who, he felt, were becoming increasingly egocentric."[34] Who is a real artist? Who decides? And on what grounds? Arnatt was acutely aware that photography, his chosen medium, wasn't taken seriously by the British establishment. In the introduction to the catalog accompanying the exhibition *I'm a Real Photographer*, Arnatt's 2007 retrospective at the Photographers' Gallery in

**Keith Arnatt**
TROUSER - WORD PIECE

'It is usually thought, and I dare say usually rightly thought, that what one might call the affirmative use of a term is basic – that, to understand 'x', we need to know what it is to be x, or to be an x, and that knowing this apprises us of what it is **not** to be x, not to be an x. But with 'real' .... it is the **negative** use that wears the trousers. That is, a definite sense attaches to the assertion that something is real, a real such-and-such, only in the light of a specific way in which it might be, or might have been, **not** real. 'A real duck' differs from the simple 'a duck' only in that it is used to exclude various ways of being not a real duck – but a dummy, a toy, a picture, a decoy, &c.; and moreover I don't know **just** how to take the assertion that it's a real duck unless I know **just** what, on that particular occasion, the speaker had it in mind to exclude .... (The) function of 'real' is not to contribute positively to the characterisation of anything, but to exclude possible ways of being **not** real – and these ways are both numerous for particular kinds of things, and liable to be quite different for things of different kinds. It is this identity of general function combined with immense diversity in specific applications which gives the word 'real' the, at first sight, baffling feature of having neither one single 'meaning', nor yet ambiguity, a number of different meanings.'
John Austin, 'Sense and Sensibilia.'

Image 40. Keith Arnatt, *Trouser-Word Piece*, 2 photographs, gelatin silver print on paper, 1972. Keith Arnatt Estate. All rights reserved. DACS / ARS 2024

London, curator Roger Hurn claimed that "there is no doubt that the art world started ignoring him as soon as he started calling himself a photographer."[35] Arnatt was onto something really powerful. His sense of humor and conceptual prowess served a left-handed blow to the system. The iconic sandwich-board-style sign asserting his creative identity undercut both the egotistical essence of the artist and the significance we place on the social ascension that others desperately crave. He mercilessly eviscerated the artist myth for everyone to see, while spilling no blood.

# Reclaiming Creativity

Art students have increasingly become more sensitized to the idea that the myth of the artist carries a dreadful patriarchal and elitist heritage. It smacks of privilege. The image of the self-indulging, tortured soul stroking their anguish across expensive canvases, with even more expensive brushes and pigments, is jarring. It tells others that, while a climate emergency is in full swing and many are victims of systemic social injustice, one can buy the peace to make luxury objects affluent people can, in turn, buy to validate themselves—oftentimes the same affluent people most responsible for killing the planet. It reminds everyone that, in the end, an artist is not down with the rest.

This cultural shift became apparent in the summer of 2020 when the *Singaporean Sunday Times* released the findings of a study on people's opinions of important occupations amid the Covid-19 epidemic. Artists topped the list of most nonessential jobs, triggering a social media storm of colossal proportions.[36] As it is with any social media controversies, misunderstandings ran amok. Many pointed out that, during the pandemic especially, musicians, film directors, and actors proved vital in keeping everyone sane. However, these were not the types of artists the sample was asked to consider. Those who took part interpreted the word "artist" in the romantic, mythical sense and responded accordingly. In the minds of most, the word failed to evoke the urgency of an ethical commitment. The word "artist" is a ruin. A crumbling monolith stuck in the past.

Numerous articles about "success addiction" also began to circulate in 2020.[37] The main tenet in all: we deem success more important than happiness. This is another symptom of a deep cultural and societal dysfunction that distorts our values and leads us to make bad life, as well as career, choices. Humankind is the victim of its own mythologizations. We ruin our lives by attempting to become protagonists in narcissistic plays where the hero is the only role worth playing. The artist myth promises anthropocentric glories that often distract from the ecosystemic interactions that make life meaningful beyond the benchmarks that institutions set for us. Social media reconfigure, often with detrimental impacts on mental health, and our sense of self-esteem. We become addicted to the dopamine highs triggered by post-likes and our happiness is shackled to a never-quenchable cycle of validation. But beneath the surface, our clicks and swipes only feed a capitalist machine driven by advertising revenue, not true cultural evolution. Can this possibly lead to long-lasting personal fulfillment? And what's left if we find the courage to strip the veneer and give up the "artist-nobiliary title"? The answer is simple: *creativity.*

Creativity is an endless and wholly generative process of *mitosis.* It knows no categories or hierarchies. It is the essence of the living that encompasses the cosmos. Stars, animals, plants, humans, fungi, bacteria, viruses—we're all made of the same matter that constantly reconfigures and reinvents itself. This planet is a creative conglomerate where everything is intimately interconnected—constant transformation is the only truth. Creativity is a process of becoming, a repurposing, and weaving.

Today, creativity, not art in the sense it was constructed in the West, has the power to change the world. Creativity, not art, bears the potential to be truly free from the constrictions of social class, race, and gender. Conceiving the art world as a vibrant and lively ecosystemic entity in which multiple organisms engage in symbiotic or coexisting relationships over time can help us envision more sustainable, creative realities.

Unfortunately, over the past century, capitalism has deeply trivialized creativity. In popular culture, creativity has become something for children, those working in "creative industries" like marketing, or product design. Besotted by the artist myth and fooled by its promises, we have lost sight of creativity. From making dinner to rallying the local community in protest or building a planter, and addressing pressing social issues, creativity is the engine of change—it's what gives life meaning. Over time, the myth of the artist has smothered creativity. It has reduced it to an elitist pursuit and has convinced us that we need an institution to validate, package, and brand our creative abilities. This is perhaps the biggest damage the romantic artist myth continues to perpetrate today.

Creativity bears the potential for true democracy. As a fluid force, it traverses bodies, media, collectives, and ideas. It is the molecular binder of life itself. Creativity is infectious; it sparks collaboration. It contaminates. It prompts us to reconfigure the world and our place within it. Most importantly, creativity does not require an audience. Creativity is humbly linked to and defined by materiality, processes, concepts, and time. Ultimately, it knows freedom that art can't. It triggers momentous change, but it is not concerned with remembrance. At its core, creativity is not bothered with posthumous glory either. It joyfully thrives in the present and is concerned with the future only as far as it can make it more livable. Architects, cooks, editors, gardeners, teachers, musicians, writers, photographers, administrators, plumbers, mechanics, and nurses, to name but a handful, harness their creative abilities in everything they do, even when they are not conscious of it. The kind of growth that only creativity can support requires patience, initiative, adaptation, trust, resilience, strength, and determination in any application—pursuing any original idea, in any medium, day after day, seeing it through to completion, investing time and resources; to believe in it when nobody else does and to obstinately push through, regardless.

Creativity takes us astray so that we can find ourselves again. It defines us in a precise moment in time and space. It connects us to the otherness of the world, linking elements and principles that might seem utterly disjointed at first. Creativity is the invisible force that gels individuals, communities, technologies, and environments. It is not a divine act of creation, a signature, or a monument but an endless field of potentialities across which we can openly encounter and embrace the alterity and diversity of the world. Our shared ability to be creative allows us to coexist and think together.

The history of art shows that even artists famous in their lifetime can easily be forgotten—their contribution deemed irrelevant, or sometimes distasteful, only one or two generations down the line. This has been particularly true of female and BIPOC artists. At the whim of a curator, artworks that brought notoriety can be relegated to the eternal darkness of the museum storage, no longer influencing, or inspiring, anyone. As the internet floods us with far more art than we can ever meaningfully engage with, at a moment in which art students and practicing artists are increasingly more concerned with their ability to make tangible positive changes, it seems necessary to rethink what being creative means beyond the culture-capital network we call art. Amid social unrest, millions of deaths, and an economic crisis, the Covid-19 pandemic also temporarily recentered our focus on the essential importance of creativity in everyday life. It invited us to rethink our careers and life journeys beyond the models we have blindly followed until then. Let's make a conscious effort not to "return to normal."

Careful consideration of the relationship between creativity and social impact might help ethically driven artists to position themselves and their professions more clearly and realistically within present situations. Making an informed choice is essential to taking control of a creative life. But most importantly, let's avoid the artist myth at all costs. Let's ask ourselves what role creativity plays in our lives and follow that lead instead, regardless of what others think. One can still be motivated by the desire to sell their work and to have their art shown in galleries and museums, but perhaps the ecosystemic model I have described in this book will also help them see how to realistically get there, or that crafting their own paths away from the validation of institutions may be just as rewarding. Abandoning whatever ill-conceived notion of being an artist is empowering. This is not the same as abandoning our dreams. If freedom is what we crave, being a professional artist, in the "artist myth sense," will bring next to none. We can keep creating in any medium and context with dignity and pride, embracing the challenges creativity bestows with the humbleness of someone who dedicates their time to life-long learning unconcerned with social rankings and the cultural markers of prestige that institutions use to constantly divide and antagonize. Institutions are what they are—colonialist, neoliberal power structures that put profit before people—always. Our desire for validation has disproportionally empowered them and it is now time to claw that power back. We have been aware of this long enough to plan a revolution, yet every attempt miserably fizzles out because, along the way, our creative journeys remain implicitly subservient to the exclusionary, elitist, and extractivist institutional models that bolster our egos with fictitious validations.

It is now time to take on the responsibility to change our mindsets first. If we do, the institutions will have to follow us. A chance to craft the new creative models that our time truly needs looms on the horizon. The good news is that this revolution can start with the small choices we all make, the paths we will decide to no longer take, and those we can invent for ourselves and others to become the artist we need to be.

The future creative minds of the art world ecosystem will not be lions, eagles, elephants, or peacocks. They will not be the charismatic megafauna, the sublime animals of hollow trophies. New creative ecosystemic modes of being in the future art world point to the adaptive resilience of cockroaches, the symbiotic interconnectedness of fungi, the regenerative deep times of lichens, the igniting properties of enzymes, the hermaphroditic joy of snails, the polymorphous unfoldings of mold, the seductive allure of moths' pheromones, the burrowing defiance of worms, or the unsteady flight of bumblebees. Composters, relentlessly breaking down decaying matter, transforming toxicity into nourishment, remodeling, delving into depths to unearth, weaving alliances, dependencies, and fostering reciprocities—always, at every opportunity:

generating,
resisting,
endlessly crafting,
constantly adapting,
most importantly, thriving.

"I'm not an artist. There, I've said it and I feel free. I'm not an artist."

David Shayne, played by John Cusack
in Woody Allen's *Bullet's on Broadway*
1994

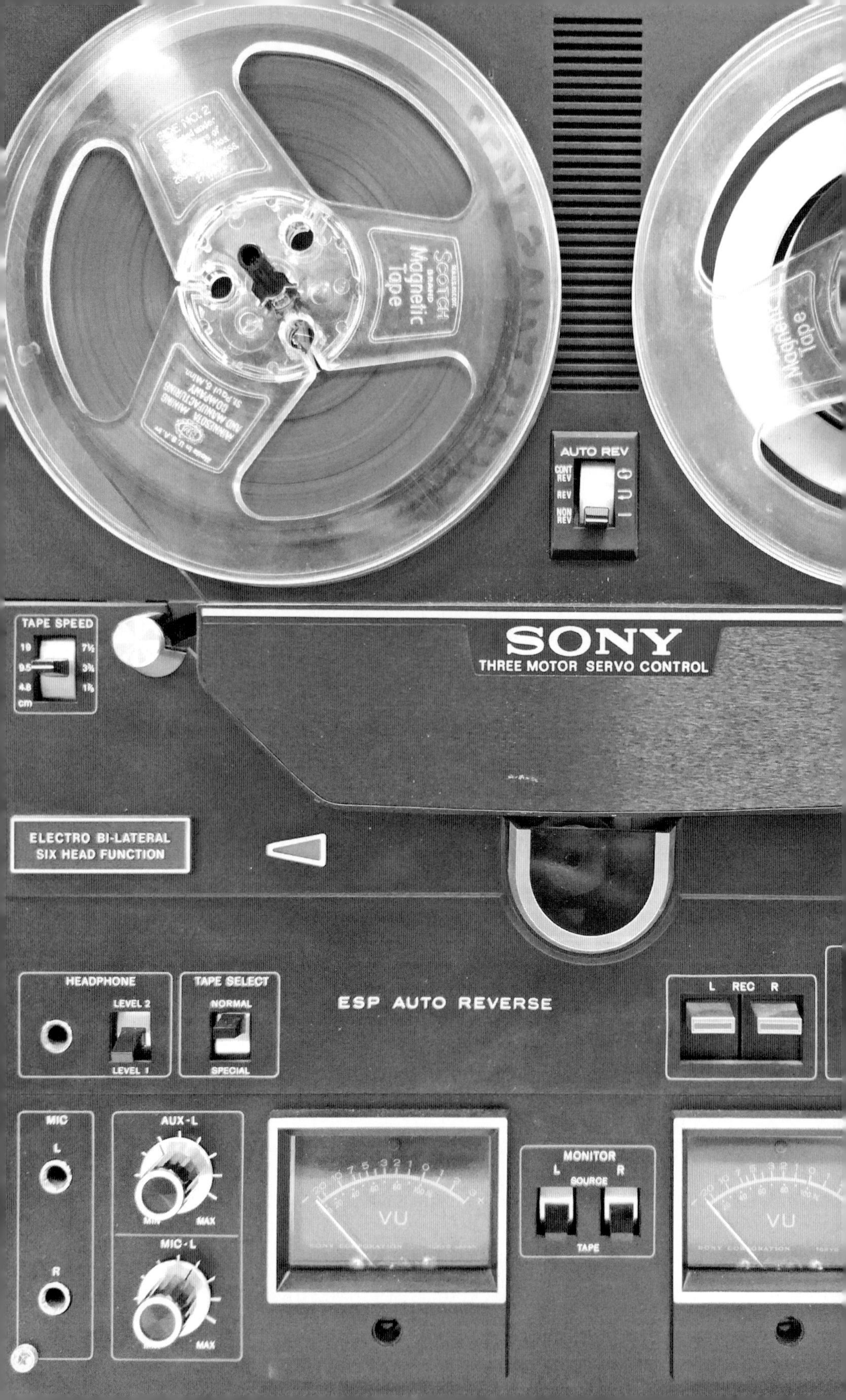

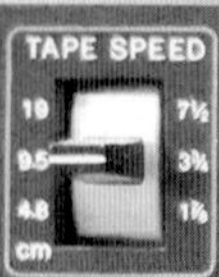

TAPE SPEED
19  7½
9.5  3¾
4.8  1⅞
cm


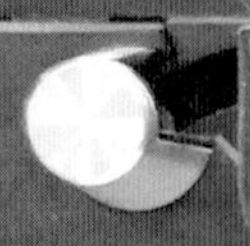

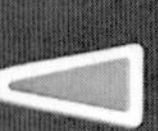

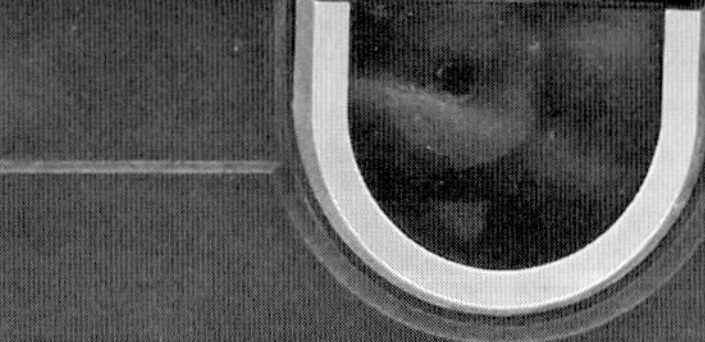

ESP AUTO REVERSE


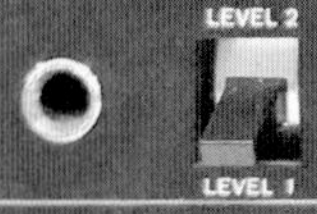

HEADPHONE
LEVEL 2
LEVEL 1


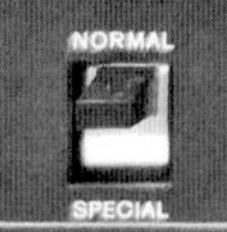

TAPE SELECT
NORMAL
SPECIAL


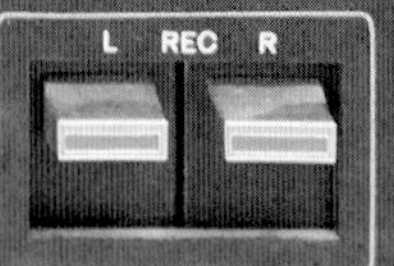

L  REC  R


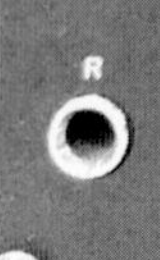

MIC
L
R


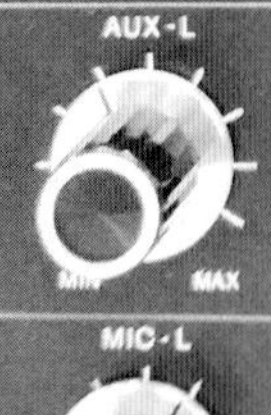

AUX-L
MIN  MAX


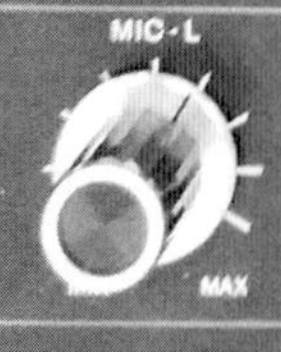

MIC-L
MAX


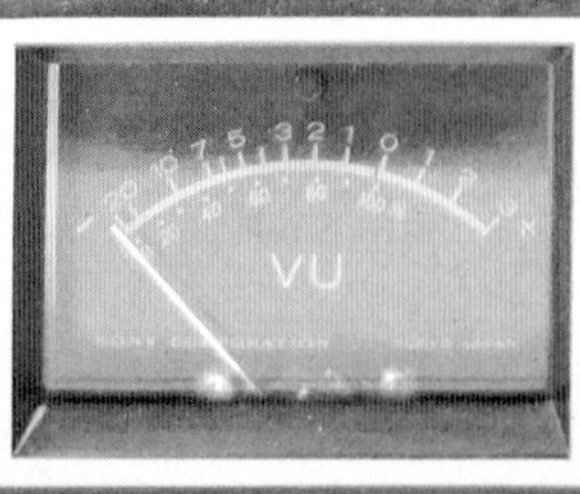

VU


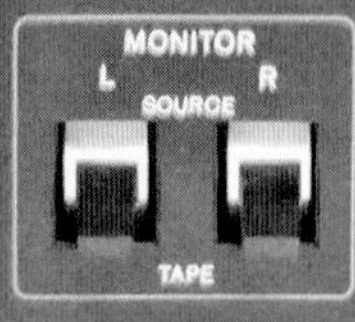

MONITOR
L  R
SOURCE
TAPE


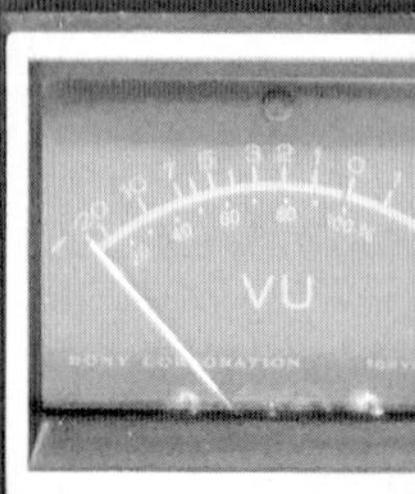

VU

# 9  In Private: Conversations

Image 41 (facing page).  SONY TC-580 Reel to Reel Tape Recorder. Photo by the author.

# Hock E Aye Vi Edgar Heap of Birds: On Building Communities

**Giovanni Aloi:** Edgar, your work has been exhibited internationally, it is in prestigious collections, and it was also featured on the front cover of *Art in America*. How does the "artist label" feel to you?

**Hock E Aye Vi Edgar Heap of Birds:** Interesting question . . . I taught art for thirty years while continuing to make my work and I found it tricky to meaningfully exist in that hybrid artist/professor zone. All along I have also served as a ceremonial leader in my tribe. The tribe leader is called "painter" because you paint people's bodies. All these identities intertwine, feed, and shape each other—so being an artist for me is about negotiating these different creative iterations.

**GA:** What was the hardest part of teaching while continuing to make work?

**HEAVEHoB:** The politics, the never-ending meetings—the majority of art professors eventually give up their practice, exhausted by institutional demands and administration duties. I survived. Being the kind of political artist that I am, in Oklahoma, has not been easy. The institution I worked for was not particularly interested in what I had to say, certainly the art history department wasn't. They weren't willing to critically address the legacy of colonialism and their conception of painting was very traditional: a brush, pigment, and a canvas. I have an expanded idea of painting as sculpture, as performance . . . It felt liberating when I finally left teaching.

**GA:** Do you think art schools equip students with the tools they need to face the art world?

**HEAVEHoB:** No. One of the most important aspects of being an artist is motivation. You have to encourage yourself, but the system makes students passive. So, they graduate and wait for the accolades to come from institutions. If they don't come or don't come quickly enough, they give up. Students are not taught how to generate and foster their own audience. Artists need to reach out to those who work outside the art world and excite them about the work they do.

**GA:** Was there ever a point in which you said "I'm an artist"?

**HEAVEHoB:** I was in 3rd grade. I could draw well, so I won a scholarship and studied academic drawing—spheres, cubes, pyramids—not particularly exciting, but I kept going. I think artists are compulsive. That's how I knew I was an artist. That drive kept me going through academia.

**GA:** How did you get to where you are today?

**HEAVEHoB:** Well, I had the opportunity to study in prestigious institutions like the Royal College of Art, London, and the Tyler School of Art, Philadelphia, but these places were also biased and limited. I knew I had to make my own headway, and build my own networks of allies in the art world. Artist-run spaces were great. I traveled and worked around the world that way and collaborated with exciting artists. The market doesn't necessarily have an interest in that. My work has been shown alongside Keith Herring, David Hammons, Jenny Holzer, and Barbara Kruger but I don't live in Chelsea because my work does not conform to the market. The model I have chosen for my career is a challenging one. But my work is in the collection of MoMA, the Whitney, and Tate Modern. I normally initiate dialogues with the institutions directly. That way I don't have to share half of the profit.

**GA:** Did you learn this along the way?

**HEAVEHoB:** Some of it I crafted myself through trial and error, but I picked up a lot from other artists.

**Giovanni Aloi:** Do you have an assistant that helps you out with the administrative part of being an artist?

**HEAVEHoB:** No, I don't. I do it all by myself and I have kind of come to like it, in a way—it is good for my brain to switch gears.

**GA:** What's the most pressing systemic challenge you have faced in the art world?

**HEAVEHoB:** The lack of sovereignty for the Native artist in the context of representation. The intermediaries are never Native people. So, your work is always culturally mediated by another. We don't have our machine. That's also why I am directly involved in all the negotiations to retain as much integrity as possible.

**GA:** Of course, this is a major issue, I agree. I often hear from students who keep in touch after graduation that they wish art school had prepared them to face these challenges and obstacles. Maybe there is only so much art school can do? What would your advice be?

**HEAVEHoB:** Well, I don't think a graduating student would like to hear this, but I would say, "Give it twenty years . . ." That's as long as it takes for things to start shaping up after graduation. So maybe that is a failure in the art school model—a doctor graduates and they are a doctor, but the artist's educational model works differently. The fact that the art world has turned into an industry does not mean that it can provide steady work. The road is much more complicated than that. When I came to Cheyenne and Arapaho Nation, Oklahoma, in 1981, I had next to nothing, so I taught primary and secondary public school, throughout Oklahoma, as a visiting artist. That taught me how to communicate clearly. I became engaged in my community. That shifted my artistic focus. I realized how important it is to make work for the people around me. One has to care for their immediate reality in order to make art that is relevant. It's not going to come from the ivory towers of exceptionalism and institutional prestige. To me, that's all about elites and exclusivity. I am not interested in that.

**Hock E Aye Vi Edgar Heap of Birds** has studied at the University of Kansas, Lawrence (BFA, 1976), undertaken graduate studies at the Royal College of Art, London (1977), and attended the Tyler School of Art, Philadelphia (MFA, 1979). He was named USA Ford Fellow in 2012 and Distinguished Alumni, University of Kansas, in 2014. Honorary Doctor of Fine Arts and Letters degrees have been awarded by the Massachusetts College of Art and Design, Boston (2008), Emily Carr University of Art and Design, Vancouver (2017), and California Institute of the Arts, Valencia (2018). His artwork has been collected by the Museum of Modern Art, Metropolitan Museum of Art, Whitney Museum of American Art, Los Angeles County Museum of Art, and the Art Institute of Chicago.

# Mandy Suzanne Wong: On Risk-Taking

**Giovanni Aloi:** What would you say is one of the hardest challenges that young creative individuals face when pursuing their careers?

**Mandy-Suzanne Wong:** The capitalist value system. It's based on hierarchies and money. This is true of the business of literature as much as it is of other arts. The business is dominated by empires: the United States, United Kingdom. So, industry insiders tell me that, because I was born in Bermuda, I've no hope of succeeding. Another misconception—because writers are almost never fairly paid—is that writing should be a hobby, a sideline that rightfully requires support from an "actual" career in teaching. Writing is, by itself, a career. It is my poorly paid profession. It's also an art. Writing is often mistaken for a mundane tool. But, for instance, I think a lot like a music composer: structure, timbre, rhythm . . . and I am very particular about writing's visual aesthetics—how words look on the page. When a page has too much dialogue, it doesn't look right. I want the dialogue to stand out visually from the rest of the text but not to break down the overall structure. The white space can be just as important as the words around it. I also think about writing as painting sometimes. You sketch something out, choose your colors, smudge, overlay . . . all in textual form.

**GA:** I completely agree with you. This is a form of ignorance that, I believe, is still rooted in the fetishization of the artist myth. We all write. Not everyone can draw or paint even if they try really hard. Painting, drawing, and sculpting in a naturalistic way still hold that classical mystique—the anointed replicating God's creation.

**MSW:** Another substantial misconception is bound to labor and how a realistic work of art is hard to execute but writing is not. You're just tapping on the keys . . .

**GA:** Can there be any freedom in a creative career?

**MSW:** I don't think you can tell an artist what to write. That's not how it works. I try to cling to that freedom as hard as I can and see if the world is going to take or leave what I create. I like to take risks. My new novel, *The Box*, is perhaps the riskiest project I have undertaken so far. I bypassed all market considerations and went for full-on weird. I never expected it to land anywhere, but it was snapped up right away. Yet, I've endured many rejections before. It's just the way it goes.

**GA:** How do you handle rejection?

**MSW:** It's so hard. Nothing I learned at school prepared me for rejection or even to submit my work in a professional way! A lot of the work involved in being a writer is sending out emails, pitching, and networking. You have to cultivate this dual personality: the artist and the admin. They're part of the same token, and nothing is likely to happen without the admin part. But rejection is hard because your work is always personal: your intuitions, perceptions, fantasies, fears—regardless of what you're writing, your writing is still you. And rejection will impact your choices. What are you going to write next? But to me, writing is a compulsion. It can be unhealthy. When I considered becoming a classical composer, a teacher said, "Don't do it unless you can't help it, unless you feel compelled to compose. Otherwise, it is going to make you miserable."

**GA:** I understand. Compulsion has come up in other conversations for this book. I feel compelled to write, too, or to play the piano, or take photographs. All in different ways. But I just can't give up. It's what makes me fulfilled and gives meaning to my life. I feel thoroughly present when I work on my projects. How long did it take you to write *The Box?*

**MSW:** About eight months.

**GA:** How often are you at the keyboard?

**MSW:** Six days a week for a minimum of six hours a day. It's like being a classical pianist. I trained as one!

**GA:** I didn't know you play piano. Do you still play?

**MSW:** No, not anymore. Musicology turned me off.

**GA:** A dear friend of mine who is very successful in the art world deliberately avoided studying film because that is their real passion and didn't want all the theory to spoil the magic.

**MSW:** I find theory beautiful and indispensable. What turned me off in universities' musicology departments is how music, theory, and history were tossed around instead of being loved.

**GA:** Do you care to be remembered?

**MSW:** That's an interesting question . . . books end up in the trash. The written word is not as permanent as people think. It's hard to know what makes a novel into a classic, and it's impossible to foresee the future. So, the question of the audience is a bit of a shot in the dark. I think I care more about the presence of my work and the joy of making it.

**MANDY-SUZANNE WONG** is a Bermudian writer of fiction and essays. Her novels include *The Box*, a *Bustle* Best Books of 2023 selection, and *Drafts of a Suicide Note*, a Foreword INDIES finalist and PEN Open Book Award nominee. She's also the author of *Listen, We All Bleed*, a PEN/Galbraith-nominated essay collection, and *Awabi*, a duet of short stories, winner of the Digging Press Chapbook Award.

# Julian Montague: On Straddling Disciplines

**Giovanni Aloi:** Julian, you have very successfully managed to straddle the line that, in the eyes of many, still separates art and design. How have you managed that?

**Julian Montague:** My father taught art history, and design history. He was skeptical of the hierarchy of fine art and craft, so I inherited some of that thinking. I didn't study art or design in college. I realized what I wanted to do at the end of my senior year. Instead of going back to school, I set out to learn on my own. It helped that computers were getting cheaper and more capable toward the end of the 1990s. The tools of graphic design were suddenly accessible to the nonprofessional. I started to create projects for myself in order to build a portfolio. That's how the *Stray Shopping Carts* project came up. That took off and I started to exhibit work.

**GA:** What does it mean to be an artist?

**JM:** I think the term might serve some purpose as a catch-all. I am a photographer, a painter, a designer . . . but I am not particularly reverential to all of the traditions associated with these media. The almost mystical level of reverence other artists have for their mediums makes me uncomfortable using certain labels. I don't often refer to myself as a "painter" for instance. I want to be free to engage with media in nonreverential ways. I don't want to get too involved with technicalities or theoretical paradigms.

**GA:** Yes, I know what you mean: the kind of professional purism that is cultivated by some. A kind of pedigree that emerges from a sort of vertical engagement with the medium.

**JM:** Correct: I don't have a lot of time for that. But I am equally disenchanted with the idea of the artist as a supernatural calling, or that the artist is an extra special being. I like to keep in mind that I am not entitled to people's attention.

**GA:** Funny you should mention that. I think there are two polarities in the spectrum of artistic personalities. At one end is the supernatural calling, and at the other seems to be the humble artist who privileges process and growth.

**JM:** Yes, I am familiar with both, and I think that in the middle is an idea of compulsion – like, if there is some kind of calling to being an artist it is only the compulsion to create.

**GA:** How important is social impact in your practice? I ask this since design is often more overtly concerned with the clarity and directness of communication while art tends to take a different route . . . How do you negotiate the two?

**JM:** As a graphic designer I can communicate a social or political message in a direct way. I want my artwork to be a space where I can deal with ideas more obliquely. Similarly, I see my client work as being very different from my artwork despite the fact that they sometimes share a visual language. I find the conceptual difference between the two to be important. But there is a gray area in between. In some of the opportunities I get involved in collaborating with companies as an "artist," creating murals in shops, graphics for clothes, etc. under my name. This work is just slightly outside of the conceptual space of my artwork, but not a straight graphic design job either. I like these projects a lot because they tend to be seen by more people than if they were in a gallery. Of course, the work of designers and illustrators is seen more than most fine artists, but are often left anonymous.

**GA:** Yes, this is another detrimental facet of the myth of the artist. The art world is full of fetishizing feedback loops. How many exhibitions of Monet, Picasso, Dali, Kahlo do we need while there are so many other exciting artists out there?

**JM:** Yes, I find it frustrating, too.

**GA:** That's why in this book I talk about the importance of exposure, which I still maintain, is the main currency in the art world. It might not pay bills today, but once you get enough, it might sustain your career for years.

**JM:** Living in Buffalo, New York, was an odd choice in the early 2000s in terms of exposure. In that time being represented by a New York City gallery made living here possible for me, but now I have 130,000 Instagram followers and only a quarter of them are even in the United States, let alone New York City. I think that's a good example of how technology can democratize the power dynamics of the art world. You can now build your own audience without gatekeepers. Ultimately, exposure is the only game in town, it's the thing that leads to the other things. No one's going to ask you to do anything if they don't know who you are and if they have not seen your work.

**GA:** What is your take on AI right now?

**JM:** I will say I'm not usually like a handwringer around new technology, but I do feel alarmed by it. I think that the illustration sector is under direct threat. The idea of AI learning and appropriating individual styles is ethically troubling, to say the least. I have less concern about fine art; it is hard to imagine that people would want to visit galleries to see AI-generated art, but who knows?

**Julian Montague** is an artist, graphic designer, and illustrator based in Buffalo, New York. Over the years, his artwork has included a wide range of mediums and approaches, from long-term conceptual projects to geometric abstraction.

# Vivien Sansour: On Not Fitting In, Ever

**Giovanni Aloi:** Vivien, you are the founder and director of the *Palestine Heirloom Seed Library*, and actively work with farmers to recover and propagate threatened heirloom varieties of vegetables. Much of your practice revolves around the creation of local and international public awareness campaigns to educate people about Palestinian agricultural heritage and biodiversity. I bet lots of people ask you if what you do classifies as art . . .

**Vivien Sansour:** Ha-ha! Once I was invited to give a talk in the Netherlands and one student insisted on asking me very category-focused questions about the role of art and artists. At some point, I just had to say, "I don't care about all that!" The art world sort of happened to me. I was doing what I believed in, and suddenly scholars would invite me to give talks and create displays for exhibitions. In 2018, I received an email from Paulo Tavares, curator of the Architecture Biennale in Chicago. At first, I didn't answer it because I thought it was phishing or an error. But from those contacts, I also understood that what I was doing could be thought of as an expanded kind of social, geographical, and ecological design practice. So, I started to see how it could be art.

But ultimately to me, art is all around us—it is not just in the museum, it is a connection with existence that manifests itself in the smallest and seemingly insignificant everyday things like a reflection on the wall, a shadow, or a sound. I don't believe in the exceptionalism of art, and more especially, I do not believe in the exceptionalism of the artist as sole genius/creator. Art is a collective practice and experience.

**GA:** Couldn't agree more. Much of what you do entails envisioning alternative models. You invite farmers to reclaim their agency as active participants in the making of national identities that reach deep into the land and ultimately into their stomachs. Are you a catalyst?

**VS:** Correct—I think it's tragic that we have made art something more valuable than life through a long process of fetishization. Life is art. Farmers are designers. They envision, they plan, and they draw layouts. We have lost our ability to see the value of everyday things because capitalism always pushes us to prefer the exceptional. But in the process, it makes us all the same—zombies addicted to a formula: disconnected, alienated, absent, unavailable.

**GA:** I always say that capitalism causes affliction in order to sell a cure. In that sense, our lives can easily become pre-encoded in feedback loops of production and consumption in which we feel powerless. How did the idea for the *Palestine Heirloom Seed Library* come about?

**VS:** My mother. I just watched what she used to do. She learned from my grandmother. I learned from family members but also from the river, the trees, the birds. I redesigned what they taught me. Being a designer, in the way I conceive it, is a form of resistance to capitalism. Today, big corporations like Monsanto reduce farmers to machines by genetically modifying seeds so that they can only be grown with the use of their products and following their processes to the point. They separate the farmer's brains from the plants and the soil. Imagining and envisioning are skills that capitalist corporations want to suppress, at least on the production level. The Haitian Revolution started from a ritual that enabled enslaved people to envision their freedom. It was that, the power to imagine, which made it possible to break the shackles the following day. Imagination can be subversive and being an artist can be subversive. This is my idea of what an artist is and does. Instead, the art world nurtures an idea of the artist's genius as a stuck-up, sophisticated intellectual who always wears black. It's a performance!

**GA:** Or maybe a farce . . . I call it "Art Drag."

**VS:** Indeed, and it suggests an unavailability of some sort. A categorical repression of feelings. If I wear colors at an opening people think I'm unsophisticated.

**GA:** And if one wears colours they'd better be intense, and the outfit preferably custom-made and geometrically awkward . . .

**VS:** Ha-ha! Correct. And you see, I am more interested in how we can create tender spaces: how do we design a world that is more inclusive and protective? I am impacted by my own grief and my grief about the world. I like to imagine something out of this. And that something can be found in a meal or a tree. You see, this is also why I wasn't happy in previous experiences with universities—I felt like to fit in, I had to surrender my imagination. Higher education institutions are often set up to reproduce a module. They also are very much about performances, and true imagination of the kind that might subvert their power scares them.

**GA:** I have experienced that, too—like in art schools that charge students astronomical fees to become artists. The institution traps us into impossible models in which contradiction is the only truth.

**VS:** Yes, correct—you love parts of it. An institution can help your career, and provide space for you to experiment but ultimately one also needs to eat. You have to live in the contradiction, in the paradox, and negotiate it within you.

**GA:** I think that's the reason I wrote this book. Because I felt the need to really negotiate what you have described in a thorough and open way rather than just groan and mumble on my own in the shower and then smile in the hallways as the performance script prescribes . . . One last question: Do you like it when people call you an artist?

**VS:** I would never go around telling people I'm an artist! It always baffles me when someone introduces themselves as such. But the world is desperate to pigeonhole you, so I let people call me an artist. It's easier. But I think students should leave this idea of becoming an artist, with all that it entails, at the door and just find their flow, their direction in a very genuine way and not become part of the performance.

**Vivien Sansour** is an artist, storyteller, researcher, and conservationist. She uses images, sketches, film, soil, seeds, and plants to enliven old cultural tales in contemporary presentations and to advocate for seed conservation and the protection of agrobiodiversity as a cultural/political act. Vivien founded the *Palestine Heirloom Seed Library* as part of this work with local farmers and has been showcased internationally, including at the Chicago Architecture Biennale, V&A Museum in London, Dutch Design Week in Eindhoven, and the Venice Art Biennale. Born in Jerusalem, Vivien lives in both Bethlehem, Palestine, and New York, NY.

# Annie Freud: On Art as Encounter

**Giovanni Aloi:** Annie, what are artists for?

**Annie Freud:** I recently watched a documentary series called *Once Upon a Time in Northern Ireland*, charting the history of the sectarian conflict in Northern Ireland in which over 3,500 people were killed. The story was told from the point of view of civilians, police, armed forces, political activists who had witnessed or committed, and lost loved ones to, acts of violence. In one episode people remembered a record shop and a club where they'd gather to listen to live music and engage in other forms of artistic expression. They would find ways to rejoice in spite of their suffering. That's what the episode was about, how an experience of art can enable one, however briefly, to transcend the grimness of daily life and resist being defined by one's circumstances. So, if one had to terribly narrow things down, I guess that would be a role of the artist.

**GA:** It sounds like you're sketching out a picture of art as social practice?

**AF:** In a sense, yes. Mexican poet Cesa A. Cruz once said: "Art should comfort the disturbed and disturb the comfortable."

**GA:** I wonder how what you just described might or not align with the commercial reality of the art world. You have been surrounded by highly successful artists all your life. Your father Lucian Freud, your mother Kitty Garman, and your grandfather Jacob Epstein . . . What challenges did that pose to your own conception of art and artists?

**AF:** Well, the most complex challenge for me has been not to be hoodwinked/subdued/annihilated by the presence of genius but to find a way of being comfortable with it—and yet—to admit its demonic power. It continues to be an essential part of my life—a constant to-ing and fro-ing. Sometimes I've found myself standing in front of a magnificent painting by my father going, GODDAMMIT!!! IT'S SO BEAUTIFUL. I CAN'T STAND IT! IT'S MAKING ME ILL. I moved house recently and I've only hung a few of his smaller works just to allow myself some sense of independence.

At other times, while traveling on the London Underground, I've looked up and noticed his painting of my mother's beautiful face staring at me from every advertisement panel. My face flushes and my heart swells with pride.

Getting comfortable with genius for me has meant opening up and seeing beyond the fetishization, in both the public and in my private world. That's something I've needed to do almost as a form of psychotherapy.

**GA:** I can only imagine how complicated that must have been. Ultimately, the classical notion of the artist is shrouded in a mystic superiority designed to induce awe and intimidate. At least that's what the romanticization of the artist entails. The monetization of art is intrinsic to this elevating process.

**AF:** A few years ago, something completely unexpected happened to me that helped me get through that. I had just returned from a tour of Ireland and my painting studio was ready. I moved in immediately and began a painting in oils of our local pub at night. It was my first painting in oils. As soon as I picked up my brushes, I found I was using my father's gestures—standing, mixing small quantities of paint, readying the brush, picking up the color, and leaning forward into the canvas, and after two brushstrokes stepping back a few paces, rinsing the brush in the glass of turpentine and starting over again, and again—observed over hundreds and hundreds of hours sitting for paintings. Even my silence was his. I have got used to it and I anticipate it returning to me whenever I start painting again. I wrote this poem some years later to mark the experience.

## Why I Am a Painter

I
In this phase of my life
I'm unable
to be serious
about much else

now I'm in bed I think
about the puppet
show of *Moby Dick*
I saw last October

in a corrugated hut
and when the sail
of the tattooed ship
unfurled on a hinge

we were on the rolling seas
and Queequeg's Yojo
jigged on the deck
and the great white whale

hung down in the spot
the harpoon was
in every scene of Ahab's
quenchless feud

which of these
I'll keep and which
not I have yet to
decide

II
I'd be unfaithful
to everything that's dear

for the sake
of my painting

I don't even
appreciate
the scrambled eggs
on my plate

I love the infinite pains
the near-madness it takes
to paint the slope
of a roof

the feeling
of intoxication
I love being
deliberate

having accidents
I love it even
when it's
hopeless

III
Sometimes I'll say
look at that rose
nothing could be
more arresting

I must admit
it's only when the subject's
already in my mind
can I be arsed

and next is Fez
its pockmarked walls
and myriad windows like
eye sockets

its crenelations
zinc roofs and cobalt rhomboids
the suggestion
of an inner courtyard

IV
And when I take
four paces back
to appraise
my work

I feel the apertures
of my pupils expanding
and contacting
in real time

and this is how
it comes to me
that lack of quality
is itself a measure

of quality
and that makes
all the difference
I hold up my palette knife

to steady myself
take infinitesimal quantities
of paint, mix them
slowly at first

and then faster
until the consistency
is perfect before
stepping into the picture

**GA:** It's wonderful, thanks for sharing it! There is something important here about the art object, its reification, and the encounter with it—the kind of encounter you describe—which transcends market values. I hope that some of the arguments in my book won't be dismissed as cynical. One of its most important aims is to disentangle the idea of art as a complex system of material negotiations from creativity. This confusion, I argue, leads to a serious misunderstanding of what being an artist entails.

**AF:** Absolutely. I hunger for the encounter.

**GA:** Yes! Poetry and painting share some interesting analogies when it comes to staging encounters. Both share an affinity: immediacy. Both present themselves in rather contracted ways—I am thinking of the brevity of poetry and the manifestation of painting as an instant image in front of the eyes of the viewer. And yet, in this sense of immediacy, they both harbor infinite depths. How do you live with the complexities this medium entails on a personal level?

**AF:** I could answer this in a hundred different ways. But one of the most important aspects for me when it comes to my creativity is to be able to find myself feeling a sense of uncomfortable desire to write. Until that space opens up, I can't put pen to paper. There are long periods of inactivity. Then, something takes you there quickly, like a rush—it's a body chemistry thing for me. You are there, in that space of urgency, caught in the desire to make and pressure to do. Sometimes poems leach out of me like gushes of saliva. Then, I see the poem on the page, and it is kind of pornographic—excretions, bursts, explosions. It is an intense encounter.

**Annie Freud** is a poet, artist, editor, and teacher. She was born in 1948 and studied English and European Literature at the University of Warwick. A pamphlet, *A Voids Officer Achieves the Tree Pose* (Donut Press, 2006), was followed by her first full collection from Picador, *The Best Man That Ever Was* (2007), which was a Poetry Book Society Recommendation and received the Glen Dimplex New Writers' Award for Poetry. Her second collection, *The Mirabelles* (Picador 2010), was a Poetry Book Society Choice and was shortlisted for the T. S. Eliot Prize. In 2014 she was named as one of the Poetry Book Society's Next Generation Poets. She is renowned for her live performances. Her poem "The Jeweller" was highly commended by the judges of the Forward Prize for Poetry in 2016. In 2012, she curated a performance of her father Lucian Freud's favourite poems at the National Portrait Gallery.

# Cannupa Hanska Luger: On Art as Process

**Giovanni Aloi:** I still love teaching, but I have lost my faith in higher education. I don't trust the model, its exclusivity, the nonprofit status that disguises neoliberalist operations, the astronomical fees . . . the relentless commodification of knowledge.

**Cannupa Hanska Luger:** I hear you. I went to school at the Institute of American Indian Arts—it's a liberal arts college. But I did not go to grad school because it was too expensive. I considered it twice and every time I did, my wife got pregnant! So, it was like "OK, we are doing this instead, I guess . . ." After the second child came, I thought it was a good idea to never even think about grad school . . .

**GA:** Do you regret not going?

**CHL:** Not at all! I spared myself getting into debt. But not taking an MFA made it harder to access the institutional network. It took me years of hard work to make up for that. But none of it is a guarantee even when you go to grad school . . . Art school is like investing with next to no guarantees. There's only one game in town and the game is crooked. My way to resist the system was to craft my own idea of "art as process" that, in some way, allows me to circumnavigate the toxicity that academic and institutional powers have ingrained in the system.

**GA:** What advice would you give to an art student today?

**CHL:** Well, have you ever heard the saying, "Shoot for the stars, aim for the moon"?

**GA:** Yes . . .

**CHL:** Not being in graduate school slowed me down. It gave me time to develop my craft in a genuine way. My advice would be to aim low and give it everything you've got, put it all in regardless of how prestigious or not it might be.

Don't perform with the safety net. When you shoot for the stars but land on the moon, you'll be disappointed that the stars are still out of reach. That frame of mind will make you overlook the importance of your real accomplishments. Putting everything you've got into everything you'll do allows you to truly grow. This slow and committed process is more likely to keep you motivated to carry on even when things get hard. Lots of my peers from school have given up too early and that's just down to their frame of mind, not a lack of talent. Being an artist is about endurance. In our social media-driven world, everyone puts forward their best lives. Success and fame seem instant. Everyone wants everything quick but that's not how it works in this field.

**GA:** The real issue is with our mental framework, and this has been compromised by the benchmarks imposed by corporativism and capitalism. The whole system is structured around exclusivity and prestige. It does not account for the strange currencies that make up the creative journey. For instance, your big moment came out of the blue in the middle of the Standing Rock protest in 2016. I suspect that's something you could have not planned, or expected, correct?

**CHL:** Yes. That project was initially only disguised as art so that the shipment of shields could bypass the checking points around North Dakota. The police, the National Guard, and private security firms would assess what classed as a weapon or not. I made a video on how to build the shields using very basic and cheap materials like plywood and rope. My friend Rory put together a crew in Minneapolis and used the video as training material. I joined him and organized a workshop to teach people how to build the shields. Since it was likely that the authorities would have classified the shields as weapons, we passed them as art.

After the shields hit the news and it became known that they were artworks, museums started to contact me asking to purchase them as cultural artifacts. But I would not sell them any. I would instead invite them to make their own and use them in support of some political action in their area. I appreciated the interest, but I kept thinking, "Where were you when we needed you to help?"

**GA:** To me, that is incredibly brave. I have seen many artists being critical of institutions but suddenly selling out when the phone starts ringing . . . ultimately, your ethical positioning could potentially curtail your career. Is it important to you that your work should be in a museum collection?

**CHL:** I am playing a long game. I am not dying to get into the institutions. Being an Indigenous person in North America is a miracle; I mean it is a miracle that I exist at all. Having any of my works exhibited in a museum is beyond any imaginal possibility. But to me, museums are of no use in the development of culture. No matter how prestigious. It's part of their nature to be slow, to show work that is a few years old already. Museums are not on the pulse of things changing. Once my work enters the museum, it becomes part of the American canon, and the American canon is chock full of holes. Up until very recently, that canon was entirely white and male, and I am aware that the canon needs me to validate its very existence. In that context, my work inevitably ends up adding value to an exclusionary art history. Instead of thinking about my significance in the institutional space, I like to think about the insignificance of the institutional space with me in it.

**GA:** Is it possible to truly decolonize the museum?

**CHL:** No. I mean, the only way we have to decolonize the museum is to put all those bricks back into the earth. Museums put capital before community and the whole art world continues to follow exclusivist models even when it claims to be changing. The inclusion of BIPOC artists in museums is often instrumental to political agendas that have little to do with empowering them. I am more interested in relationships of generosity.

Born on the Standing Rock Reservation in North Dakota, New Mexico-based artist **Cannupa Hanska Luger** is an enrolled member of the Three Affiliated Tribes of Fort Berthold and is of Mandan, Hidatsa, Arikara, and Lakota heritage. Creating monumental installations, sculpture, and performance to communicate urgent stories about twenty-first-century Indigeneity, Luger incorporates ceramics, steel, fiber, video, and repurposed materials to activate speculative fiction, engage land-based actions of repair, and practice empathetic response through social collaboration.

# Anicka Yi: On the Laws of Impermanence

**Anicka Yi:** I have just returned from a ten-day Vipassana meditation retreat. Vipassana is an Indian-Buddhist traditional meditation technique. It is meant to provide a heightened sense of clarity. There were a hundred meditators—we could not speak, touch, or even glance at each other. No book reading, no writing. We had to agree to no lying, no killing, no sex. You live like a monk: one and a half meals a day; wake up at 4 a.m. and meditate until 9 p.m. It's a purification of the mind or, as they refer to it, you're doing a kind of self-surgery to pierce yourself at the deepest level, to really uncover the layers and layers of sludge and accumulated garbage that life deposits upon you over time.

The meditation process is quite straightforward. You close your eyes and focus on a sensation that comes through your body. You are meant to observe with equanimity and balance their fluctuations.

**Giovanni Aloi:** Interesting . . . and were you approached to go there, or did you inflict this upon yourself?

**AY:** Ha-ha! I was adamant to go. It's very competitive to get in, especially in some of the Hotspots in California, Southern California, where I went in the desert. Thousands of people apply each year.

**GA:** Meditation is so important to the creative mind. You are a trailblazer artist working at the intersection of art and science who engages through often radical approaches to aesthetics with bacteria, fungi, insects, tempura-fried flowers, and odors. I often talk to my students about you as an incredible success story, especially in the context of your utter unconventionality. So, how do you navigate the challenges involved in collaborating with institutions of all kinds?

**AY:** Yes, that's the difficult part of being an artist that does not get talked about very much. On the one hand, you have to be able to take risks, think out of the box, and push the boundaries of disciplines and institutions. On the other, you also have to be very pragmatic and insanely razor-sharp if you want to successfully bring those visions to fruition. If artists have a superpower, then that's the ability to live through uncertainty. Through all stages: inspiration, ideation communication, actualization—uncertainty is the baseline. One has to come to terms with the "laws of impermanence." That's also why the meditation retreat was important to me. There's nothing but infinite change, cascades of change, and I think that, as an artist dealing with institutions or any other kind of structure or systems, one has to learn to ride those waves of change and uncertainty. That has helped me tremendously, and if anything, that's where I draw a lot of strength from.

**GA:** I think that's a great piece of advice, especially since art schools do not prepare students to navigate institutions at all . . . the focus is all on finding your inner voice as an artist.

**AY:** I find that very problematic. The notion of the artist is romantic and still wildly popular in mainstream culture, and is attached to a fictitious conception of the autonomous self. The artist has a unique personality, the irreplicable individual—it's all fiction.

**GA:** I couldn't agree more. In this book, I discuss the artist myth as purely narcissistic, and I see around me how that archetype ruins people's lives. The myth of the artist is so ingrained in society that we often fail to recognize how deeply it permeates our thinking and sense of existence.

**AY:** Much of that, I believe, is down to the compartmentalization of knowledge that came with the Enlightenment. Indigenous epistemologies and Eastern philosophies have handled the production of knowledge differently, in different ways. The Western conception is highly individualistic, and it has been disastrous for our planetary survival and other humans, too.

**GA:** Yes, and that cultural matrix has fed into the capitalist/neoliberalist blueprint upon which our cultural institutions are founded. The mindset you have just described is relentlessly reinforced and perpetuated by cultural institutions that constantly claim to map free and revolutionary creative pathways. I find that baffling and problematic.

**AY:** One of the most important factors in life on this planet in a biological sense is mutation and evolution. If we don't evolve, we don't survive. Adaptability is another important skill that artists must master—the ability to shape shift, change, and let go. You can't get too comfortable even when you are successful. You have to be light on your feet, and you have to just keep moving. An artistic manifestation of this is a project I started in 2019 called *Metaspore:* based on nomadic research, it aims to bring together arts, science, and technology communities into conversation in order to create a shared social space and trust between disciplines.

**GA:** Through your practice, you are seriously expanding the conception of what art is and what it can do. I see in your work a model for the artist as agent of change, as a catalyst able to challenge and recontextualize well beyond the remit of the art world.

**AY:** Thank you. That means a lot. You know, sometimes a student comes up to me at the end of a lecture and says, "How did you do this? You didn't go to art school . . ." and I always respond, "You don't want to follow my path. It's not for the faint of heart. It's lonely. There's a reason why people go to school. On the one hand, they want to get a good education, but on the other, a school provides a pathway and access to a network. My path was hard. I had to carve it. It was excruciating. It was divergent at every turn. There was no real map. I think the one most valuable thing art schools do that I did not benefit from was being part of a community. So, I don't think I would be a good model for anybody else in that sense, but if I were to give a word of advice, I would tell students to ask themselves about the urgency of their message. Upon that hinges the very question of why you want to be an artist, what your role, your purpose is.

Informed by scientific research, biology, and perfumers, **Anicka Yi** has produced a unique body of work over the past decade at the intersection of politics and macrobiotics. Her practice questions the increasingly hazy taxonomic distinctions between what is human, animal, plant, and machine, and is the result of an alchemical process of experimentation that explores often incompatible materials. She collaborates with researchers to create media that are often inherently political, and delves into the cultural conditioning of sense and perception in a way she describes as a "biopolitics of the senses." Yi's work has been the subject of numerous solo exhibitions at institutions around the world.

# Derrick Woods-Morrow: On the Nature of Success

**Giovanni Aloi:** What does the label "artist" mean to you?

**Derrick Woods-Morrow:** Labels are always complicated. I think it was through grad school that I realized how important they can be to communities. Personally, I've always tried to evade labels, but capitalism is built on them, so, inevitably, they matter. The "artist" label is also very elusive. I clearly remember one time driving to work in Chicago and finding myself stuck in traffic on Lakeshore Drive. I thought I'd call my mom, and during the conversation she asked me, "How is work?" I started to tell her about the courses I was teaching and the students, but she stopped to say, "No, I mean *your work*: you're an artist! What about your work . . ." Well, that mattered to me. I guess that's when you can call yourself an artist, when your family and the people who care for you agree that you are one? There's also a ridiculous application called Limna that draws information about you from online data and uses it to produce a profile that charts your career as well as investment potential. It produces valuations of your work and charts your momentum. Maybe you're an artist when you are listed there? [laughs]. It's one of the scariest things I have ever seen. My profile claims that I am a mid-career, ultra-contemporary artist. What is mid-career? What is ultra-contemporary anyway? The fact that a website like that exists says a lot about the roles artists play in society today.

**GA:** How do you think that impacts artists?

**DWM:** Horribly—being an artist involves so much pressure and stress as it is. And so here we are . . . and our society founded upon a weird panopticism is now governed by algorhythms—social media and other websites, too, distort our perception of who we see and what they are seeing. It all far too easily becomes a performance for the algorhythm. We all post our achievements. The anxiety is inescapable, not just for those who watch but for the watcher, too. There's an urge to keep the game going, to support a steady rhythm of accomplishments.

**GA:** Do you think social media have helped your career?

**DWM:** Probably. But I think that going to parties half naked and getting drunk has worked much better. That's when I've run into curators and spoken to them about my work. That kind of sweaty nonsense generally has worked wonders for me.

**GA:** That's precious advice!
Do you feel that art school prepared you to be successful in the art world?

**DWM:** Well, yes and no . . . I think that art school might have given me a taste of the hypocrisy that I'd eventually encounter in the art world. For instance, during grad school it became obvious to me that my professors and peers had clear expectations of the kind of work I was meant to do based on my skin color and gender. To a certain degree, I would often perform to their expectations in order to fit in. This resulted in my work being liked. But I would not recommend anyone else do that. That kind of coercive pressure is awful, especially for minority and black artists. I eventually came around to focusing on my particular interests and finding success on my terms (I'm still working on that)—equally, I also expected art school to be much more welcoming and safer (rainbows and unicorns), but it wasn't that at all. If anything, I did have a few lovely advisors, and I learned how hard it would be to teach and lead a career as an artist that was immensely helpful. I tell my students that all the time.

**GA:** Well, I am glad that at least you had that kind of experience. Most professors at art school glide over the very important detail that teaching is their only or main source of income and that, without it, their work would not exist. I think we have a responsibility to talk to students about the financial complications inherent to their career choice.

**DWM:** Yes, there's a lack of clarity about that and it can be misleading. Many of my professors at art school were well-known "successful" artists but they still needed a teaching job to support themselves. There was rarely a conversation about the sustainability of their careers. I try to bring a different form of vulnerability to teaching at Rhode Island School of Design.

**GA:** Derrick, what is success?

**DWM:** Success is a very volatile notion. Sometimes I feel successful for a minute, and then not the next . But all in all, I have come to the conclusion that success is a kind of happiness. I am done for the most part with the "comparison game" or at least I try very hard not to compare myself to my peers and their achievements in a way that is destructive. Comparison over comparison, really always from here on out. It won't be perfect, and surely, I'll get jealous, but I think I have learned to choose me and be kind to myself and others.

**GA:** And how did you get there?

**DWM:** Well, I guess it took me a long while to learn to live with anxiety and then to renegotiate my ambition so that it might not break me. I know far too many people who burnt out really hard because they put too much into one project or invested too much into a fictitious idea of success. It's important to have a small number of people around you that you can rely on and who understand you. The world is so unkind otherwise. It is important to have some genuine support. I might seem successful in the eyes of other people, but I am still negotiating what success means to me in the context of the work that I'd like to make. I think I am getting there and that I am finding my way. But people might not like the work that might come out of it. We'll see how that goes, and I'll navigate it accordingly. But it all feels more authentic.

**Derrick Woods-Morrow** engages in process-oriented collaborative projects with Queer Black Fol(x) across a wide variety of media. His work has been presented across the United States including at the 2019 Whitney Biennial (in collaboration with Paul Mpagi Sepuya), the Modern Museum of Art, the Contemporary Art Center (New Orleans), the Museum of Contemporary Art Chicago and the Smart Museum (Chicago), and internationally, in Sweden, the Netherlands, and Berlin. Woods-Morrow is a member of the Chicago-based collective Concerned Black ImageMakers and serves on the Board of Directors of the Fire Island Artist Residency. He holds an MFA from the School of Art Institute of Chicago and completed a Post-Baccalaureate at the Massachusetts College of Art Design. He is a 2023 3arts Camargo Foundation Residency Recipient, 2022 Rhode Island Foundation MacColl Johnson Fellow, and 2021 Edith and Philip Leonian fellow at the Center of Photography Woodstock and is Assistant Professor of Sculpture, Painting & Textiles at the Rhode Island School of Design where he holds a Schiller Family Assistant Professorship in Race and Design. Originally from Greensboro, NC, he splits his time between Chicago and Rhode Island.

# Pamela Sneed: On Art as Poetry

**Giovanni Aloi:** You've had a stellar career—award-winning author, comedian, poet, painter . . . What does it mean to you to work in so many different media and fields?

**Pamela Sneed:** Well, there's something spiritual to it. Nature and the cosmos are filled with different creative dimensions all somehow linked to each other. That entwinement is natural, so you are a poet performing, an activist, an educator teaching through poetry, and so on . . . Poetry was my first medium. I don't believe in hierarchies of media. I started to write poetry when I was 8 or 9 years old. A few years back, I wrote an essay title, "It's All Poetry to Me." Poets and poetry are everywhere; they are the essence of things. Poetry is considered the finest accomplishment in creativity. People love to separate things and label, but it does not work that way.

My creative journey entailed studying art therapy and thirteen years ago I completed an MFA in new media art performance. When I finished that, I started to feel the urge to make things with my hands. So, I took on painting and drawing but they also feel like forms of poetry to me.

**GA:** Can you give us an example of how you bring different art forms together?

**PS:** Well, before the pandemic I was commissioned by Denison Hill to do a show. I could've done a poetry show, but I said no. I want to do a tribute to Big Mama Thornton and I wanted to expand to music and so on . . . It was postponed so many times because of Covid, so I ended up working on it for three years. It debuted at Denison Hill in Manhattan at Park Avenue, Armory, and we sold out a month in advance. We broke a record. I sang, and I wrote the whole set. The BBC interviewed me . . . I bring all my artforms together on the stage. In 2020, for Funeral Diva I started to paint all the men in my life that I lost. I am just as committed with watercolor as I am with words to recover the visibility of those who have been erased and reclaim visual histories.

**GA:** You have taken an MFA program as a student and also teach on one. Can you tell us about your experience in the art and education?

**PS:** Well, art schools are not easy places. My experience as a student was complicated because of jealousy from faculties . . . but I love learning and I am inquisitive, so I enjoyed the environment. I think I chose well—I wanted to study new media, art, and performance and the program put me in conversation with a lot of what was going on at the very cusp. That was really important.

**GA:** Do you recall when someone called you an artist for the first time? How did that feel?

**PS:** No. But I recall how chuffed I was when someone called me a *writer* for the first time. I was an undergrad at the New School, and Ann Barr Snitow, a famous feminist scholar, called me a writer after I read her some of my work. That was the first time and it felt good.

**GA:** Do you care to be called an artist?

**PS:** Yes and no . . . maybe it mattered more when I was younger? Growing up queer, coming out at 19. Some labels matter because they help you nurture a sense of cultural and social place, a kind of belonging. But I am not that keen on it now. My identity does not depend on it. Maybe it is so ingrained in my DNA that I don't have to say it anymore. In "America Ain't Ready," I say, "The real freedom will come when these terms don't make or break us." Labels of all kinds box us. Lesbian: does it mean that I am always going to be attracted to women? I think at my age labels begin to feel confining.

**GA:** You have worked in so many different fields. What advice would you give to someone who would like to follow in your footsteps?

**PS:** Follow your instincts. Stick to it and don't believe in the idea that you should wait to be discovered. Make yourself visible. Take risks. I see that a lot with the young people I work with. They don't take risks. Be vulnerable but go wild. Go for it. Get to know yourself and take responsibility but go for it, 100 percent.

**GA:** With all that you do, how do you manage your creativity?

**PS:** I'm a night owl. Unless I am working on a deadline, I am pretty free-flowing. When I paint, I always write—I process things. But I work every day. I stay up till 3 or 4 in the morning. I love it because everyone is asleep and it can be me time, uninterrupted. That's very important. It's precious.

**GA:** It's my impression that art schools do not prepare students to handle the emotional toll of a creative career. How have you learned to negotiate the highs and lows of your creative journey?

**PS:** I have always tried to be as self-sufficient as possible. I like to preserve my integrity and it takes time and effort to do that. So doing what I do is about survival. Now it's starting to pay off, but my journey has been long. My creativity is everything; it's what gives me joy. The process is what helps me to be alive. I need to do it. It's compulsive. I had a pretty difficult life and the thing that has kept me here is writing, poetry, painting—art.

**Pamela Sneed** is an American poet, performance artist, actress, activist, and teacher. Her book, *Funeral Diva*, is a memoir in poetry and prose about growing up during the AIDS crisis, and the winner of the 2021 Lambda Literary Award for lesbian poetry. Sneed earned a Bachelor of Arts degree from Lang College at The New School and a Masters of Fine Arts degree in New Media Art and Performance in 2008 at Long Island University.

# Frances Whitehead: On Following Meaningfulness

**Giovanni Aloi:** Yesterday, I interviewed Vivien Sansour and she mentioned the idea of the art world uniform, you know, that existentialist posturing that requires people to wear black . . .

**Frances Whitehead:** Well, you know where that came from, right? Ad Reinhardt wearing those black turtlenecks and his black paintings . . . We used to joke that the colors of the School of the Art Institute of Chicago (SAIC) were black and black . . . But these clichés became even more obsolete as I moved away from being a gallery artist and into public and environmental practice. I realized that what I wanted to do was not commerce but *meaningfulness.* I began to follow meaning instead of making objects. The world does not need more objects. Everyone's got stuff coming out of their ears.

**GA:** Is there a specific event that triggered that realization? Or was it just this kind of sum of events that led you to decide that the gallery space, the institutional domain, was not where you want it to be anymore?

**FW:** It was psychological. I went through a major crisis in my 40s. I woke up one day and nothing made sense any longer. I was living with a partner I had no business living with who would never understand me. I was living an obscured life, hiding from myself and my true ambitions. I was performing someone else's life. That was my career. That was my private life, that was everything. And it threw me into a clinical depression. I was in that for about a year and a half. When I came out of it, I just couldn't pick up where I left off. What I had done before was no longer my work. At that point, I turned to the garden as a laboratory, and what I learned from it was "complexity." The garden taught me how to become a system thinker. Ecological awareness allowed me to see the interconnectedness of everything. This was a significant shift in my worldview because it challenged my own art historical position, which was driven by conceptualism, not materiality.

**GA:** What you describe sounds like the beginning of the type of thinking that is finally gaining traction today?

**FW:** Yes, it is—it was the end of a hundred years of art talking to itself about itself.

**GA:** Does it still make sense to call someone an artist?

**FW:** It's become a form of branding. Over time, I have realized that I am participating in a kind of reverse engineering of the Enlightenment because that specialization has disconnected everything. It is dis-integrative. Artists operate laterally. We are able to connect Ariadne's thread, moving through disconnected systems and epistemes of other disciplines. Artists can do that because we are trained in seeing patterns and systems of recognition, making the invisible, seeing the invisible—to find the question that has been obscured by the answer. Artists are disruptive and connective.

**GA:** Do you think art schools prepare students to become the type of artist you are describing?

**FW:** No. I tried more than once to start new, experimental programs along these lines, but the institution always obstructed them in the end.

**GA:** Why is there so much resistance toward this type of change? That's also why I decided to write this book, because the conversation at SAIC could not even start . . .

**FW:** A lot of what I do involves taking risks, and the capitalist format that art schools have adopted entails the opposite. Students have been rendered passive by a system that never truly challenges them. So, there is no more risk of a real revolution. They are no longer real critical thinkers. The school is too afraid to be sued to take risks. Teaching has become a service they buy and as a result students do not absorb by osmosis, by experience. It's a different transaction and it has become monodimensional and thin.

But the art world is also self-absorbed with its categories and currencies. For instance, in 2012, I was appointed Lead Artist for "The 606" redevelopment project in Chicago—an elevated greenway built over an abandoned rail line. It was a massive project with a $100 million budget, and it took four years to complete. It was incredibly complex, but we pulled it off, and it is such a success. But I don't think that massive undertaking, which has made a major difference to the city of Chicago and its people, has won me any credit in the art world. It's just not what it cares about.

**GA:** That must have been a difficult situation . . . I mean to work with the municipality, the architects, the lawyers. It is hard enough to exhibit in a museum. What did that experience mean to you?

**FW:** I came out a different person than I went in. It was a steep learning curve on so many levels. Economies, negotiations, communications, contractors. I had to learn the lingo of "civic speak." It was extremely stressful, but it was life-changing. These practice ideas—civic art practice, the artist urbanist, the embedded artist, the public artist—are something I've been working with for a long time, and I was finally able to enact these ideas fully. There's also a question of duration in this positioning of the artist that is very important: the understanding that processes have their own time frames and durationality. This kind of engagement and this way to conceive of the artist is an opportunity to open up another art world, one that is bigger and more permeable. But that's not what art schools are interested in. At stake is the prestige of the institution and its positioning in the market, or so "management" believes. That comes first. And that's a really big problem.

**Frances Whitehead** is a civic practice artist bringing the methods, mindsets, and strategies of contemporary art practice to the process of shaping the future. Connecting emerging art practices to discourses of sustainability, heritage, just-transition, and remediation, she works as a Public Artist, expanding the role of artists in society and within multiple ecologies, asking, *What do Artists Know?* Whitehead has worked professionally as an artist since the early 1980s and has worked collaboratively as ARTetal Studio since 2001. She is Professor Emerit of Sculpture at the School of the Art Institute of Chicago.

# Cecilia Vicuña: On a World of Precarity

**Cecilia Vicuña:** Could you just hold on a second? I have olive on my hands—I need to wash them.

**Giovanni Aloi:** Olive oil?

**CV:** Yes, I love olive oil.

**GA:** My parents are from the south of Italy, so olive trees are pretty iconic in my personal mythology.

**CV:** Where from in the south of Italy?

**GA:** Calabria.

**CV:** My grandfather in Chile grew many olive trees and made olive oil, so this tree is also very special to me. They have so much character.

**GA:** Yes! My parents moved to Milan in the 1960s looking for work. I would spend school time in Milan and summer in the south. The contrast was so stark—Milan was so grey while the south brimmed with animal and plant life. Returning to city living was traumatic.

**CV:** I knew there had to be something to why you are interested in my work!

**GA:** Yes, I am very fond of your work, and your *Sidewalk Forests*, especially. Like you, I was looking for nature everywhere, and to my surprise, I was able to find it in places nobody thought it might be. I found frogs, fish, and newts in a canal close to my home that everyone thought was dead because of pollution. It became my secret world. One just had to look.

**CV:** I've had a similar experience. I was born in the south part of the valley in Santiago and then I moved to the mountain foothills. I was surrounded by nature. But New York was a different environment altogether. I looked very hard for nature. That's where the *Sidewalk Forests* came from. There's something special about children, you see. They are more readily connected to nature and a lot of what Western society has done well is to sever that connection. This, in turn, prevents humans from being humans. So, good advice from me to all art students is to keep that connection and knowledge alive. It's a form of resistance. Media communication and social media especially distort our perception and reduce our attention span. They alienate. To retain that wild element, one has to practice meditation. I find wilderness by laying on the floor to attune myself to the planet. It is mostly a practice of listening to many dimensions at once. First listening to your body and then opening up to the world.

Everything in the universe is telepathically connected and being connected is what enables a deep sense of serenity to emerge. I would recommend that exercise to anyone but most especially art students.

**GA:** It would be interesting to implement that meditative exercise at the beginning of classes. Students rush in from chaotic environments and they find it hard to focus or feel grounded in the practice and learning. Art school can be a bit like a mall where one moves from class to class as from one shop to another.

**CV:** Yes, I think art schools trap students in many ways. Telling them there's someone who knows best. Make them fearful and needy of others' validation and approval.

That can be terribly destructive for young artists especially. I see that when I am invited to art schools to do studio visits. You can see the suffering. How hard it is for them to be themselves or find themselves in that structure.

Let me read you something I wrote in 1973 for my exhibition at the ICA:

The real explanations of my paintings are lost in Santiago.

I regard my act of painting as a ritual. Any object that this activity produces exists beyond art history. As if art history was already dead, or it could have never existed. In my paintings, I need every form to irritate, disgust, or disturb. They issue from a convulsed state in which images elicit forms moving as propellers for their way out. What are those images I yearn to capture in a poem? A painting, a conversation, or a concept?

This relationship to your own work as an unknown is very important, and it is a relationship of total respect. The relationship with the wilderness of your imagination is infinite, like the cosmos may be infinite. We're really cosmic creatures, and that means that our imagination and our sensations, our emotions are wild and we, as conscious people, become observers and caretakers, gardeners in that wilderness. For example, if you look at Indigenous cultures, and if you look closely, it becomes visible that taking care of the wilderness means gardening. We now know that the Amazon rainforest is not the result of an absence but of a 10,000-year-long, close interaction with Indigenous people. And this applies to practically every forest in the world. There is intense co-creativity that exists between our images, lines, drawings, or whatever medium we choose to work in. This is true of every art.

So, I'm an old person. I'm 75 years old, and this relationship of amazement and awareness is just as alive in my mind as when I was 4 years old. I consider this a true mastery. To resist the forces that incessantly push you onto the pre-encoded professional tracks that people in the art world want you to be on. That's one of the dangers especially if in their eyes you are a failure—and I was a failure for most of my life—and I am thankful for that because it allowed me to find some freedom. But if I had. I did not abandon my state of failure to follow a pre-encoded success formula. Mastery is always relative. The process is uncomfortable and it makes you afraid but mastery entails staying with that instead of pleasing others.

**GA:** What you say is so meaningful to me. One of the aspects that I am interested in the most about your work is the idea of precarity and how it plays in your positioning of yourself as an artist as well as your work. I think art students are not prepared to contemplate that as a perpetual state of their existence, also because institutions have removed the word "failure" from our exchanges. It has pretty much become taboo.

**CV:** I guess my expectation was the opposite of the expectation of young artists. I did not expect or seek success. I wanted to practice freedom. I think that's integrity. We talk a lot about colonialism today, but colonialism is not just what the West did to South America, Africa, or Asia; it is also this alienation from the natural world that every child is subjected to. My defense from this was to observe and bond with nature and culture, to observe carefully but not to categorize. That's where the concept of "precarious" or *basurita* emerged. They are assemblages of fragile, ephemeral, rough, and playful objects I collected from the beach. The concept of "precariousness" is intrinsic to the way the world, not the work of art, is. Everything is in transformation, and without the concept of the precarious we cannot be human because we are the most precarious creatures. We are so fragile, but that's our strength.

**Cecilia Vicuña** was born in 1948 and raised in Santiago, Chile. A visual artist and a poet, she began painting at an early age, and her first poems appeared in a bilingual quarterly out of Mexico City in 1967. She studied art at the Universidad de Chile from 1966 to 1971, and in 1972 she moved to London to pursue postgraduate studies at the Slade School of Fine Arts.

# List of Illustrations

# Notes

1. Saar, Betye (2021) "How I became an artist: Betye Saar," interview with Janelle Zara, in *Art Basel, Stories* online https://www.artbasel.com/stories/betye-saar-interview-ica-miami

2. Ruggenberg, Luke (2020) *Plants are Terrible People* (independently published) p. 15.


## Introduction

1. Good, K. (2017) *Elephant Artists? Here's Why Making an Elephant Paint is Cruel, Not Cute*. One Green Planet, July 23. https://www.onegreenplanet.org/animalsandnature/why-making-an-elephant-paint-is-cruel-not-cute/

2. Desmond, Adrian, Charles Darwin, and James Moore (2017) *The Descent of Man* (London: Penguin).

3. Adams, Laurie Schneider (2009) *The Methodologies of Art: An Introduction* (2nd ed.; London: Routledge) p. 9.

4. Adams, *The Methodologies of Art*, p. 9.

5. "Every morning the *Scenopoetes dentirostris* [or stagemaker bowerbird], a bird of the Australian rain forest, cuts leaves, makes them fall to the ground, and turns them over so that the paler, internal side contrasts with the earth. In this way it constructs a stage for itself like a ready-made; and directly above, on a creeper or a branch, while fluffing out the feathers beneath its beak to reveal their yellow roots, it sings a complex song made up from its own notes and, at intervals, those of other birds that it imitates: it is a complete artist." From Deleuze and Guattari, *What is Philosophy?*, p. 184.

6. Jarman, Derek (1996) *Derek Jarman's Garden* (New York: Overlook Books).

7. For an argumentation of the philosophical currents that have devalued animal intelligence see: Andrews, Kristin, and Jacob Beck, eds. (2017) *The Routledge Handbook of Philosophy of Animal Minds* (New York: Routledge); Carruthers, Peter (2019) *Human and Animal Minds: The Consciousness Questions Laid to Rest* (Oxford: Oxford University Press); Cavalieri, Paola, and Peter Singer (1993) *The Great Ape Project: Equality Beyond Humanity* (London: Fourth Estate).

8. Bazin, André (1960) "The Ontology of the Photographic Image" *Film Quarterly* 13(4): 4–9.

9. Grant, Catherine, and Dorothy Price (2020) "Decolonizing Art History" *Art History* 43(1): 8–66.

10. Enwezor, Okwui (2007) "The Production of Social Space as Artwork" in Blake Stimson and Gregory Sholette (eds.), *Collectivism after Modernism: The Art of Social Imagination after 1945* (Minneapolis: University of Minnesota Press) pp. 223–51; quote on p. 225.

11. Solomon, T. (2023). *The Year in Activism: Israel-Palestine Shatters Art World Consensus*. ARTnews.com, December 21. https://www.artnews.com/art-news/news/2023-activism-israel-palestine-shatters-art-world-consensus-1234690406/

12. Jung, Carl G., and R. A. Segal (1998) *Jung on Mythology* (Princeton: Princeton University Press).

13. Jung, Carl G. (1991) *The Archetypes and the Collective Unconscious* (London: Routledge) p. 5.

14. Jung, Carl G., G. Adler, and R. F. C. Hull (1971) *The Spirit in Man, Art, & Literature* (Princeton: Princeton University Press).

15. Gaensheimer, Susanne, Isabelle Malz, Catherine Nichols, Eugen Blume, and Kunstsammlung Nordrhein-Westfalen (2021) *Everyone Is an Artist—Cosmopolitical Exercises with Joseph Beuys: [Exhibition, Düsseldorf, Kunstsammlung Nordrhein-Westfalen, March 27 - August 15, 2021]* (Düsseldorf: Kunstsammlung Nordrhein-Westfalen; Berlin).

16. Heartfield, John, and George Grosz (1920) "Der Kunstlump" *Der Gegner* 1(10–12): 48–56, translated and reprinted in Kaes, A., M. Jay, and E. Dimendberg (1995) *The Weimar Republic Sourcebook* (Berkeley: University of California Press) p. 485.

17. Mbembe, Achille (2021) *Out of the Dark Night* (Amsterdam: Amsterdam University Press).

18. Lokko, Lesley (2023) "The Laboratory of the Future: Agents of Change" *18th Venice Biennale of Architecture* 2023. https://www.labiennale.org/en/architecture/2023/introduction-lesley-lokko

19. Fraser, Andrea (2005) "From the Critique of Institution to an Institution of Critique" in *Art Forum* (September) pp. 100–6.

20. Elkins, J. (2001) *Why Art Cannot be Taught: A Handbook for Art Students* (Urbana: University Of Illinois Press).

21. Seltzer, R. (2023) "Why So Many Independent Art Colleges are Shutting Their Doors." *The Observer*, September 11. https://observer.com/2023/09/independent-art-colleges-closing/

22. Sandford, Mariellen (2003) *Happenings and Other Acts* (London: Routledge) p. 288.

23. Among others: Aloi, Giovanni (2011) *Art & Animals* (London: I.B. Tauris); (2018) *Speculative Taxidermy* (New York: Columbia University Press); (2019) *Why Look at Plants?* (Leiden: Brill); coedited with Susan McHugh (2021) *Posthumanism in Art and Science* (New York: Columbia University Press).

24. Haraway, Donna (2016) *Staying with the Trouble: Making Kin in the Chthulucene* (Durham, NC: Duke University Press); hooks, bell (1995) *Art on My Mind: Visual Politics* (New York: New Press); Ghosh, Amitav (2017) *The Great Derangement: Climate Change and the Unthinkable* (Chicago: University Of Chicago Press); Kimmerer, Robin Wall (2013) *Braiding Sweetgrass: Indigenous Wisdom, Scientific Knowledge and the Teachings of Plants* (Minneapolis: Milkweed Editions); Shiva, Vandana (2016) *Staying Alive: Women, Ecology, and Development* (Berkeley: North Atlantic Books); Morton, Timothy (2012) *The Ecological Thought* (Cambridge, MA, and London: Harvard University Press).

25. Guattari, Félix (1995) *Chaosmosis: An Ethico-Aesthetic Paradigm* (Sydney: Power) pp. 119–20.

26. Morton, *The Ecological Thought*, p. 7.

27. This "alternative art history" is in part inspired by the now often overlooked and underrated social art history of Arnold Hauser. Hauser, Arnold (1951) *Social History of Art* (New York: Vintage).

## 1 Becoming Artist: Constraints and Freedom

1. Dawson, Raymond (2000) *The Chinese Experience* (London: Orion).

2. Pei, Fang Jing (1997) *Treasures of the Chinese Scholar* (Toronto: Weatherhill) p. 6.

3. Bush, Susan (2012) *The Chinese Literati on Painting: Su Shih (1037–1101) to Tung Ch'i-ch'ang (1555–1636)* (Hong Kong: Hong Kong University Press) p. 10; Jenyns, Soame (1996) *A Background to Chinese Painting* (New York: Schocken Books) p. 134.

4. Bush, *The Chinese Literati on Painting*, pp. 13–15.

5. Elman, Benjamin (2002) *A Cultural History of Civil Examinations in Late Imperial China* (Berkeley: University of California Press) pp. 405–6.

6. The word comes from the Portuguese *mandarin* and Malay *Mantri,* a counselor or minister of state; the ultimate origin of the word is the Sanskrit root *man-*, meaning "to think." Britannica, The Editors of Encyclopaedia (2010). "Mandarin." *Encyclopedia Britannica*, August 30. https://www.britannica.com/topic/mandarin

7. Weidner, M. S. (1988) *Views From Jade Terrace: Chinese Women Artists 1300–1912* (New York and Milan: Rizzoli) p. 13.

8. Bose, M. B. (2018) *Women, Gender and Art in Asia, c. 1500–1900* (London: Routledge); Weidner, Marsha, ed., (1991) *Flowering in the Shadows: Women in the History of Chinese and Japanese Painting (English, Chinese and Japanese Edition)* (Honolulu: University of Hawai'i Press) p. 11.

9. Yü, Chienhua (1981) *Chungkuo meishuchia jenming tz'utien* (Biographical dictionary of Chinese artists) (Shanghai: Jenmin meishu ch'u pan she); Morris, Rossab (1986) "Kuan Tao Sheng: Women Artist in Yuan China" *Bulletin of Sung and Yuan Studies, No. 2*, pp. 67–84.

10. Weidner, *Views From Jade Terrace*, p. 67; a concise history detailing the careers of more Chinese female artists is featured in Marsha Weidner's essay "Women in the History of Chinese Painting" included in Weidner, *Views from Jade Terrace*, pp. 13–29.

11. Martin, Therese, ed. (2012) *Reassessing the Roles of Women as 'Makers' of Medieval Art and Architecture* (Leiden: Brill) pp. 5–7.

12. Zhang Yanyuan (Tang Dynasty) 1992 *Li Dai Ming Hua Ji* (A Record of the Famous Paintings of All the Dynasties) (Shanghai: Han Fen Lou).

13. Vasari, Giorgio, Peter Bondanella, and Julia Conway (2008) *The Lives of the Artists (Oxford World's Classics)* (Oxford: Oxford University Press) 1550

14. Ragg, Laura Maria (1907) *The Women Artists of Bologna* (London: Methuen) pp. 170–1.

15. Shiner, L. E. (2001) *The Invention of Art: A Cultural History* (Chicago: University of Chicago Press).

16. Cennino, Cennini (1400) *Il Libro dell'Arte, o Trattato della Pittura di Cennino Cennini da Colle di Valdelsa; di nuovo pubblicato, con molte correzioni e coll'aggiunta di più capitoli, tratti dai codici fiorentini, per cura di Milanesi, Gaetano e Milanesi, Carlo* (Florence: Felice Le Monnier Editore) 1859

17. Cennino, *Il Libro dell'Arte*.

18. Vasari et al., *The Lives of the Artistis*.

19. Alighieri, Dante, D. M. Black, and Robert Harrison (2021) *Purgatorio* (New York: NYRB Classics) p. 134.

20. MacCullogh, John (1908) "Hastings, James; Selbie, John Alexander; & Gray, Louis Herbert" *Encyclopaedia of Religion and Ethics* (Edinburgh: T. & T. Clark) vol. 11, p. 445.

21. Maddox, John Lee, and Albert Galloway Keller (2010) *The Medicine Man: A Sociological Study of the Character and Evolution of Shamanism* (Whitefish, MT: Kessinger Publishing).

22. Adam, Leonhard (1940) *Primitive Art* (London: Penguin Books).

23. Wardwell, Allen (2009) *Tangible Visions: Northwest Coast Indian Shamanism and Its Art* (New York: The Monacelli Press).

24. Wardwell, *Tangible Visions*, p. 20. In the late 1980s, a PBS TV series by Professor Joseph Campbell titled *The Power of Myth* went so far as to claim that shamanism links all artists across time and that contemporary artists are descendants of shamans. Campbell, Joseph (1988) *The Power of Myth* [TV series] PBS.

25. Plato (1964) *The Works of Plato*, trans. B. Jowett (Oxford: Clarendon Press) *Rep.* X, p. 598.

26. In this context, it is important to remember that, as argued by Jeremy Tanner in 1999, "Recent contributions to the debate on the role, status, and autonomy of the artist in Greece remain polarised in terms which have remained largely unchanged for a century. On one side, we find 'modernisers' who hold that the role of the function of art and the social structure of the Greek art world was more similar to the modem western art world than different. On the other side are ranged the 'primitivists' who argue that modern conceptions of artistic autonomy and creativity are an anachronistic imposition on ancient Greek art, which was a largely anonymous craft, performing traditional functions and oriented to the reproduction of traditional artistic forms rather than the individualistic innovation held to be characteristic of western European art since the Renaissance. The modernisers look back to Winckelmann's neo-classical view of the Greek artist as free and autonomous creator, whilst the primitivists ultimately draw their inspiration from Jacob Burckhardt's alternative account of the Greek artist as a mechanical craftsman or banausos." Tanner, Jeremy (1999) "Culture, Social Structure and the Status of Visual Artists in Classical Greece" *Proceedings of the Cambridge Philological Society* no. 45, pp. 136–75.

27. Benedictow, Ole Jørgen (2021) *Black Death 1346–1353 The Complete History* (Woodbridge: Boydell Press).

28. Hinds, Kathryn (2009) *Everyday Life in the Renaissance* (New York: Marshall Cavendish Benchmark) pp. 94–5.

29. Kemp, Martin (2011) *Leonardo: Revised Edition* (Oxford: Oxford University Press).

30. Burke, Peter (1994) "Italian Artist and His Role" in Peter Burke, Ellen Bianchini, and Claire Dorey (eds.), *History of Italian Art, Volume I* (Cambridge: Polity Press) pp. 1–28.

31. Vasari et al., *The Lives of the Artists*.

32. Dean, Trevor, and Kate Lowe, eds. (1994) *Crime, Society and the Law in Renaissance Italy* (Cambridge: Cambridge University Press).

33. Barker, Sheila, ed. (2016) *Women Artists in Early Modern Italy: Careers, Fame, and Collectors* (Turnhout: Brepols).

34. Barker, Emma, Nick Webb, and Kim Woods, eds. (1999) *The Changing Status of the Artist* (New Haven: Yale University Press).

35. Kempers, Bram (1992) *Painting, Power and Patronage: The Rise of the Professional Artist in the Italian Renaissance* (London: Allen Lane).

36. Beltramme, Marcello (1990) "Le teoriche del Paleotti e il riformismo dell'Accademia di San Luca nella politica artistica di Clemente VIII, 1592–1605" *Storia dell'arte* 69, pp. 201–33.

37. Koerner, Leo J. (2008) *The Reformation of the Image* (Chicago: University of Chicago Press).

38. Wietse de Boer(2021). *Art in Dispute* (Leiden: Brill).

39. Stunkel, Kenneth R. (2011) *Ideas and Art in Asian Civilizations: India, China, and Japan* (London and New York: Routledge) pp. 92–3.

40. Tsuda, Noritake, and Patricia Graham (2009) *A History of Japanese Art: From Prehistory to the Taisho Period* (Clarendon: Tuttle Publishing) p. 200.

41. Seyller, John (1999) "Workshop and Patron in Mughal India: The Freer Rāmāyaṇa and Other Illustrated Manuscripts of 'Abd al-Raḥīm" *Artibus Asiae. Supplementum* 42: 3–344.

42. Tazi, Abdelhadi (1980) *Eleven Centuries in the History of Al-Qarawiyyin University On Occasion of the Campaign for Saving and Repairing the Fes City* (Fes: Ministry of Information).

43. Bonafede, Carolina (1845) *Cenni biografici e ritratti d'insigni donne bolognesi: raccolti dagli storici più accreditati* (1977) (Bologna: Atesa Editrici) p. 11.

44. Chadwick, Whitney (1990) *Women, Art, and Society* (New York and London: Thames & Hudson) p. 28.

45. Berg, Gary A. (2019) *The Rise of Women in Higher Education: How, Why, and What's Next* (Lanham, MD: Rowman & Littlefield).

46. Nochlin, Linda (1971) "Why Have There Been No Great Women Artists" in Vivian Gornick and BarbaraMoran (eds.), *Woman in Sexist Society: Studies in Power and Powerlessness* (New York: Basic Books).

47. André Félibien quoted in Paul Duro (2007) "Imitation and Authority: The Creation of the Academic Canon in French Art 1648–1870," in Anna Brzysky (ed.0, *Partisan Canons* (Durham, NC: Duke University Press) pp. 95–113; quote on p. 96.

48. Yi, Song Mi (2000) "Sin Saimdang: The Foremost Woman Painter of the Choson Dynasty" *Oriental Art* 46(1).

49. Borzello, Francis (2000) *A World of Our Own: Women as Artists Since the Renaissance* (New York: Watson-Guptill Publications) p. 55.

50. Gombrich, E. H. (1950) *The Story of Art* (London: Phaidon).

51. Gipson, Ferren (2022) *Women's Work: From Feminine Arts to Feminist Art* (London: Frances Lincoln); Hessel, Katy (2022) *The Story of Art without Men* (New York: W. W. Norton & Co.); Chadwick, Whitney (2020) *Women, Art, and Society* (London: Thames & Hudson); McCormack, Catherine (2021) *Women in the Picture Women, Art and the Power of Looking* (London: Icon Books).

52. Bennett, Tony (1995) *The Birth of the Museum: History, Theory, Politics* (London: Routledge).

53. Gardner, Victoria C., and Jon L. Seydl (2007) *Antiquity Recovered: The Legacy of Pompeii and Herculaneum* (Los Angeles: J. Paul Getty Museum).


## 2  The Modern Artist: A Rebel Without a Cause?

1. Brown, Christopher Lesley, Jan Kelch, and Pieter Van Thiel (1991) *Rembrandt: The Master and His Workshop: Paintings* (New Haven: Yale University Press).

2. Baxandall, Michael (1988) *Painting and Experience in Fifteenth-Century Italy: A Primer in the Social History of Pictorial Style* (Oxford: Oxford University Press).

3. Links, J. G. (1983) *Canaletto and His Patrons* (New York: Hacker Art Books) p. 21.

4. Van Slujter, Eric (2009) *Art Market and Connoisseurship: A Closer Look at Paintings by Rembrandt, Rubens and Their Contemporaries* (Amsterdam: Amsterdam University Press) p. 14.

5. It is important to note that Géricault was ordered by the organizers of the Salon to change the title of his painting to *Scéne de Naufrage* in order to avoid any direct reference to the shipwreck of the *Medusa*.

6. Alhadeff, Albert (2002) *The Raft of the Medusa: Géricault, Art and Race* (New York: Prestel).

7. Riding, Christine (2003) "The Fatal Raft: Christine Riding Looks at British Reaction to the French Tragedy at Sea Immortalised in Gericault's Masterpiece 'The Raft of the Medusa'" *History Today*, February.

8. Hamilton, James (2008) *London Lights: The Minds that Moved the City That Shook the World* (London: John Murray) p. 179.

9. Snell, Robert (2016) *Portraits of the Insane: Theodore Géricault and the Subject of Psychotherapy* (London: Routledge).

10. Brylowe, Thora (2019) *Romantic Art in Practice : Cultural Work and the Sister Arts, 1760–1820* (Cambridge: Cambridge University Press).

11. Hirsch, Robert (2017) *Seizing the Light: A Social & Aesthetic History of Photography* (3rd ed; London: Routledge).

12. Sturgis, Alexander (2006) *Rebels and Martyrs: The Image of the Artist in the Nineteenth Century* (New Haven: Yale University Press; London: The National Gallery) p. 96.

13. Boime, A. (2008) *Art in an Age of Civil Struggle, 1848–1871* (Chicago: University of Chicago Press) p. 170.

14. Courbet, Gustave and Petra ten-Doesschate Chu (1992) *Letters of Gustave Courbet* (Chicago: University of Chicago Press).

15. Courbet and Chu, *Letters of Gustave Courbet*, p. 58.

16. Milza, Pierre (2009) *L'année terrible – La Commune* (Paris: Perrin) pp. 296–7.

17. Mainardi, Patricia (1991) "Courbet's Exhibitionism" *Gazette des Beaux-Arts* no. 118, pp. 256–65.

18. Paradoxically, later in life, as his art lost political bite, Courbet became a true political activist. By 1870, he had finally become deeply involved in the Paris Commune; he was arrested and briefly imprisoned following the disastrous end of this short-lived political movement. Upon his release, he fled to Switzerland in self-imposed exile to avoid the enormous fines imposed upon him by the French government.

19. Mainardi, "Courbet's Exhibitionism," pp. 256–65.

20. Baudelaire, Charles (1846) "The Salon of 1846: On the Heroism of Modern Life" in Francis Frascina and Charles Harrison (eds.), *Modern Art and Modernism: A Critical Anthology* (London: Routledge) 1982.

21. Meneglier, Hervé (1990) *Paris impérial: La vie quotidienne sous le Second Empire* (Paris: Armand Colin) p. 173.

22. Hewitt, Catherine (2020) *Art Is a Tyrant: The Unconventional Life of Rosa Bonheur* (London: Icon Books).

23. Gross, Daniel A., and Karen Chernick (2018) "160 Years before the Frida Kahlo Barbie, a Rosa Bonheur Doll Celebrated a Queer Woman Painter." *Hyperallergic*, March 22. https://hyperallergic.com/433726/frida-kahlo-barbie-rosa-bonheur-doll/

24. Sciolino, Elaine (2022) "Rich, Famous and Then Forgotten: The Art of Rosa Bonheur." *The New York Times*, October 17, sec. Arts. https://www.nytimes.com/2022/10/17/arts/design/rosa-bonheur.html

25. Hewitt, *Art Is a Tyrant*.

26. Baudelaire, Charles (1964) *The Painter of Modern Life*. New York: Da Capo Press. Originally published, in French, in *Le Figaro*, 1863.

27. Baudelaire, *The Painter of Modern Life*.

28. Clark, T. J. (1999) *The Painting of Modern Life: Paris in the Art of Manet and his Followers* (Princeton: Princeton University Press) p. 82.

29. Pollock, Griselda (1994) "Modernity and the space of femininity" in *Vision & Difference: Feminity, Feminism, and the Histories of Art* (London: Routledge) pp. 50–90.

30. Roe, Sue (2007) *The Private Lives of the Impressionists* (New York: Harper Perennial).

31. Tinterow, Gary, and Henri Loyrette (1994) *Origins of Impressionism* (New York: Harry N. Abrams).

32. Zarobell, J. (2015) "Paul Durand-Ruel and the market for modern art, 1870–1873" in Sylvie Patry (ed.), *Inventing Impressionism: Paul Durand-Ruel and the Modern Art Market*, (London: National Gallery), 76–97.

33. Zarobell, "Paul Durand-Ruel and the market for modern art, 1870–1873," pp. 76–97.

34. Wolff, Albert (1876) quoted in Francis Haskell (1987) *Past and Present in Art and Taste: Selected Essays* (New Haven: Yale University Press) p. 207.

35. Bennett, Jackie (2019) *The Artist's Garden* (New York: White Lion Publishing).

## 3 Modern Ecologies: Markets, Marketeers, and Alliances


1. Kift, Dagmar (1996) *The Victorian Music Hall: Culture, Class and Conflict* (Cambridge: Cambridge University Press).
2. Baudelaire, Charles (1859) *On Photography*, in *The Salon of 1859* (New York: Doubleday Anchor Books) p. 232.
3. Baudelaire, "The Salon of 1846," p. 18.
4. Benjamin, Walter (2006) *The Writer of Modern Life: Essays on Charles Baudelaire* (Cambridge, MA: Harvard University Press) pp. 61–6.
5. Montias, John Michael (1988) "Art Dealers in the Seventeenth-Century Netherlands" *Simiolus: Netherlands Quarterly for the History of Art* 18(4): 244–56.
6. Weill, Berth, et al., (2022) *Pow! Right in the Eye! Thirty Years behind the Scenes of Modern French Painting* (Chicago: University of Chicago Press).
7. Wertheim, Lucy Carrington (2022) *Adventure in Art* (Lewes: Unicorn).
8. Fleming, G. H. (1998) *John Everett Millais: A Biography* (London: Constable).
9. Ketner, Joseph D. (1993) *The Emergence of the African-American Artist: Robert S. Duncanson, 1821–1872* (Columbia, MO: University of Missouri Press).
10. Bill Hodges Gallery (2003) *Robert Duncanson 1821–1872: Landscape, 1870* (New York: Bill Hodges Gallery & Merton D. Simpson Gallery, Inc.).
11. Barr, Alfred H. (1967) *Van Gogh* (New York: Taylor & Francis) p. 36.
12. Heinich, Nathalie (1996) *The Glory of van Gogh: An Anthropology of Admiration* (Princeton: Princeton University Press).
13. Heinich, *The Glory of van Gogh*.
14. Gogh-Bonger, V. Jo., and Martin Gayford (2018) *A Memoir of Vincent van Gogh* (Los Angeles: J. Paul Getty Museum).
15. Fry, Roger, and Christopher Reed (1996) *A Roger Fry Reader* (Chicago: University of Chicago Press).
16. Gowing, Lawrence (2005) *Facts on File Encyclopedia of Art*: 5 (New York: Facts on File) p. 804.
17. Bashkoff, Tracey (2018) *Hilma Af Klint: Paintings for the Future* (New York: Guggenheim Museum Publishing).
18. Steinhauer, Jillian (2014) "The Vivian Maier 'Discovery' Is More Complicated than We Thought." *Hyperallergic*, July 21. https://hyperallergic.com/138816/the-vivian-maier-discovery-is-more-complicated-than-we-thought/
19. Wilson, Paul (2018) "How Much Was Pablo Picasso Worth When He Died?" in *Celebrity Net Worth*, online: https://www.celebritynetworth.com/articles/how-much-does/happens-estate-valued-billion-dollars-dont-leave-will-children-pablo-picasso-found-hard-way/
20. Kramer, Hilton (1990) "The Man Who Held the Cubists Together." *The New York Times*, September 2, online: https://www.nytimes.com/1990/09/02/books/the-man-who-held-the-cubists-together.html
21. Andrews, Wayne, and James Laughlin (1990) *The Surrealist Parade*. New Directions, p. 144.

22. Eldredge, C. Charles (1996) *Georgia O'Keeffe: American And Modern* (New Haven: Yale University Press).

23. de Burca, Jackie (2018) *Salvador Dalí at Home* (North Brabant: Van Haren Publishing).

24. Shanes, Eric (2014) *Salvador Dalí* (New York: Parkstone International) pp. 17–18.

25. Shanes, *Salvador Dalí*, p. 32.

26. Shank, Ian (2017) "How Salvador Dalí Accidentally Sabotaged His Own Market for Prints" in *Artsy.net*, online: https://www.artsy.net/article/artsy-editorial-salvador-Dalí-accidentally-sabotaged-market-prints

27. Solomon, Deborah (2001) *Jackson Pollock: A Biography* (London: Cooper Square Press).

28. Saunders, Frances Stonor (2013) *The Cultural Cold War the CIA and the World of Arts and Letters* (New York: New Press).

29. Benjamin, Walter (1935) "Work of Art in the Age of Mechanical Reproduction" in *Illuminations* (New York: Schocken Books) 1977.

30. Gopnik, Blake (2020) *Warhol* (New York: Ecco).

31. Mitali, Banerjee, and Paul L. Ingram (2018) "Fame as an Illusion of Creativity: Evidence from the Pioneers of Abstract Art" (HEC Paris Research Paper No. SPE-2018-1305, *Columbia Business School Research Paper* No. 18-74, available at SSRN: https://ssrn.com/abstract=3258318 or http://dx.doi.org/10.2139/ssrn.3258318; Lesser, Casey (2019) "Study Finds Artists Become Famous through Their Friends, Not the Originality of Their Work" in *Artsy.net*, online: https://www.artsy.net/article/artsy-editorial-artists-famous-friends-originality-work accessed on 07/15/2021; Edlund, Carolyn (2019) "Why Artists Must Develop a Network" in *Artsy Shark*, online: https://www.artsyshark.com/2019/11/27/why-artists-must-develop-a-network/

32. Danto, Arthur (1964) "The Artworld" *The Journal of Philosophy* 16(19): 571–84.

33. Motley, Willard (1947) *Knock on Any Door* (Chicago: Northern Illinois University Press) 1998.

34. Saggese, J. M. (2021) *The Jean-Michel Basquiat Reader: Writings, Interviews, and Critical Responses* (Berkeley: University of California Press) p. 208.

35. Ault, Julie (2003) *Alternative Art New York, 1965–1985* (Minneapolis: University of Minnesota Press).

36. Ricard, Rene (1981) "The Radiant Child" in *Art Forum*, pp. 35–43.

37. Deitch, Jeffrey (1982) "Jean-Michel Basquiat: Annina Nosei" in *Flash Art* (May), p. 50.

38. Harring, Keith, quoted in Jordan M. Saggese (2021) *The Jean-Michel Basquiat Reader: Writings, Interviews, and Critical Responses* (Berkeley: University of California Press) p. 208.

39. Cascone, Sarah (2018) "5 Things We Learned about Yayoi Kusama from the New Documentary about Her Extraordinary Life." Artnet News, September 6. https://news.artnet.com/art-world/yayoi-kusama-documentary-1343456#:~:text=Georgia%20O

40. Kusama, Yayoi, and Ralph McCarthy (2021) *Infinity Net: The Autobiography of Yayoi Kusama by Yayoi Kusama* (London: Tate Publishing).

41. Cutler, Jody (2011) "Narcissus, Narcosis, Neurosis: The Visions of Yayoi Kusama" in Isabelle Loring Wallace and Jennie Hirsh (eds.), *Contemporary Art and Classical Myth* (Farnham: Ashgate Publishing).

42. Warhol, Andy, quoted in Louis Cicotello and Raphael Sassower (2000) *The Golden Avant-garde* (Charlottesville and London: University Press of Virginia).

43. Clyde, Jacqueline (2023) "Who Are the Richest Artists in the World Today?" in *Widewalls*, online: https://www.widewalls.ch/magazine/richest-artists-in-the-world

## 4 Responsibility: Art that Builds Better Worlds

1. Scotti, R. A. (2009) *Vanished Smile: The Mysterious Theft of Mona Lisa* (New York: Knopf).

2. Scotti, *Vanished Smile*.

3. Hales, D. (2015) *Mona Lisa: A Life Discovered* (New York: Simon & Schuster).

4. Samuels, Ernest, and Jayne Samuels (1987) *Bernard Berenson, the Making of a Legend* (Cambridge, MA: Harvard University Press) p. 215.

5. Roosevelt, Theodore (1913) "Mr. Rosevelt on the Cubists" in *The Literary Digest* (April 5), p. 772.

6. Godfrey, B. Tony (1998) *Conceptual Art* (London: Phaidon).

7. Dachy, Marc (2006) *Dada: The Revolt of Art* (London: Thames & Hudson) pp. 11–14.

8. Höch, Hannah, in Édouard Roditi (1959) "Interview with Hannah Höch" *Arts Magazine* 34(3): 29.

9. Leperlier, Francois (1999) *Claude Cahun* (London: Verso).

10. Gammel, Irene (2003) *Baroness Elsa: Gender, Dada, and Everyday Modernity—A Cultural* (Cambridge, MA: MIT Press).

11. Gammel, *Baroness Elsa*, quote on p. 219.

12. Gammel, *Baroness Elsa*, p. 180.

13. Gammel, *Baroness Elsa*.

14. Livezeanu, Irina (2005) "'From Dada to Gaga': The Peripatetic Romanian Avant-Garde Confronts Communism" in Mihai Dinu Gheorghiu and Lucia Dragomir (eds.), *Littératures et pouvoir symbolique. Colloque tenu à Bucarest (Roumanie), 30 et 31 mai 2003* (Paris: Maison des sciences de l'homme).

15. Witham, Larry (2013) *Picasso and the Chess Player: Pablo Picasso, Marcel Duchamp, and the Battle for the Soul of Modern Art* (Hanover, NH, and London: University Press Of New England).

16. Duchamp, Marcel (1956) *A Conversation with Marcel Duchamp*, The National Broadcasting Company, Philadelphia Museum of Art.

17. Pertsov, Viktor (1922) "At the junction of art and production" in John Bowlt (ed.), *Russian Art of the Avant-Garde: Theory and Criticism, 1902–1934* (New York: Viking) 1976, p. 236.

18. Klutsis, Gustav (1931) "Photomontage as a new kind of agitation art" in *Photomontage Between the Wars: 1918–1939* (Ottawa: Carleton University Art Gallery) p. 117.

19. Kuc, Kamila, and Michael O'Pray (2014) *The Struggle for Form: Perspectives on Polish Avant-Garde Film, 1916–1989* (New York: Wallflower Press).

20. Fox Weber, Nicholas (2011) *The Bauhaus Group: Six Masters of Modernism* (New Haven: Yale University Press) pp. 33–4.

21. Fox Weber, *The Bauhaus Group*, pp. 33–4.

22. Fox Weber, *The Bauhaus Group*, pp. 136–7.

23. Buick, K. Pai (2010) *Child of the Fire: Mary Edmonia Lewis and the Problem of Art History's Black and Indian Subject* (Durham, NC: Duke University Press).

24. Locke, Alain (1997) *The New Negro* (New York: Simon & Schuster).

25. Hayes, Jeffreen M., Kirsten Pai Buick, and Bridget R. Cooks (2021) *Augusta Savage: Renaissance Woman* (Lewes: Giles).

26. Poston, T. R. (1935) "Augusta Savage" *Metropolitan Magazine* (January) n.p.

27. Antal, Lara (2017) *James Van Der Zee: Photographer* (New York: Cavendish Square Publishing).

28. Christian, Shawn Anthony (2016) *The Harlem Renaissance and the Idea of a New Negro Reader* (Amherst, MA: University Of Massachusetts Press).

29. Motely, Archibald (1918) "The Negro in Art" in *The Chicago Defender*, July 6.

30. Huggins, Nathan (2007) *Harlem Renaissance* (Oxford: Oxford University Press).

31. Brenner, Anita (1938) "America Creates American Murals" in *The New York Times*, 10 April. https://www.nytimes.com/1938/04/10/archives/american-creates-american-murals-to-bid-for-the-favor-of-a-new-mass.html

32. Grieve, Virginia (2009) *The Federal Art Project and the Creation of Middlebrow Culture* (Champaign: University of Illinois Press).

33. Grieve, *The Federal Art Project*, p. 84.

34. Dana, John Cotton, M. S. S. Price, and S. E. Weil (1999) *The New Museum: Selected Writings by John Cotton Dana* (Washington DC: American Alliance of Museums).

35. Cohen, Alina (2018), 'When Paul Cadmus's Homoerotic Military Painting Launched a National Scandal' in *Artsy*, online: https://www.artsy.net/article/artsy-editorial-paul-cadmuss-homoerotic-military-painting-launched-national-scandal

36. McLerran, Jennifer (2009) *A New Deal for Native Art: Indian Arts and Federal Policy, 1933–1943* (Tucson: University of Arizona Press).

37. Elderfield, John, ed. (2011) *De Kooning: A Retrospective* (New York: Museum of Modern Art).

38. Rivera, Diego. quoted in Caistor, Nick (2021) *Mexico City* (Oxford: Signal Books) p. 168.

39. Overtly political art is often in danger of veering toward propaganda. At times artists are aware of ideologies and consciously express it. At others, ideologies have naturalized—they become a default aesthetic approach and go unquestioned. Mexican muralism was defined by a strong dose of machismo—men posed as revolutionary heroes; examples to emulate. Women were often relegated to the background, comparatively passive, or cast as mothers and teachers or posed naked as allegorical figures. For more see: Deffebach, Nancy (2015) *María Izquierdo and Frida Kahlo: Challenging Visions in Modern Mexican Art* (Latin American and Caribbean Arts and Culture Publication Initiative, Mellon Foundation) (Austin: University of Texas Press) p. 126.

40. Low, Trisha (2019) *Socialist Realism* (Brooklyn: Coffee House Press).

41. Juraga, Dubravka, and Keith M. Booker (2002) *Socialist Cultures East and West* (Westport, CT: Praeger) p. 68.

42. Spotts, Frederic (2002) *Hitler and the Power of Aesthetics* (New York: The Overlook Press) pp. 151–68.

43. Levi, Neil (2013) *Modernist Form and the Myth of Jewification* (New York: Fordham University Press), p. 64.


## 5  Art Capital: The Infinity of Currencies

1. Battino, Freddy, and Luca Palazzoli (1991) *Piero Manzoni*: *Catalogue raisonné*, Milan, pp. 123–8, 472–5, catalogue no. 1053/4, reproduced p. 472.

2. Redazione ANSA, "Manzoni's *Artist Shit* Goes for 275,000 Euros" in *ANSA Arts & Culture*, online: https://www.ansa.it/english/news/lifestyle/arts/2016/12/07/manzoni-artists-shit-goes-for-275000_baab4664-23a7-40c3-8eb5-a6012d06e95d.html

3. Villa, Angelica (2021) "The Most Expensive Artworks by Pablo Picasso Ever Sold at Auction" in *Art News*, online: https://www.artnews.com/list/art-news/artists/pablo-picasso-highest-auction-records-1234594915/femme-assise-1909/

4. Adorno, Theodor W., Samuel Weber, and Shierry Weber (1981) *Prisms* (Cambridge, MA: MIT Press).

5. Miang, Tiampo (2011) *Gutai decentering modernism* (Chicago: University of Chicago Press).

6. Celant, Germano (1985) *Arte povera* (Milan: Electa).

7. McWilliams, J. C. (2020). *The 1960s Cultural Revolution* (New York: Bloomsbury).

8. Pelkey, Jamin (2023) *Bloomsbury Semiotics Volume 1: History and Semiosis* (London: Bloomsbury).

9. Berman, Art (1988) *From the New Criticism to Deconstruction: The Reception of Structuralism and Post-Structuralism* (Urbana: University Of Illinois Press).

10. Jones, Jonathan (2018) "Carl Andre's Equivalent VIII: The Most Boring Controversial Artwork Ever" *The Guardian*, February 22. https://www.theguardian.com/artanddesign/jonathanjonesblog/2016/sep/20/carl-andre-equivalent-viii-bricks

11. Danto, Arthur (1998) *After the End of Art: Contemporary Art and the Pale of History* (Princeton: Princeton University Press).

12. Danto, *After the End of Art*, p. 47.

13. Gelfand, Aleksandr (2013) "Today in MET History: February 4th" in *The Met*, online: https://www.metmuseum.org/blogs/now-at-the-met/features/2013/today-in-met-history-february-4

14. Hughes, Robert (2008) *The Mona Lisa Curse*, documentary, dir. Mandy Chang.

15. Hook, Phillip (2018) *Rogues Galleries: A History of Art and Its Dealers* (London: Profile Books) p. 256.

16. Jasper Johns, Robert Rauschenberg, Frank Stella, Cy Twombly, Lee Bontecou, Roy Lichtenstein, John Chamberlain, Andy Warhol, James Rosenquist, Donald Judd, Christo, Edward Higgins, Robert Morris, Joseph Kosuth, Dan Flavin, Bruce Nauman, Keith Sonnier, Richard Serra, Richard Artschwager, Ed Ruscha, Claes Oldenburg, Lawrence Weiner, Ellsworth Kelly, Hanne Darboven, Kenneth Noland, James Turrell, Julian Schnabel, and David Salle in Hook, *Rogues Galleries*.

17. Findlay, Michael (2014) *The Value of Art : Money, Power, Beauty* (Munich: Prestel).

18. Scull, Robert (1973) *A Selection of Fifty Works from the Collection of Robert C. Scull* (New York: Sotheby Parker Barnet Inc.).

19. Rose, Barbara (1973) "Profit Without Honor" in *The New York Magazine*, November 5, pp. 80–1.

20. Boucher, B. (2012). "Resale Royalty Legislation Under Discussion" In *ARTnews.com*, October 22. https://www.artnews.com/art-in-america/features/resale-royalty-legislation-under-discussion-58076/

21. Hughes, *The Mona Lisa Curse*.

22. Rauschenberg, Robert, in conversation with Jason Kaufman (1997) "Robert Rauschenberg: 'Business sure screwed up the art world universally'" in *The Arts Newspaper*, online: https://www.theartnewspaper.com/1997/09/01/robert-rauschenberg-business-sure-screwed-up-the-art-world-universally

23. Kinsella, Eileen (2018) "The Dung-Adorned Madonna That Giuliani Once Tried to Ban Has Been Donated to MoMA by Steve Cohen" in *Artnet*, online: https://news.artnet.com/art-world/steve-cohen-chris-ofili-virgin-mary-moma-1269002

24. Muir, Gregor (2012) *Lunky Kunst: The Rise and Fall of Young British Art* (London: Aurum Press).

25. The movement included Jake and Dinos Chapman, Tracey Emin, Anya Gallaccio, Damien Hirst, Gary Hume, Sarah Lucas, Chris Ofili, Marc Quinn, Sam Taylor-Johnson, Mark Wallinger, and Rachel Whiteread.

26. Hirst, Damien (n.d.) *Freeze* in Damien Hirst official website, online: https://www.damienhirst.com/exhibitions/group/1988/freeze

27. Editors (2020) "Top 10 World's Richest Artists" in *Design Museum*, online: http://www.designmuseum.me/artists/top-10-worlds-richest-living-artists-nowadays/

28. Als, Hilton, Sadie Coles, Pauline Daly, Tracey Emin, Sarah Lucas, Gregor Muir, and Ceirth Wyn Evans (2021) "Remembering Tracey Emin and Sarah Lucas's *The Shop*" in *Frieze*, online: https://www.frieze.com/article/tracey-emin-and-sarah-lucas-shop

## 6 Institutional Dissociative Identity Disorders

1. Among the most recent, I recommend Deresiewicz, William (2015) *Excellent Sheep: The Miseducation of the American Elite and the Way to a Meaningful Life* (New York: Free Press); Fleming, Peter (2021) *Dark Academia: How Universities Die* (London: Pluto Press); Carey, Kevin (2016) *The End of College: Creating the Future of Learning and the University of Everywhere* (New York: Riverhead Books).

2. Fleming, Peter (2021) *Dark Academia: How Universities Die* (London: Pluto Press).

3. Vyletel, Brenda, Erin Voichoski, Sarah Lipson, and Justin Heinze (2023) *Exploring faculty burnout through the 2022-23 HMS faculty/staff survey.* August 31. https://www.apa.org/ed/precollege/psychology-teacher-network/introductory-psychology/faculty-burnout-survey

4. Palmer, Laure (2015) "Back to School: 10 Famous Art Professors We Wish We Had as Teachers in College" in *Artnews*, online: https://news.artnet.com/art-world/best-art-professors-around-the-world-330870

5. The sentences originated in George Bernard Shaw's 1905 play *Man and Superman* and it has since become a staple in popular culture.

6. Gallant, Leah (2020) "Breaking Down Faculty Demographics" in *FNMagazine*, online: https://fnewsmagazine.com/images/issues/2020-08-Summer.pdf/breaking-down-faculty-demographics.html

7. Bhopal, Kalwant (2020) "UK's white female academics are being privileged above women – and men – of colour" in *The Guardian*, online: https://www.theguardian.com/education/2020/jul/28/uks-white-female-academics-are-being-privileged-above-women-and-men-of-colour

8. Beardsley, J. (2002) *The quilts of Gee's Bend* (Atlanta: Tinwood Books in Association with the Museum Of Fine Arts, Houston).

9. Maneker, Marion (2022) "The Magical Modernism of Gee's Bend." *LiveArt*, July 18. https://liveart.io/stories/blogs/editorials/the-magical-modernism-of-gee-s-bend

10. Artprice editors (2016) "The Contemporary Art Market, 2016" in *Artprice.com*, online: https://www.artprice.com/artprice-reports/the-contemporary-art-market-report-2016/market-geography

11. The World Bank editors, (2021) "Overview" in *The World Bank*, online: https://www.worldbank.org/en/country/china/overview#3

12. Quemin, Alain (2015) "The impact of Nationality in the Contemporary Art Market" in *Scielo Brazil*, online: https://www.scielo.br/j/sant/a/p3cbxHS9yGx7zNFY5wqFtxM/?lang=en

13. Marlow, Tim, John Tancock, Daniel Rosbottom, A. Locke, and W. Ai (2015) *Ai Weiwei* (London: Royal Academy Publications).

14. Kusama, Yayoi, and Ralph McCarthy (2021) *Infinity Net: The Autobiography of Yayoi Kusama by Yayoi Kusama*.

15. Schad, Ed, Shirin Neshat, and Godfrey Cheshire (2019) *Shirin Neshat* (Los Angeles: The Broad).

16. Casparie, Sabine (2021) "Understanding Njideka Akunyili Crosby in 10 Works of Art" in *The Collector*, online: https://www.thecollector.com/njideka-akunyili-crosby-10-works-of-art/

17. Younge, G. (2014) "Theaster Gates, the artist whose latest project is regenerating Chicago". *The Guardian*, October 6. https://www.theguardian.com/society/2014/oct/06/theaster-gates-artist-latest-project-is-regenerating-chicago-artes-mundi

18. It is important to distinguish commercial galleries that sell paintings and sculptures by artists who do not engage with current discussion in the art world and those who do. The majority of commercial art galleries sell paintings and sculptures of pleasing subjects like ballerinas, flowers, and animals predominantly made as interior decoration. This type of art is modern in style and classical in essence. It does not challenge the viewer. It is not the art critics review, art historians write about, and museums end up showing.

19. Fanon, Frantz (1968) *The Wretched of the Earth* (New York: Grove Press).

20. Taylor, Nora A. (2005) "Why have there not been great Vietnamese artists?" in *Michigan Quarterly Review* XLIV(1): *Viet Nam: Beyond the Frame (Part Two)*, Winter.

21. Ayres, P. G. (2012). *Shaping Ecology: The Life of Arthur Tansley* (Malden, MA: Wiley-Blackwell).

22. Masaharu, Tsujimoto, Kajikawa Yuya,, Tomita Junichi,, and Matsumoto Yoichi (2018) "A review of the ecosystem concept — Towards coherent ecosystem design" *Technological Forecasting and Social Change* 136(November): 49–58. doi: 10.1016/J.TECHFORE.2017.06.032

23. Reyburn, Scott (2015) "A Tug of War over Art-Sales Transparency" *The New York Times*, September 25, sec. Arts. https://www.nytimes.com/2015/09/28/arts/international/a-tug-of-war-over-art-sales-transparency.html?_r=0

24. Kazakina, Katya (2022) "Musicians and Movie Stars Have Had Managers Forever. Now, It's Becoming Big Business to Manage Artists, Too." *Artnet News*, August 26. https://news.artnet.com/market/artist-managers-art-detective-2166044

25. https://www.theartnewspaper.com/authors/anny-shaw. "'Pay-To-Play' Galleries—Which Charge Artists Thousands to Exhibit—Are on the Rise." *The Art Newspaper – International art news and events*, October 26, 2022. https://www.theartnewspaper.com/2022/10/26/pay-to-play-galleries-are-on-the-risebut-how-ethical-are-they?utm_source=The+Art+Newspaper+Newsletters&ut.

26. Battcock, Gregory, quoted in "Gregory Battcock: 'The Art World Is Corrupt in the Following Ways . . .'" in Russeth, Andrew (2016) *ArtNews*, July 27. https://www.artnews.com/art-news/news/gregory-battcock-the-art-world-is-corrupt-in-the-following-ways-6729/

27. Russeth, "Gregory Battcock"

28. Salisbury, Laurel Wickersham (2019) "It's Not That Easy: Artist Resale Royalty Rights and The ART Act" in *Center for Art Law*, online: https://itsartlaw.org/2019/07/01/its-not-that-easy-artist-resale-royalty-rights-and-the-art-act/

29. Nadler, et al. (2018) Press Release: "Nadler, Hatch, Leahy & Collins Introduce Bipartisan, Bicameral American Royalties Too Act" (September 25). See also Hanoch Sheps (2013), *Artist Resale Royalty Rights – Is a US Droite de Suite in our Future?*, Center for Art Law (December 2).

30. Adam, Georgina (2020) "The Turn of the Screw: Will Tighter Regulations Impact the Art Market?" *The Art Newspaper*, November 25. https://www.theartnewspaper.com/2020/11/25/the-turn-of-the-screw-will-tighter-regulations-impact-the-art-market

31. UBS Editors (2023) "The Art Market 2019" in *Artbasel.com*, online: https://www.ubs.com/global/en/our-firm/art/collecting/art-market-survey/download-report-2023.html

32. Berniker, Talia (2020) "Behind Closed Doors: A Look At Freeports" in *Center for Art Law*, online: https://itsartlaw.org/2020/11/03/behind-closed-doors-a-look-at-freeports/#post-56093-footnote-15

33. Grindon, Gavin (2020) "Opinion  This Exhibition Was Brought to You by Guns and Big Oil" in *The New York Times*, May 26, sec. Opinion. https://www.nytimes.com/2020/05/26/opinion/sunday/museums-investors-art.html

34. Sutton, Benjamin (2015) "Artists from Five Galleries Dominate US Museum Shows" in *Hyperallergic*, online: https://hyperallergic.com/195752/artists-from-five-galleries-dominate-us-museum-shows/

35. Tremayne-Pengelly, Alexandra (2022) "New York's Metropolitan Museum of Art Is Now One of the Most Expensive Museums in the World." *The Observer*, June 30. https://observer.com/2022/06/new-yorks-metropolitan-museum-of-art-is-now-one-of-the-most-expensive-museums-in-the-world/

36. Luke, Ben (2019) "Here are 2019's most visited contemporary art exhibitions" in *The Art Newspaper*, online: https://www.theartnewspaper.com/2020/03/31/here-are-2019s-most-visited-contemporary-art-exhibitions

37. Solsman, Joan E. (2021) "Netflix's Squid Game was even bigger than you thought – 2.1B hours big" in *Cnet.com*, online: https://www.cnet.com/news/netflix-squid-game-is-even-bigger-than-you-thought-2-billion-hours-big/

38. Postcommodity, *Through the Repellent Fence*, https://www.throughtherepellentfence.com/

39. Times Higher Education Editors (2017) "The Cost of Studying at a University in the United States." *Times Higher Education* (THE), November 28. https://www.timeshighereducation.com/student/advice/cost-studying-university-united-states.

40. Jones, C., and Maoret Massimo (2018) *Frontiers of Creative Industries: Exploring Structural and Categorical Dynamics* (Bingley: Emerald Publishing) p. 74.

41. Weaton, Wil (2015) "You can't pay your rent with 'the unique platform and reach our site provides'" in *Wil Weaton dot net*, online: http://wilwheaton.net/2015/10/you-cant-pay-your-rent-with-the-unique-platform-and-reach-our-site-provides/

42. MEAA Editors (2016) "MEAA appalled by AIM and Warner Bros. seeking musicians to work for free" in *Media Entertainment & Arts Alliance*, online: https://www.meaa.org/news/meaa-appalled-by-aim-and-warner-bros-seeking-musicians-to-work-for-free/

43. Resch, Magnus (2016) *The Global Art Gallery Report 2016* (London: Phaidon) p. 12.

44. Chubb Editors, "New Chubb Survey Measures Americans' Attitudes Toward Collecting Valuables and Purchasing Decisions Amid the Pandemic" in *Chubb*, online: https://www.prnewswire.com/news-releases/new-chubb-survey-measures-americans-attitudes-toward-collecting-valuables-and-purchasing-decisions-amid-the-pandemic-301422308.html

45. Shaw, Anny (2021) "Who is Beeple? The art world disruptor at the heart of the NFT boom" in *The Art Newspaper*, online: https://www.theartnewspaper.com/2021/03/05/who-is-beeple-the-art-world-disruptor-at-the-heart-of-the-nft-boom

46. Shaw, "Who is Beeple?".

47. Mattei, Shanti Escalante-De (2022) "After 2022'S Crypto Crash, the Future Vision of NFTs Is Looking Far More Banal." *ARTnews.com*, December 27. https://www.artnews.com/art-news/news/future-of-nfts-2022-opensea-royalties-1234651990/

48. Malloy, Judy (2003) *Women, Art, and Technology* (Cambridge, MA: MIT Press).

49. Greenberger, Alex (2023) "Artist Wins Photography Contest after Submitting AI-Generated Image, Then Forfeits Prize." *ARTnews.com*, April 17. https://www.artnews.

com/art-news/news/ai-generated-image-world-photography-organization-contest-artist-declines-award-1234664549/

50. Mattei, Shanti Escalante-De (2023) "Artists Are Suing Artificial Intelligence Companies and the Lawsuit Could Upend Legal Precedents around Art." *ARTnews.com*, May 5. http://www.artnews.com/art-in-america/features/midjourney-ai-art-image-generators-lawsuit-1234665579/

51. Gervais, Thierry, Gaëlle Morel, and John Tittenson (2017) *The Making of Visual News: A History of Photography in the Press* (London: Bloomsbury) p. 14.

## 7 Outsiders and Professional Amateurs

1. Bey, Dawoud, quoted in Clint Smith (2023) *One Book One Northwestern 2022–23: How the Word is Passed* (Chicago: Northwestern University Press).

2. Bann, S (2002) "Entre philosophie et critique: Victor Cousin, Théophile Gautier et l'art pour l'art" in P.-H. Frangne and J.-M. Poinsot (eds.), *L'Invention de la critique d'art* () (Rennes: Presses Universitaires de Rennes) pp. 137–44.

3. Sutherland, Daniel E. (2014) *Whistler: A Life for Art's Sake* (New Haven: Yale University Press).

4. Nietzsche, Friedrich Wilhelm, and Duncan Large (2008) *Twilight of the Idols: Or How to Philosophize with a Hammer* (Oxford: Oxford University Press).

5. Tsong-Zung, Chang (2011) "Ink Painting in the Age of New Wave" in Jörg Huber and Zhao Chuan (eds.), *A New Thoughtfulness in Contemporary China* (London: Transaction Publishers) p. 7.

6. Khomami, N. (2023) "Nan Goldin named art world's most influential figure." *The Guardian*, December 1. https://www.theguardian.com/artanddesign/2023/dec/01/nan-goldin-photographer-artreview-power-100-list-art-world-most-influential-figure#:~:text=ArtReview%20said%20Goldin

7. Enwezor, Okwui (2003) "The Postcolonial Constellation: Contemporary Art in a State of Permanent Transition" in *Research in African Literatures* 34(4): 57–82.

8. Hunt, Joshua (2022) "Cannupa Hanska Luger Is Turning the Tables on the Art World." *The New York Times*, June 16. https://www.nytimes.com/2022/06/16/magazine/cannupa-hanska-luger-profile.html

9. Okeke-Agulu, C. (2006) "The Challenge of the Modern: An Introduction" *African Arts* 39(1): 14–91. http://www.jstor.org/stable/20447747

10. McAndrew, Clare, and Charlotte Burns (2020) *The Bulletin with UBS, a podcast from Monocle*, online: https://www.ubs.com/global/en/our-firm/art/2020/racial-and-gender-diversity.html

11. Jaeger, P. T., N. A. Cooke, C. Feltis, M. Hamiel, F. Jardine, and K. Shilton (2015) "The Virtuous Circle Revisited: Injecting Diversity, Inclusion, Rights, Justice, and Equity into LIS from Education to Advocacy" *The Library Quarterly: Information, Community, Policy* 85(2): 150–71. https://doi.org/10.1086/680154

12. Dubuffet, Jean (1949) "Art Brut in Preference to the Cultural Arts" in *Art and Text 27* (December–February 1988): 31–3, quote on p. 33.

13. Cardinal, Roger (1972) *Outsider Art* (New York: Praeger) pp. 24–30.

14. Outsider Art Fair Organizers (n.d.) "What is Outsider Art?" in *Outsider Art Fair*, online: https://www.outsiderartfair.com/the-field

15. Selz, Peter (1962). *The Work of Jean Dubuffet, with Texts by the Artist* (New York: New York Museum of Modern Art).

16. D'Souza, Aruna (1997) "I Think Your Work Looks A Lot Like Dubuffet: Dubuffet and America, 1946–1962" *Oxford Art Journal* 20(2): 61.

17. Wisniewski, Gene (2020) *The Art of Looking at Art* (Lanham, MD: Rowman & Littlefield) p. 226.

18. Pholdhampalit, Khetsirin (2019) "Art in Its Purest Form" in *The Nation: Thailand*, online: https://www.nationthailand.com/life/30373871

19. Yentob, Alan (2013) *Turning the Art World Inside Out*, [documentary] BBC, online: https://www.youtube.com/watch?v=98RUUhVgLR0&t=5s

20. Erlanger, Steven (2010) "A French Castle Built of Stone and Dreams" in *The New York Times*, online: https://www.nytimes.com/2010/08/01/world/europe/01castle.htmlaccessed

21. Schuster, Clayton (2020) "In NYC, a Fair Dedicated to Outsider Art Cultivates an Interest in the Eccentric" in *The Observer*, online: https://observer.com/2020/01/outsider-art-fair-market-growth-in-new-york

22. Cardinal, Roger, and Victor Musgrov (1979) *Outsiders: An art without precedent or tradition* (London: Arts Council of Great Britain).

23. Rexer, Lyle (2005) *How to Look at Outsider Art* (New York: Harry N. Abrams).

24. Thompson, John, and Monika Kinley (2006) *Inner Worlds Outside at the Whitechapel Gallery* (London: Whitechapel Art Gallery).

25. Gioni, Massimiliano, interviewed by M. Andrew Goldstein (2013) "Massimiliano Gioni on His Venice Biennale Show, and 'Trying to See More'" in *Artspace*, online: https://www.artspace.com/magazine/interviews_features/qa/massimiliano_gioni_venice_biennale_interview-51106

26. Grant, C., and D. Price (2020) "Decolonizing Art History" *Art History* 43: 8–66.

27. Hooks, B. (1995) *Art on My Mind: Visual Politics* (New York: The New Press) p. 163.

## 8 I'm Not an Artist

1. Dubuffet, Jean (1979) quote from text wall in *Outsiders* exhibition at Hayward Gallery, London.

2. In "The Trouble with (the term) art" Carolyn Dear offers a comprehensive list of the many authoritative essays and books published on the subject: Morris Weitz, "The Role of Theory in Aesthetics," *Journal of Aesthetics and Art Criticism* 15, no. I (1956): 27–35; James Carney, "Defining Art," *British Journal of Aesthetics* 15(1975): 191–206; Robert Matthews, "Traditional Aesthetics Defended," *Journal of Aesthetics and Art Criticism* 38, no. I (1979): 39–50; Thomas Leddy, "Rigid Designation in Defining Art," *Journal of Aesthetics and Art Criticism* 45, no. 3 (Spring 1987): 263–72; Jerrold Levinson, "Refining Art Historically," *Journal of Aesthetics and Art Criticism* 47, no. I (Winter 1989): 21–33; and David Novitz, "Disputes about An," *Journal of Aesthetics and Art Criticism* 54, no. 2

(Spring 1996): 153–63. See also W. B. Gallie, "Art as an Essentially Contested Concept," *Philosophical Quarterly* 6, no. 23 (April 1956): 97–114.

3. Fanon, F. (1963) *The Wretched of the Earth* (Cape Town: Kwela Books); Deleuze, G., F. Guattari, R. Hurley, M. Seem, H. R. Lane, amd M. Foucault (2009). *Anti-Oedipus: Capitalism and Schizophrenia (Penguin Classics)* (Illustrated ed.) (London: Penguin Classics); Wynter, S. (2003) "Unsettling the coloniality of being/power/truth/freedom: Toward the human, after man, its overrepresentation— an argument" in *New Centennial Review* 3(3): 257–337; Jameson, F. (1992) *Postmodernism, or, The Cultural Logic of Late Capitalism* (Durham, NC: Duke University Press); Zizek, S. (2017). *Trouble in Paradise: From the End of History to the End of Capitalism* (New York: Melville House); Robinson, Cedric (1983) *Black Marxism* (Chapel Hill: University of North Carolina Press); Fisher, Mark (2009) *Capitalist Realism* (London: Zero Books).

4. Fischer, *Capitalist Realism*, p. 6.

5. Fischer, *Capitalist Realism*, p. 15.

6. Eames, Charles, quoted in Scott Berkun (2010) "Why You Are Not an Artist" in *Scott Berkun*, online: https://scottberkun.com/2010/why-are-not-an-artist/

7. See, for example, the collection of real estate developer Harry Mack Lowe's and his ex-wife Linda, which as I write is breaking records at Sotheby's. So far, the most expensive art collection sold at auction is that of banker David Rockefeller, whose art sold for $835.1 million in 2018 at Christie's. See also Shivani, Vora (2021) "Sotheby's Auction to Sell Warring Macklowe Art Collection Brings in Record $676 Million" in *Architectural Digest*, online: https://www.architecturaldigest.com/story/macklowe-auction-sothebys

8. Wood, M. Ellen (2017) *The Origin of Capitalism: A Longer View* (New York: Verso).

9. Eliot, T. S., C. Ricks, and J. McCue (2018) *The poems of T.S. Eliot. Volume I, Collected and uncollected poems* (New York: Farrar, Straus & Giroux).

10. Alberge, D. (2012) "Resurrected: Dracula author Bram Stoker's first attempts at Gothic horror." *The Observer*, December 16. https://www.theguardian.com/books/2012/dec/16/bram-stoker-dracula-lost-stories

11. Waldman, Kathy (2018) "Does Having a Day Job Mean Making Better Art?" in *The New York Times Style Magazine*, online: https://www.nytimes.com/2018/03/22/t-magazine/art/artist-day-job.html

12. Donnell, Courtney Graham, S. Weininger, and R. Cozzolino (1997) *Ivan Albright* (New York: Hudson Hills Press).

13. Kosut, M. (2012) *Encyclopedia of Gender in Media* (Thousand Oaks: Sage Publications).

14. Harvey, Michelle (2010) "MoMA  'ART WORK': Famous Former Staff." www.moma.org, July 10. https://www.moma.org/explore/inside_out/2010/07/01/art-work-famous-former-staff/#:~:text=In%201960%2C%20artist%20Sol%20LeWitt

15. Guggenheim Editors, "Dan Flavin" Guggenheim Museum website, Collection Online. https://www.guggenheim.org/artwork/artist/dan-flavin

16. Morril, Rebecca, and Sara Bader, eds. (2022) *Artifacts: fascinating facts about art, artists, and the art world* (London: Phaidon).

17. Glickman, K. (2020) "Julie Mehretu takes East Lansing roots to key spot in art world." *Lansing State Journal*, December 23. https://www.lansingstatejournal.com/story/

entertainment/arts/2020/12/23/julie-mehretu-takes-east-lansing-roots-key-spot-art-world/115211830/

18. Morril and Bader, eds., *Artifacts.*

19. Alston, Charles Henry, and Al Murray (1968) "An interview of Charles Henry Alston" *Archives of American Art*, October 19. https://www.aaa.si.edu/collections/interviews/oral-history-interview-charles-henry-alston-11460

20. Waldam, Kathy (2018) "Does Having a Day Job Mean Making Better Art?" in *The New York Times Style Magazine*, online: https://www.nytimes.com/2018/03/22/t-magazine/art/artist-day-job.html

21. Saar, Betye (2021) "How I became an artist" in *Roberts Projects*, online: https://www.robertsprojectsla.com/news/how-i-became-an-artist-betye-saar

22. "Hobby" in *Merriam-Webster.com Dictionary*, Merriam-Webster, https://www.merriam-webster.com/dictionary/hobby.

23. Scanlan, Joe (2017) "Not Knowing: Contemporary Art and the Amateur" in *Joe Scanlan artist website*, online: https://joescanlan.biz/not-knowing-contemporary-art-and-the-amateur/

24. Nesbitt, Judith, ed., (2008) *Peter Doig* (London: Tate) p. 114.

25. Saltz, Jerry (2020) "My Life as a Failed Artist" in *Vulture*, online: https://www.vulture.com/2017/04/jerry-saltz-my-life-as-a-failed-artist.html

26. Saltz, "My Life as a Failed Artist."

27. Le Feuvre, Lisa (2010) "If at first you don't succeed, celebrate" in *Tate, Etc.*, online: https://www.tate.org.uk/tate-etc/issue-18-spring-2010/if-first-you-dont-succeed-celebrate

28. Baldessari, John, quoted in Sarah Thornton (2008) *Seven Days in the Art World* (New York: W. W. Norton & Co.) p. 52.

29. Flaherty, C. (2020) "Even 'Valid' Student Evaluations Are 'Unfair'." *Inside Higher Ed.*, online: https://www.insidehighered.com/news/2020/02/27/study-student-evaluations-teaching-are-deeply-flawed#:~:text=Student%20evaluations%20of%20teaching%20reflect

30. Krizan, Z., and A. D. Herlache (February 2018). ""The Narcissism Spectrum Model: A Synthetic View of Narcissistic Personality" in *Personality and Social Psychology Review* 22(1): 3–31.

31. Kundera, Milan (2020) *The Unbearable Lightness of Being* (London: Faber & Faber) p. 141.

32. Picasso, Pablo, quoted in John Richardson (2009) *A Life of Picasso – Volume 3* (London: Pimlico) p. 499.

33. Freud, Sigmund, quoted in D. Craufurd Goodwin (1998) *Art and the Market: Roger Fry on Commerce in Art, Selected Writings, Edited with an Interpretation* (Ann Arbor: University of Michigan Press) p. 130.

34. Mellor, David Alan (1998) *Chemical Traces: Photography and Conceptual Art*, exhibition catalog (Kingston upon Hull: Ferens Art Gallery) p. 5.

35. Hurn, David, and Claire Grafik (2007) *I'm a Real Photographer* (London: Chris Boot).

36. Lui, John (2020) "Essentially no one is saying that painters, actors, singers, and writers contribute nothing" in *The Straits Times*, online: https://chaseonline.chase.com/Secure/OSL.aspx?newstoken=false&LOB=RBGLogon&Referer=https%3A%2F%2Fwww.chase.com%2F&resId=success&

37. Brooks, Arthur (2020) "'Success Addicts' Choose Being Special Over Being Happy" in *The Atlantic*, July 30. Online: https://www.theatlantic.com/family/archive/2020/07/why-success-wont-make-you-happy/614731/

# Bibliography

Adam, Leonhard (1940) *Primitive Art* (London: Pelican / Penguin Books).

Adams, Laurie Schneider (2009) *The Methodologies of Art: An Introduction* (Second edition, London: Routledge).

Adorno, Theodor W., Samuel Weber, and Shierry Weber (1981) *Prisms* (Cambridge, MA: MIT Press).

Alhadeff, Albert (2002) *The Raft of the Medusa: Géricault, Art and Race* (New York: Prestel).

Alighieri, Dante, D. M. Black, and Robert Harrison (2021) *Purgatorio.* (New York: NYRB Classics).

Andrews, Wayne, and James Laughlin (1990) *The Surrealist Parade.* New Directions, p. 144.

Art Basel Editors, "The Art Market 2019" in *Artbasel.com*.

Artfinder (2017) "The Artfinder Independent Art Market Report: 2017" in *Artfinder.com online*: www.Artfinder.com/powertotheartist.

Artprice eds. (2016) "The Contemporary Art Market, 2016" in *Artprice.com*.

Ault, Julie (2003) *Alternative Art New York, 1965–1985* (Minneapolis: University of Minnesota Press).

Baldessari, John, quoted in Sarah Thornton (2008) *Seven Days in the Art World* (New York: W. W. Norton & Co.).

Bann, S. (2002) "Entre philosophie et critique: Victor Cousin, Théophile Gautier et l'art pour l'art" in P.-H. Frangne and J.-M. Poinsot (eds.), *L'Invention de la critique d'art* (Rennes: Presses Universitaires de Rennes) pp. 137–44.

Barker, Emma, Nick Webb, and Kim Woods, eds. (1999) *The Changing Status of the Artist* (New Haven: Yale University Press).

Barker, Sheila, ed. (2016) *Women Artists in Early Modern Italy: Careers, Fame, and Collectors* (Turnhout: Brepols).

Barr, Alfred H. (1967) *Van Gogh* (New York: Taylor & Francis).

Battino, Freddy, and Luca Palazzoli (1991) *Piero Manzoni: Catalogue raisonné*, Milan, pp. 123–8, 472–5, catalogue no. 1053/4.

Baudelaire, Charles (1846) "The Salon of 1846: On the Heroism of Modern Life" in Francis Frascina and Charles Harrison (eds.), *Modern Art and Modernism: A Critical Anthology* (London: Routledge) 1982.

Baudelaire, Charles (1859) *On Photography*, in *The Salon of 1859* (New York: Doubleday Anchor).

Baudelaire, Charles (1964) *The Painter of Modern Life* (New York: Da Capo Press). Originally published, in French, in *Le Figaro*, 1863.

Baxandall, Michael (1988) *Painting and Experience in Fifteenth-Century Italy: A Primer in the Social History of Pictorial Style* (Oxford: Oxford University Press).

Bazin, André (1960) "The Ontology of the Photographic Image" *Film Quarterly* 13(4): 4–9.

Beltramme, Marcello (1990) "Le teoriche del Paleotti e il riformismo dell'Accademia di San Luca nella politica artistica di Clemente VIII, 1592–1605" in *Storia dell'arte* 69, pp. 201–33.

Benedictow, Ole Jørgen (2021) *Black Death 1346–1353 The Complete History* (Woodbridge: Boydell Press).

Benjamin, Walter (1935) "Work of Art in the Age of Mechanical Reproduction" in *Illuminations* (New York: Schocken Books) 1977.

Benjamin, Walter (2006) *The Writer of Modern Life: Essays on Charles Baudelaire* (Cambridge, MA: Harvard University Press).

Berg, Gary A. (2019) *The Rise of Women in Higher Education: How, Why, and What's Next* (Lanham, MD: Rowman & Littlefield).

Berniker, Talia (2020) "Behind Closed Doors: A Look At Freeports" in *Center for Art Law*, online: https://itsartlaw.org/2020/11/03/behind-closed-doors-a-look-at-freeports/#post-56093-footnote-15.

Bhopal, Kalwant (2020) "UK's white female academics are being privileged above women – and men – of colour" in *The Guardian*, online: https://www.theguardian.com/education/2020/jul/28/uks-white-female-academics-are-being-privileged-above-women-and-men-of-colour.

Bishar, Hakim (2019) "Hilma Af Klint Breaks Records at the Guggenheim Museum" in *Hyperallergic*, online: https://hyperallergic.com/496326/hilma-af-klint-breaks-records-at-the-guggenheim-museum/.

Boime, A. (2008) *Art in an Age of Civil Struggle, 1848–1871* (Chicago: University of Chicago Press).

Bonafede, Carolina (1845) *Cenni biografici e ritratti d'insigni donne bolognesi: raccolti dagli storici più accreditati* (Bologna: Atesa Editrice) 1977.

Borzello, Francis (2000) *A World of Our Own: Women as Artists Since the Renaissance* (New York: Watson-Guptill Publications).

Bose, M. B. (2018) *Women, Gender and Art in Asia, c. 1500–1900* (London: Routledge); Weidner, Marsha, ed. (1991) *Flowering in the Shadows: Women in the History of Chinese and Japanese Painting (English, Chinese and Japanese Edition)* (Honolulu: University of Hawai'i Press).

Brenner, Anita (1938) "America Creates American Murals" in *The New York Times*, 10 April, online: https://www.nytimes.com/1938/04/10/archives/american-creates-american-murals-to-bid-for-the-favor-of-a-new-mass.html.

Britannica, The Editors of Encyclopaedia (2010) "Mandarin" *Encyclopedia Britannica*, August 30, online: https://www.britannica.com/topic/mandarin.

Brooks, Arthur (2020) "Success Addicts' Choose Being Special Over Being Happy" in *The Atlantic*, July 30, online: https://www.theatlantic.com/family/archive/2020/07/why-success-wont-make-you-happy/614731/.

Brown, Christopher Lesley, Jan Kelch, and Pieter van Thiel (1991) *Rembrandt: The Master and His Workshop: Paintings* (New Haven: Yale University Press).

Buick, K. Pai (2010) *Child of the Fire: Mary Edmonia Lewis and the Problem of Art History's Black and Indian Subject* (Durham, NC: Duke University Press).

Burke, Peter (1994) "Italian Artist and His Role" in Peter Burke Ellen Bianchini, and Claire Dorey (eds.), *History of Italian Art, Volume I* (Cambridge: Polity Press) pp. 1–28.

Bush, Susan (2012) *The Chinese Literati on Painting: Su Shih (1037–1101) to Tung Ch'i-ch'ang (1555–1636)* (Hong Kong: Hong Kong University Press).

Campbell, Joseph (1988) *The Power of Myth* [TV series] PBS.

Cardinal, Roger (1972) *Outsider Art* (New York: Praeger).

Cardinal, Roger, and Victor Musgrov (1979) *Outsiders: An art without precedent or tradition* (London: Arts Council of Great Britain).

Carey, Kevin (2016) *The End of College: Creating the Future of Learning and the University of Everywhere* (New York: Riverhead Books).

Carney, James (1975) "Defining Art" *British Journal of Aesthetics* 15: 191–206; Matthews, Robert (1979) "Traditional Aesthetics Defended" *Journal of Aesthetics and Art Criticism* 38(1): 39–50.

Casparie, Sabine (2021) "Understanding Njideka Akunyili Crosby in 10 Works of Art" in *The Collector*, online: https://www.thecollector.com/njideka-akunyili-crosby-10-works-of-art/.

Cennino, Cennini (1400) *Il Libro dell'Arte, o Trattato della Pittura di Cennino Cennini da Colle di Valdelsa*.

Chadwick, Whitney (1990) *Women, Art, and Society* (New York and London: Thames & Hudson).

Charles Eames quoted in Berkun, Scott (2010) "Why You Are Not an Artist" in *Scott Berkun*, online: https://scottberkun.com/2010/why-you-are-not-an-artist/.

Cohen, Alina (2018) "When Paul Cadmus's Homoerotic Military Painting Launched a National Scandal" in *Artsy*, online: https://www.artsy.net/article/artsy-editorial-paul-cadmuss-homoerotic-military-painting-launched-national-scandal.

Chubb Editors, "New Chubb Survey Measures Americans' Attitudes Toward Collecting Valuables and Purchasing Decisions Amid the Pandemic" in *Chubb*, online: https://www.prnewswire.com/news-releases/new-chubb-survey-measures-americans-attitudes-toward-collecting-valuables-and-purchasing-decisions-amid-the-pandemic-301422308.html.

Clark, T. J. (1999) *The Painting of Modern Life: Paris in the Art of Manet and his Followers* (Princeton: Princeton University Press).

Courbet, Gustave, and Petra ten-Doesschate Chu (1992) *Letters of Gustave Courbet* (Chicago: University of Chicago Press).

Craig-Martin, M. (2019) *On being an artist* (New York: Art Books).

Dachy, Marc (2006) *Dada: The Revolt of Art* (London: Thames & Hudson).

Dana, John Cotton, M. S. S. Price, and S. E. Weil (1999) *The New Museum: Selected Writings by John Cotton Dana* (Washington DC: American Alliance of Museums).

Danto, Arthur (1964) "The Artworld" in *The Journal of Philosophy* 16(19): 571–84.

Danto, Arthur (1998) *After the End of Art: Contemporary Art and the Pale of History* (Princeton: Princeton University Press).

Davis, R., and A. Tilley (2019) *What They Didn't Teach You in Art School: What You Actually Need to Know to Succeed in the Industry* (Banbury: Ilex).

Dawson, Raymond (2000) *The Chinese Experience* (Phoenix: Orion).

de Burca, Jackie (2018) *Salvador Dalí at Home* (North Brabant: Van Haren Publishing).

De Duve, Thierry, and Rosalind Krauss (1989) "Andy Warhol or the machine perfected" *October* 48(Spring): 3–14.

Dean, Trevor, and Kate Lowe, eds. (1994) *Crime, Society and the Law in Renaissance Italy* (Cambridge: Cambridge University Press).

Deffebach, Nancy (2015) *María Izquierdo and Frida Kahlo: Challenging Visions in Modern Mexican Art* (Latin American and Caribbean Arts and Culture Publication Initiative, Mellon Foundation) (Austin: University of Texas Press).

Deitch, Jeffrey (1982) "Jean-Michel Basquiat: Annina Nosei" in *Flash Art*, May.

Deleuze, G., F. Guattari, R. Hurley, M. Seem, H. R. Lane, and M. Foucault (2009) *Anti-Oedipus: Capitalism and Schizophrenia* (London: Penguin Classics).

Dercon, Chris (2015) *The World Goes Pop* (London: Tate Publishing).

Deresiewicz, William (2015) *Excellent Sheep: The Miseducation of the American Elite and the Way to a Meaningful Life* (New York: Free Press).

Dimendberg, E. (1995) *The Weimar Republic Sourcebook* (Berkeley: University of California Press) p. 485.

Droste, Magdalen (2019) *Bauhaus* (Berlin: Taschen).

D'Souza, Aruna (1997) "I Think Your Work Looks a Lot Like Dubuffet: Dubuffet and America, 1946–1962" *Oxford Art Journal* 20(2): 61.

Dubuffet, Jean (1949) "Art Brut in Preference to the Cultural Arts" *Art and Text 27* (December–February 1988): 31–3.

Dubuffet, Jean (1979) quote from text wall in *Outsiders* exhibition at Hayward Gallery, London.

Duchamp, Marcel (1956) *A Conversation with Marcel Duchamp*, The National Broadcasting Company, Philadelphia Museum of Art.

Duro, Paul (2007) "Imitation and Authority: The Creation of the Academic Canon in French Art 1648–1870" in Anna Brzysky (ed.), *Partisan Canons* (Durham, NC: Duke University Press).

Elderfield, John, ed. (2011) *De Kooning: A Retrospective* (New York: Museum of Modern Art).

Eldredge, C. Charles (1996) *Georgia O'Keeffe: American And Modern* (New Haven: Yale University Press).

Elman, Benjamin (2002) *A Cultural History of Civil Examinations in Late Imperial China* (Berkeley: University of California Press).

Enwezor, Okwui (2003) "The Postcolonial Constellation: Contemporary Art in a State of Permanent Transition" *Research in African Literatures* 34(4): 57–82.

Enwezor, Okwui (2007) "The Production of Social Space as Artwork" in Blake Stimson and Gregory Sholette (eds.) *Collectivism after Modernism: The Art of Social Imagination after 1945* (Minneapolis: University of Minnesota Press) pp. 223–51.

Erlanger, Steven (2010) "A French Castle Built of Stone and Dreams" in *The New York Times*, online: https://www.nytimes.com/2010/08/01/world/europe/01castle.htmlaccessed.

Fanon, Frantz (1968) *The Wretched of the Earth* (New York: Grove Press).

Fisher, Mark (2009) *Capitalist Realism* (London: Zero Books).

Fleming, G. H. (1998) *John Everett Millais: A Biography* (London: Constable).

Fleming, Peter (2021) *Dark Academia: How Universities Die* (London: Pluto Press).

Fox Weber, Nicholas (2011) *The Bauhaus Group: Six Masters of Modernism*. (New Haven: Yale University Press).

Frascina, Francis, and Charles Harrison (1982) *Modern Art and Modernism: A Critical Anthology* (London: Routledge).

Fraser, Andrea (2005) "From the Critique of Institution to an Institution of Critique" in *Art Forum*, September, pp. 100–6.

Freud, Sigmund, quoted in Goodwin, D. Craufurd (1998). *Art and the Market: Roger Fry on Commerce in Art, Selected Writings, Edited with an Interpretation* (Ann Arbor: University of Michigan Press) p. 130.

Freud, Sigmund, and James Strachey (1910) *Leonardo da Vinci and a Memory of His Childhood (Complete Psychological Works of Sigmund Freud)* (New York: W. W. Norton & Co.) p. 67.

Friedman, Zack (2002) "Student Loan Debt Statistics In 2020: A Record $1.6 Trillion" in *Forbes*, online: https://www.forbes.com/sites/zackfriedman/2020/02/03/student-loan-debt-statistics/?sh=4a5a0537281f.

Fry, Roger, and Christopher Reed (1996) *A Roger Fry Reader* (Chicago: University of Chicago Press).

Gablik, Suzie (1985) *Has Modernism Failed?* (London: Thames & Hudson).

Gaensheimer, Susanne, Isabelle Malz, Catherine Nichols, Eugen Blume, and Kunstsammlung Nordrhein-Westfalen (2021) *Everyone Is an Artist : Cosmopolitical Exercises with Joseph Beuys : [Exhibition, Düsseldorf, Kunstsammlung Nordrhein-Westfalen, March 27 – August 15, 2021].* (Düsseldorf: Kunstsammlung Nordrhein-Westfalen; Berlin).

Gallant, Leah (2020) "Breaking Down Faculty Demographics" in *FNMagazine*, online: https://fnewsmagazine.com/images/issues/2020-08-Summer.pdf/breaking-down-faculty-demographics.html accessed 12/05/2020.

Gallie, W. B. (1956) "Art as an Essentially Contested Concept" *Philosophical Quarterly* 6(23): 97–114.

Gammel, Irene (2003) *Baroness Elsa: Gender, Dada, and Everyday Modernity—A Cultural* (Cambridge: MIT Press).

Gelfand, Aleksandr (2013) "Today in MET History: February 4th", in *The Met*, online: https://www.metmuseum.org/blogs/now-at-the-met/features/2013/today-in-met-history-february-4.

Gewin, Virginia (2021) "Pandemic burnout is rampant in academia" in *Nature*, online: https://www.nature.com/articles/d41586-021-00663-2.

Gioni, Massimiliano, interviewed by M. Andrew Goldstein (2013) "Massimiliano Gioni on His Venice Biennale Show, and "Trying to See More" in *Artspace*, online: https://www.artspace.com/magazine/interviews_features/qa/massimiliano_gioni_venice_biennale_interview-51106.

Godfrey, B. Tony (1998) *Conceptual Art* (London: Phaidon).

Gogh-Bonger, V. Jo., and Martin Gayford (2018) *A Memoir of Vincent van Gogh* (Los Angeles: J. Paul Getty Museum).

Gombrich, H. E. (1950) *The Story of Art* (London: Phaidon).

Gopnik, Blake (2020) *Warhol* (New York: Ecco).

Ghosh, Amitav (2017) *The Great Derangement: Climate Change and the Unthinkable* (Chicago: University of Chicago Press).

Gipson, Ferren (2022) *Women's Work: From Feminine Arts to Feminist Art* (London: Frances Lincoln).

Gowing, Lawrence (2005) *Facts on File Encyclopedia of Art*: 5 (New York: Facts on File).

Grant, C., and D. Price (2020) "Decolonizing Art History" *Art History* 43, pp. 8–66.

Grieve, Virginia (2009) *The Federal Art Project and the Creation of Middlebrow Culture* (Champaign: University of Illinois Press).

Guattari, Félix (1995) *Chaosmosis: An Ethico-Aesthetic Paradigm* (Sydney: Power).

Hales, D. (2015) *Mona Lisa: A Life Discovered* (New York: Simon & Schuster).

Hamilton, James (2008) *London Lights: The Minds that Moved the City That Shook the World* (London: John Murray).

Haraway, Donna (2016) *Staying with the Trouble: Making Kin in the Chthulucene* (Durham, NC: Duke University Press).

Harring, Keith, quoted in Jordan M. Saggese (2021) *The Jean-Michel Basquiat Reader: Writings, Interviews, and Critical Responses* (Berkeley: University of California Press).

Hauser, Arnold (1951) *Social History of Art* (New York: Vintage).

Hayes, Jeffreen M., Kirsten Pai Buick, and Bridget R. Cooks (2021) *Augusta Savage: Renaissance Woman* (Lewes: Giles).

Hartfield, John, and George Grosz (1920) "Der Kunstlump" *Der Gegner* 1(10–12): 48–56.

Heinich, Nathalie (1996) *The Glory of van Gogh: An Anthropology of Admiration* (Princeton: Princeton University Press).

Hewitt, Catherine (2020) *Art Is a Tyrant: The Unconventional Life of Rosa Bonheur* (London: Icon Books).

HiHo Kids (2017) "100 Kids Tell Us What They Want to Be When They Grow Up" online: https://www.youtube.com/watch?v=RUup841pZrs.

Hilma Af Klint Foundation: https://www.hilmaafklint.se/en.

Hinds, Kathryn (2009) *Everyday Life in the Renaissance* (New York: Marshall Cavendish Benchmark).

Hirsch, Robert (2017). *Seizing the Light: A Social & Aesthetic History of Photography* (London: Routledge).

Hirst, Damien (n.d.) *Freeze* in Damien Hirst official website, online: https://www.damienhirst.com/exhibitions/group/1988/freeze.

Höch, Hannah, in Édouard Roditi (1959) "Interview with Hannah Höch" *Arts Magazine* 34(3).

Honnef, Klaus, and Andy Warhol (2000) *Andy Warhol: Commerce Into Art* (London: Taschen).

Hook, Phillip (2018) *Rogues Galleries: A History of Art and Its Dealers* (London: Profile Books).

hooks, bell (1995) *Art on My Mind: Visual Politics* (New York: The New Press).

Huggins, Nathan (2007) *Harlem Renaissance* (Oxford: Oxford University Press).

Hughes, Robert (2008) *The Mona Lisa Curse*, documentary, dir. Mandy Chang.

Hurn, David, and Claire Grafik (2007) *I'm a Real Photographer* (London: Chris Boot).

Jameson, F. (1992) *Postmodernism, or, The Cultural Logic of Late Capitalism* (Durham, NC: Duke University Press).

Jung, Carl. G. (1991) *The Archetypes and the Collective Unconscious* (London: Routledge).

Jung, Carl. G., and R. A. Segal (1998) *Jung on Mythology* (Princeton: Princeton University Press).

Jung, Carl. G., G. Adler, and R. F. C. Hull (1971) *The Spirit in Man, Art, & Literature*) (Princeton: Princeton University Press).

Juraga, Dubravka, and Keith M. Booker (2002) *Socialist Cultures East and West* (Westport, CT: Praeger).

Kellaway, Kate (2016) "Hilma Af Klint: a painter possessed" in *The Guardian*, February 21, online: https://www.theguardian.com/artanddesign/2016/feb/21/hilma-af-klint-occult-spiritualism-abstract-serpentine-gallery on 07/07/2021.

Kemp, Martin (2011) *Leonardo: Revised Edition* (Oxford: Oxford University Press).

Kempers, Bram (1992) *Painting, Power and Patronage: The Rise of the Professional Artist in the Italian Renaissance* (London: Allen Lane).

Kift, Dagmar (1996) *The Victorian Music Hall: Culture, Class and Conflict* (Cambridge: Cambridge University Press).

Kinsella, Eileen (2018) "The Dung-Adorned Madonna That Giuliani Once Tried to Ban Has Been Donated to MoMA by Steve Cohen" in *Artnet*, online: https://news.artnet.com/art-world/steve-cohen-chris-ofili-virgin-mary-moma-1269002.

Kimmerer, Robin Wall (2013) *Braiding Sweetgrass: Indigenous Wisdom, Scientific Knowledge and the Teachings of Plants* (Minneapolis: Milkweed Editions).

Klutsis, Gustav (1931) "Photomontage as a new kind of agitation art" in *Photomontage Between the Wars: 1918–1939* (Ottawa: Carleton University Art Gallery).

Koerner, Leo J. (2008) *The Reformation of the Image* (Chicago: University of Chicago Press).

Kramer, Hilton (1990) "The Man Who Held the Cubists Together" in *The New York Times*, September 2, online: https://www.nytimes.com/1990/09/02/books/the-man-who-held-the-cubists-together.html accessed on 07/11/2021.

Kuc, Kamila, and Michael O'Pray (2014) *The Struggle for Form: Perspectives on Polish Avant-Garde Film, 1916–1989* (New York: Wallflower Press).

Kundera, Milan (2020) *The Unbearable Lightness of Being.* (London: Faber & Faber).

Kusama, Yayoi, and Ralph McCarthy (2021) *Infinity Net: The Autobiography of Yayoi Kusama by Yayoi Kusama* (London: Tate Publishing).

Le Feuvre, Lisa (2010) "If at first you don't succeed, celebrate" in *Tate, Etc.*, online: https://www.tate.org.uk/tate-etc/issue-18-spring-2010/if-first-you-dont-succeed-celebrate accessed 12/26/2021.

Leddy, Thomas (1987) "Rigid Designation in Defining Art" *Journal of Aesthetics and Art Criticism* 45(3): 263–72.

Leperlier, Francois (1999) *Claude Cahun* (London: Verso).

Levi, Neil (2013) *Modernist Form and the Myth of Jewification*, (New York: Fordham University Press).

Levinson, Jerrold (1989) "Refining Art Historically" *Journal of Aesthetics and Art Criticism* 47(I): 21–33.

Links, J. G. (1983) *Canaletto and His Patrons* (New York: Hacker Art Books).

Livezeanu, Irina (2005) "'From Dada to Gaga': The Peripatetic Romanian Avant-Garde Confronts Communism" in Mihai Dinu Gheorghiu and Lucia Dragomir (eds.), *Littératures et pouvoir symbolique. Colloque tenu à Bucarest (Roumanie), 30 et 31 mai 2003* (Paris: Maison des sciences de l'homme).

Locke, Alain (1997) *The New Negro* (New York: Simon & Schuster).

Lui, John (2020) "Essentially no one is saying that painters, actors, singers, and writers contribute nothing" in *The Straits Times*, online: https://chaseonline.chase.com/Secure/OSL.aspx?newstoken=false&LOB=RBGLogon&Referer=https%3A%2F%2Fwww.chase.com%2F&resId=success&.

Luke, Ben (2019) "Here are 2019's most visited contemporary art exhibitions" in *The Art Newspaper*, online: https://www.theartnewspaper.com/2020/03/31/here-are-2019s-most-visited-contemporary-art-exhibitions.

MacCullogh, John (1908) "Hastings, James; Selble, John Alexander; & Gray, Louis Herbert" *Encyclopaedia of Religion and Ethics* (Edinburgh: T. & T. Clark) vol. 11, p. 445.

Maddox, John Lee, and Albert Galloway Keller (2010) *The Medicine Man: A Sociological Study of the Character and Evolution of Shamanism* (Whitefish, MT: Kessinger Publishing).

Mainardi, Patricia (1991) "Courbet's Exhibitionism" *Gazette des Beaux-Arts* no. 118, pp. 256–65.

Marlow, Tim, John Tancock Daniel Rosbottom, A. Locke, and W. Ai (2015) *Ai Weiwei* (London: Royal Academy Publications).

Martin, Therese, ed. (2012) *Reassessing the Roles of Women as 'Makers' of Medieval Art and Architecture* (Leiden: Brill).

Mbembe, Achille (2021) *Out of the Dark Night* (Amsterdam: Amsterdam University Press).

McAndrew, Clare, and Charlotte Burns (2020) *The Bulletin with UBS, a podcast from Monocle*, online: https://www.ubs.com/global/en/our-firm/art/2020/racial-and-gender-diversity.html.

McCormack, Catherine (2021) *Women in the Picture Women, Art and the Power of Looking* (London: Icon Books).

McLerran, Jennifer (2009) *A New Deal for Native Art: Indian Arts and Federal Policy, 1933–1943* (Tucson: University of Arizona Press).

MEAA Editors (2016) "MEAA appalled by AIM and Warner Bros. seeking musicians to work for free" in *Media Entertainment & Arts Alliance*, online: https://www.meaa.org/news/meaa-appalled-by-aim-and-warner-bros-seeking-musicians-to-work-for-free/.

Mellor, David Alan (1998) *Chemical Traces: Photography and Conceptual Art*, exhibition catalog (Ferens Art Gallery, Kingston upon Hull).

Meneglier, Hervé (1990) *Paris impérial: La vie quotidienne sous le Second Empire* (Paris: Armand Colin).

Milanesi, Gaetano, and Carlo Milanesi (Florence: Felice Le Monnier Editore) 1859.

Milza, Pierre (2009) *L'année terrible – La Commune* (Paris: Perrin).

Mitali, Banerjee, and Paul L. Ingram (2018 "Fame as an Illusion of Creativity: Evidence from the Pioneers of Abstract Art" (HEC Paris Research Paper No. SPE-2018-1305, *Columbia Business School Research Paper* No. 18-74, available at SSRN: https://ssrn.com/abstract=3258318 or http://dx.doi.org/10.2139/ssrn.3258318.

Montias, John Michael (1988) "Art Dealers in the Seventeenth-Century Netherlands" *Simiolus: Netherlands Quarterly for the History of Art* 18(4): 244–56.

Morgan, Marcyliena H. (2014) *Speech Communities* (Cambridge: Cambridge University Press).

Morton, Timothy (2012) *The Ecological Thought* (Cambridge, MA, and London: Harvard University Press).

Motely, Archibald (1918) "The Negro in Art" in *The Chicago Defender*, July 6.

Motley, Willard (1947) *Knock on Any Door*, 1998 (Chicago: Northern Illinois University Press).

Muir, Gregor (2012) *Lunky Kunst: The Rise and Fall of Young British Art* (London: Aurum Press).

Nadler, et al. (2018) Press Release: "Nadler, Hatch, Leahy & Collins Introduce Bipartisan, Bicameral American Royalties Too Act" (September 25); see also Hanoch Sheps (2013) *Artist Resale Royalty Rights – Is a US Droite de Suite in our Future?*, *Center for Art Law* (December 2).

Nerburn, K. (2020). *The Artist's Journey* (Edinburgh: Canongate Books).

Nesbitt, Judith, ed. (2008) *Peter Doig* (London: Tate).

Nietzsche, Friedrich Wilhelm, and Duncan Large (2008) *Twilight of the Idols: Or How to Philosophize with a Hammer* (Oxford: Oxford University Press).

Nochlin, Linda (1971) "Why Have There Been No Great Women Artists" in Vivian Gornick and Barbar Moran (eds.), *Woman in Sexist Society: Studies in Power and Powerlessness* (New York: Basic Books).

Novitz, David (1996) "Disputes about An" *Journal of Aesthetics and Art Criticism* 54(2): 153–63.

Outsider Art Fair Organizers (n.d.) "What is Outsider Art?" in *Outsider Art Fair*, online: https://www.outsiderartfair.com/the-field.

Palmer, Laure (2015) "Back to School: 10 Famous Art Professors We Wish We Had as Teachers in College" in *Artnews*, online: https://news.artnet.com/art-world/best-art-professors-around-the-world-330870.

Pei, Fang Jing (1997) *Treasures Of The Chinese Scholar* (Toronto: Weatherhill) p. 6.

Pertsov, Viktor (1922) "At the junction of art and production" in John Bowlt (ed.) *Russian Art of the Avant-Garde: Theory and Criticism, 1902–1934* (New York: Viking) 1976.

Pholdhampalit, Khetsirin (2019) "Art in Its Purest Form" in *The Nation: Thailand*, online: https://www.nationthailand.com/life/30373871.

Picasso, Pablo, quoted in John Richardson (2009) *A Life of Picasso – Volume 3* (London: Pimlico).

Plato (1964) *The Works of Plato*, trans. B. Jowett (Oxford: Clarendon Press) *Republic* X.

Pollock, Griselda (1994) "Modernity and the space of femininity" in *Vision & Difference: Feminity, Feminism, and the Histories of Art* (London: Routledge).

Price, Dorothy, and Patrick Grant (2020) "Decolonizing Art History" in *Art History* (February), pp. 8–66.

Postcommodity, *Through the Repellent Fence*, online https://www. throughtherepellentfence.com/.

Quemin, Alain (2015) "The impact of Nationality in the Contemporary Art Market" in *Scielo Brazil*, online: https://www.scielo.br/j/sant/a/p3cbxHS9yGx7zNFY5wqFtxM/?lang=en.

Ragg, Laura Maria (1907) *The Women Artists of Bologna* (London: Methuen).

Rauschenberg, Robert, in conversation with Jason Kaufman (1997) "Robert Rauschenberg: 'Business sure screwed up the art world universally'" in *The Arts Newspaper*, online: https://www.theartnewspaper.com/1997/09/01/robert-rauschenberg-business-sure-screwed-up-the-art-world-universally.

Redazione ANSA, "Manzoni's *Artist Shit* Goes for 275,000 Euros" in *ANSA Arts & Culture*, online: https://www.ansa.it/english/news/lifestyle/arts/2016/12/07/manzoni-artists-shit-goes-for-275000_baab4664-23a7-40c3-8eb5-a6012d06e95d.html.

Resch, Magnus (2016) *The Global Art Gallery Report 2016* (London: Phaidon).

Resch, Magnus (2021) *How to Become a Successful Artist* (London: Phaidon).

Rexer, Lyle (2005) *How to Look at Outsider Art* (New York: Harry N. Abrams).

Ricard, Rene (1981) "The Radiant Child" in *Art Forum*, pp. 35–43.

Riding, Christine (2003) "The Fatal Raft: Christine Riding Looks at British Reaction to the French Tragedy at Sea Immortalised in Gericault's Masterpiece 'The Raft of the Medusa'" in *History Today* (February).

Rivera, Diego, quoted in Nick Caistor (2021) *Mexico City* (Oxford: Signal Books) p. 168.

Robinson, Cedric (1983) *Black Marxism* (Chapel Hill: University of North Carolina Press).

Roe, Sue (2007) *The Private Lives of the Impressionists* (New York: Harper Perennial).

Roosevelt, Theodore (1913) "Mr. Rosevelt on the Cubists" in *The Literary Digest*, April 5, p. 772.

Rose, Barbara (1973) "Profit Without Honor" in *The New York Magazine*, November 5, pp. 80–1.

Rossab, Morris (1986) "Kuan Tao Sheng: Women Artist in Yuan China" in *Bulletin of Sung and Yuan Studies, No. 2*, pp. 67–84.

Ruggenberg, Luke (2020) *Plants are Terrible People* (independently published).

Saar, Betye (2021) "How I became an artist" in *Roberts Projects*, online: https://www.robertsprojectsla.com/news/how-i-became-an-artist-betye-saar.

Saggese, J. M. (2021) *The Jean-Michel Basquiat Reader: Writings, Interviews, and Critical Responses* (Berkeley: University of California Press).

Salisbury, Laurel Wickersham (2019) "It's Not That Easy: Artist Resale Royalty Rights and The ART Act" in *Center for Art Law*, online: https://itsartlaw.org/2019/07/01/its-not-that-easy-artist-resale-royalty-rights-and-the-art-act/.

Saltz, Jerry (2020) "My Life as a Failed Artist" in *Vulture*, online: https://www.vulture.com/2017/04/erry-saltz-my-life-as-a-failed-artist.html.

Samuels, Ernest, and Jayne Samuels (1987) *Bernard Berenson, the Making of a Legend* (Cambridge, MA: Harvard University Press).

Scanlan, Joe (2017) "Not Knowing: Contemporary Art and the Amateur" in *Joe Scanlan artist website*, online: https://joescanlan.biz/not-knowing-contemporary-art-and-the-amateur/.

Schad, Ed, Shirin Neshat, and Godfrey Cheshire (2019) *Shirin Neshat* (Los Angeles: The Broad).

Schuster, Clayton (2020) "In NYC, a Fair Dedicated to Outsider Art Cultivates an Interest in the Eccentric" in *The Observer*, online: https://observer.com/2020/01/outsider-art-fair-market-growth-in-new-york.

Scotti, R. A. (2009) *Vanished Smile: The Mysterious Theft of Mona Lisa* (New York: Knopf).

Scull, Robert (1973) *A Selection of Fifty Works from the Collection of Robert C. Scull* (New York: Sotheby Parker Barnet Inc.).

Selz, Peter (1962) *The Work of Jean Dubuffet, with Texts by the Artist* (New York: New York Museum of Modern Art).

Seyller, John (1999) "Workshop and Patron in Mughal India: The Freer Rāmāyaṇa and Other Illustrated Manuscripts of 'Abd al-Raḥīm'" in *Artibus Asiae. Supplementum* 42: 3–344.

Shanes, Eric (2014) *Salvador Dalí* (New York: Parkstone International).

Shank, Ian (2017) "How Salvador Dalí Accidentally Sabotaged His Own Market for Prints" in *Artsy.net*, online: https://www.artsy.net/article/artsy-editorial-salvador-Dalí-accidentally-sabotaged-market-prints.

Shaw, Anny (2021) "Who is Beeple? The art world disruptor at the heart of the NFT boom" in *The Art Newspaper*, online: https://www.theartnewspaper.com/2021/03/05/who-is-beeple-the-art-world-disruptor-at-the-heart-of-the-nft-boom.

Sherwin, Brian (2007) "Art Space Talk: Michael Craig-Martin" *Myartspace*, August 16.

Shiva, Vandana (2016) *Staying Alive: Women, Ecology, and Development* (Berkeley: North Atlantic Books).

Shivani, Vora (2021) "Sotheby's Auction to Sell Warring Macklowe Art Collection Brings in Record $676 Million" in *Architectural Digest*, online: https://www.architecturaldigest.com/story/macklowe-auction-sothebys.

Smith, B., and R. Smith (2020) *You are an Artist* (London and New York: Thames & Hudson).

Smith, Clint (2023) *One Book One Northwestern 2022–23: How the Word is Passed* (Chicago: Northwestern University Press).

Snell, Robert (2016) *Portraits of the Insane: Theodore Gericault and the Subject of Psychotherapy* (London: Routledge).

Solomon, Deborah (2001) *Jackson Pollock: A Biography* (London: Cooper Square Press).

Solsman, Joan E. (2021) "Netflix's Squid Game was even bigger than you thought – 2.1B hours big" in *Cnet.com*, online: https://www.cnet.com/news/netflix-squid-game-is-even-bigger-than-you-thought-2-billion-hours-big/.

Spotts, Frederic (2002) *Hitler and the Power of Aesthetics* (New York: The Overlook Press).

Stunkel, Kenneth R. (2011) *Ideas and Art in Asian Civilizations: India, China, and Japan* (London and New York: Routledge).

Sturgis, Alexander (2006) *Rebels and Martyrs: The Image of the Artist in the Nineteenth Century* (New Haven: Yale University Press; London: The National Gallery).

Sutherland, Daniel E. (2014) *Whistler: A Life for Art's Sake* (New Haven: Yale University Press).

Sutton, Benjamin (2015) "Artists from Five Galleries Dominate US Museum Shows" in *Hyperallergic*, online: https://hyperallergic.com/195752/artists-from-five-galleries-dominate-us-museum-shows/.

Tanner, Jeremy (1999) "Culture, Social Structure and the Status of Visual Artists in Classical Greece" in *Proceedings of the Cambridge Philological Society* no. 45, pp. 136–75.

Tazi, Abdelhadi (1980) *Eleven Centuries in the History of Al-Qarawiyyin University On Occasion of the Campaign for Saving and Repairing the Fes City* (Fes: Ministry of Information).

Taylor, Mark C. (2012) *Refiguring the Spiritual* (New York: Columbia University Press).

Taylor, Nora A. (2005) "Why have there not been great Vietnamese artists?" *Michigan Quarterly Review* XLIV(1): *Viet Nam: Beyond the Frame (Part Two)*.

The World Bank editors (2021) "Overview" in *The World Bank*, online: https://www.worldbank.org/en/country/china/overview#3.

Thompson, John, and Monika Kinley (2006) *Inner Worlds Outside at the Whitechapel Gallery* (London: Whitechapel Art Gallery).

Tinterow, Gary, and Henri Loyrette (1994) *Origins of Impressionism* (New York: Harry N. Abrams).

Tsong-Zung, Chang (2011) "Ink Painting in the Age of New Wave" in Jörg Huber and Zhao Chuan (eds.), *A New Thoughtfulness in Contemporary China* (London: Transaction Publishers).

Tsuda, Noritake, and Patrician Graham (2009) *A History of Japanese Art: From Prehistory to the Taisho Period* (Clarendon: Tuttle Publishing).

Van Slujter, Eric (2009) *Art Market and Connoisseurship: A Closer Look at Paintings by Rembrandt, Rubens and Their Contemporaries* (Amsterdam: Amsterdam University Press).

Vasari, Giorgio, Peter Bondanella, and Julia Conway (2008) *The Lives of the Artists (Oxford World's Classics)* (Oxford: Oxford University Press) 1550.

Villa, Angelica (2021) "The Most Expensive Artworks by Pablo Picasso Ever Sold at Auction" in *Art News*, online: https://www.artnews.com/list/art-news/artists/pablo-picasso-highest-auction-records-1234594915/femme-assise-1909/.

Waldam, Kathy (2018) "Does Having a Day Job Mean Making Better Art?" in *The New York Times Style Magazine*, online: https://www.nytimes.com/2018/03/22/t-magazine/art/artist-day-job.html.

Wallace, Isabelle Loring, and Jennie Hirsh (2011) *Contemporary Art and Classical Myth* (Farnham: Ashgate).

Wardwell, Allen (2009) *Tangible Visions: Northwest Coast Indian Shamanism and Its Art* (New York: The Monacelli Press).

Weaton, Wil (2015) "You can't pay your rent with 'the unique platform and reach our site provides'" in *Wil Weaton dot net*, online: http://wilwheaton.net/2015/10/you-cant-pay-your-rent-with-the-unique-platform-and-reach-our-site-provides/.

Weidner, M. S. (1988) *Views From Jade Terrace: Chinese Women Artists 1300 –1912* (New York and Milan: Rizzoli).

Weitz, Morris (1956) "The Role of Theory in Aesthetics" *Journal of Aesthetics and Art Criticism* 15(I): 27–35.

Weill, Berth, et al. (2022) *Pow! Right in the Eye! Thirty Years behind the Scenes of Modern French Painting* (Chicago: University of Chicago Press).

Wertheim, Lucy Carrington (2022) *Adventure in Art* (Lewes: Unicorn).

Wilhelm, Alex (2021) "Amazon stock falls on revenue miss, rising costs due to macroeconomic conditions" in *Techurch.com*, online: https://techcrunch.com/2021/10/28/amazon-stock-falls-on-revenue-miss-rising-costs-due-to-macroeconomic-conditions/.

Wilson, Paul (2018) "How Much Was Pablo Picasso Worth When He Died?" in *Celebrity Net Worth*, online: https://www.celebritynetworth.com/articles/how-much-does/happens-estate-valued-billion-dollars-dont-leave-will-children-pablo-picasso-found-hard-way/.

Wisniewski, Gene (2020) *The Art of Looking at Art* (Lanham, MD: Rowman & Littlefield).

Wolff, Albert (1876) quoted in Haskell, Francis (1987) *Past and Present in Art and Taste: Selected Essays* (New Haven: Yale University Press).

Wood, M. Ellen (2017) *The Origin of Capitalism: A Longer View* (New York: Verso).

Yentob, Alan (2013) *Turning the Art World Inside Out* [documentary] BBC, online: https://www.youtube.com/watch?v=98RUUhVgLR0&t=5s.

Yi, Song Mi (2000) "Sin Saimdang: The Foremost Woman Painter of the Choson Dynasty" *Oriental Art* 46(1).

Yü, Chienhua (1981) *Chungkuo meishuchia jenming tz'utien* (Biographical dictionary of Chinese artists) (Shanghai: Jenmin meishu ch'u pan she).

Zarobell, J. (2015) "Paul Durand-Ruel and the market for modern art, 1870–873" in Sylvie Patrry (ed.), *Inventing Impressionism: Paul Durand-Ruel and the Modern Art Market* (London: National Gallery) pp. 76–97.

Zhang Yanyuan (Tang Dynasty) (1992) *Li Dai Ming Hua Ji* (A Record of the Famous Paintings of All the Dynasties) (Shanghai: Han Fen Lou).

Zizek, S. (2017) *Trouble in Paradise: From the End of History to the End of Capitalism* (New York: Melville House)

# Index